The Eleven Comedies

[Second Volume]

ARISTOPHANES

(Playwright)

[ZHINGOORA BOOKS]

This edition is published by
Zhingoora Books.

CONTENTS OF THE SECOND VOLUME

THE WASPS

INTRODUCTION

"This Comedy, which was produced by its Author the year after the performance of 'The Clouds,' may be taken as in some sort a companion picture to that piece. Here the satire is directed against the passion of the Athenians for the excitement of the law-courts, as in the former its object was the new philosophy. And as the younger generation—the modern school of thought—were there the subjects of the caricature, so here the older citizens, who took their seats in court as jurymen day by day, to the neglect of their private affairs and the encouragement of a litigious disposition, appear in their turn in the mirror which the satirist holds up."

There are only two characters of any importance to the action—Philocleon ('friend of Cleon') and his son Bdelycleon ('enemy of Cleon'). The plot is soon told. Philocleon is a bigoted devotee of the malady of litigiousness so typical of his countrymen and an enthusiastic attendant at the Courts in his capacity of 'dicast' or juryman. Bdelycleon endeavours to persuade his father by every means in his power to change this unsatisfactory manner of life for something nobler and more profitable; but all in vain. As a last resource he keeps his father a prisoner indoors, so that he cannot attend the tribunals.

The old man tries to escape, and these attempts are conceived in the wildest vein of extravaganza. He endeavours to get out by the chimney, pretending he is "only the smoke"; and all hands rush to clap a cover on the chimney-top, and a big stone on that. He slips through a hole in the tiles, and sits on the roof, pretending to be "only a sparrow"; and they have to set a net to catch him. Then the Chorus of Wasps, representing Philocleon"s fellow 'dicasts,' appear on the scene to rescue him. A battle royal takes place on the stage; the Wasps, with their formidable stings, trying to storm the house, while the son and his retainers defend their position with desperate courage. Finally the assailants are repulsed, and father and son agree upon a compromise. Bdelycleon promises, on condition that his father gives up attending the public trails, to set up a mock tribunal for him in his own house.

4

Presently the theft of a Sicilian cheese by the house-dog Labes gives the old fellow an opportunity of exercising his judicial functions. Labes is duly arraigned and witnesses examines. But alas! Philocleon inadvertently casts his vote for the defendant's *acquittal*, the first time in his life "such a thing has ever occurred," and the old man nearly dies of vexation.

At this point follows the 'Parabasis,' or Author's personal address to the audience, after which the concluding portion of the play has little connection with the main theme. This is a fault, according to modern ideas, common to many of these Comedies, but it is especially marked in this particular instance. The final part might almost be a separate play, under the title perhaps of 'The dicast turned gentleman,' and relates various ridiculous mistakes and laughable blunders committed by Philocleon, who, having given up his attendance on the law-courts, has set up for playing a part in polite society.

The drama, as was very often the case, takes its title from the Chorus—a band of old men dressed up as wasps, who acrimonious, stinging, exasperated temper is meant to typify the character fostered among Athenian citizens by excessive addiction to forensic business.

Racine, in the only comedy he attempted, 'Les Plaideurs,' borrows the incident of the mock trial of the house-dog, amplifying and adding further diverting features.

Perhaps 'The Wasps' is the least amusing of all our Author's pieces which have come down to us—at any rate to a modern reader. The theme of its satire, the litigious spirit of the Athenians, is after all purely local and temporary, while the fun often strikes us as thin and forced. Schlegel writes in his 'Dramatic Literature': "The subject is too limited, the folly it ridicules appears a disease of too singular a description, without a sufficient universality of application, and the action is too much drawn out."

* * * * *

THE WASPS

DRAMATIS PERSONAE

PHILOCLEON, a Dicast.
BDELYCLEON, his Son.
SOSIAS, House-servant of Philocleon.
XANTHIAS, House-servant of Philocleon.
BOYS.
A DOG.
A BAKER'S WIFE.
ACCUSER.
CHORUS OF ELDERS, costumed as Wasps.

SCENE: Philocleon's house at Athens.

* * * * *

THE WASPS

SOSIAS. Why, Xanthias! what are you doing, wretched man?

XANTHIAS. I am teaching myself how to rest; I have been awake and on watch the whole night.

SOSIAS. So you want to earn trouble for your ribs,[1] eh? Don't you know what sort of an animal we are guarding here?

XANTHIAS. Aye indeed! but I want to put my cares to sleep for a while.

SOSIAS. Beware what you do. I too feel soft sleep spreading over my eyes. Resist it, for you must be as mad as a Corybant if you fall asleep.[2]

XANTHIAS. No! 'Tis Bacchus who lulls me off.

SOSIAS. Then you serve the same god as myself. Just now a heavy slumber settled on my eyelids like a hostile Mede; A nodded and, faith! I had a wondrous dream.

XANTHIAS. Indeed! and so had I. A dream such as I never had before. But first tell me yours.

SOSIAS. Methinks I saw an eagle, a gigantic bird, descend upon the market-place; it seized a brazen buckler with its talons and bore it away into the highest heavens; then I saw 'twas Cleonymus had thrown it away.

XANTHIAS. This Cleonymus is a riddle worth propounding among guests. How can one and the same animal have cast away his buckler both on land, in the sky and at sea?[3]

SOSIAS. Alas! what ill does such a dream portend for me?

XANTHIAS. Rest undisturbed! An it please the gods, no evil will befall you.

SOSIAS. Nevertheless, 'tis a fatal omen when a man throws away his weapons. But what was your dream? Let me hear.

XANTHIAS. Oh! it is a dream of high import. It has reference to the hull of the State; to nothing less.

SOSIAS. Tell it me quickly; show me its very keel.

XANTHIAS. In my first slumber I thought I saw sheep, wearing cloaks and carrying staves,[4] met in assembly on the Pnyx; a rapacious whale was haranguing them and screaming like a pig that is being grilled.

SOSIAS. Faugh! faugh!

XANTHIAS. What's the matter?

SOSIAS. Enough, enough, spare me. Your dream stinks vilely of old leather.[5]

XANTHIAS. Then this scoundrelly whale seized a balance and set to weighing ox-fat.[6]

SOSIAS. Alas! 'tis our poor Athenian people, whom this accursed beast wished to cut up and despoil of their fat.

XANTHIAS. Seated on the ground close to it, I saw Theorus,[7] who had the head of a crow. The Alcibiades said to me in his lisping way, "Do you thee? Theoruth hath a crow'th head."[8]

SOSIAS. Ah! 'twas very well lisped indeed!

XANTHIAS. This is might strange; Theorus turning into a crow!

SOSIAS. No, it is glorious.

XANTHIAS. Why?

SOSIAS. Why? He was a man and now he has suddenly become a crow; does it not foretoken that he will take his flight from here and go to the crows?[9]

XANTHIAS. Interpreting dreams so aptly certainly deserves two obols.[10]

SOSIAS. Come, I must explain the matter to the spectators. But first a few words of preamble: expect nothing very high-flown from us, nor any jests stolen from Megara;[11] we have no slaves, who throw baskets of nuts[12] to the spectators, nor any Heracles to be robbed of his dinner,[13] nor is Euripides loaded with contumely; and despite the happy chance that gave Cleon his fame[14] we shall not go out of our way to belabour him again. Our little subject is not wanting in sense; it is well within your capacity and at the same time cleverer than many vulgar Comedies.—We have a master of great renown, who is now sleeping up there on the other story. He has bidden us keep guard over his father, whom he has locked in, so that he may not go out. This father has a curious complaint; not one of you could hit upon or guess it, if I did not tell you.—Well then, try! I hear Amynias, the son of Pronapus, over there, saying, "He is addicted to gambling."

XANTHIAS. He's wrong! He is imputing his own malady to others.

SOSIAS. No, yet love is indeed the principal part of his disease. Ah! here is Sosias telling Dercylus, "He loves drinking."

XANTHIAS. Not at all! The love of wine is the complaint of good men.

SOSIAS. "Well then," says Nicostratus of the Scambonian deme, "he either loves sacrifices or else strangers."

XANTHIAS. Ah! great gods! no, he is not fond of strangers, Nicostratus, for he who says "Philoxenus" means a dirty fellow.[15]

SOSIAS. 'Tis mere waste of time, you will not find it out. If you want to know it, keep silence! I will tell you our master's complaint: of all men, it is he who is fondest of the Heliaea.[16] Thus, to be judging is his hobby, and he groans if he is not sitting on the first seat. He does not close an eye at night, and if he dozes off for an instant his mind flies instantly to the clepsydra.[17] He is so accustomed to hold the balloting pebble, that he awakes with his three fingers pinched together[18] as if he were offering incense to the new moon. If he sees scribbled on some doorway, "How charming is Demos,[19] the son of Pyrilampes!" he will write beneath it, "How charming is Cemos!"[20] His cock crowed one evening; said he, "He has had money from the accused to awaken me too late."[21] As soon as he rises from supper he bawls for his shoes and away he rushes down there before dawn to sleep beforehand, glued fast to the column like an oyster.[22] He is a merciless judge, never failing to draw the convicting line[23] and return home with his nails full of wax like a bumble-bee. Fearing he might run short of pebbles[24] he keeps enough at home to cover a sea-beach, so that he may have the means of recording his sentence. Such is his madness, and all advice is useless; he only judges the more each day. So we keep him under lock and key, to prevent his going out; for his son is broken-hearted over this mania. At first he tried him with gentleness, wanted to persuade him to wear the cloak no longer,[25] to go out no more; unable to convince him, he had him bathed and purified according to the ritual[26] without any greater success, and then handed him over the the Corybantes;[27] but the old man escaped them, and carrying off the kettle-drum,[28] rushed right into the midst of the Heliasts. As Cybelé could do nothing with her rites, his son took him again to Aegina and forcibly made him lie one night in the temple of Asclepius, the God of Healing, but before daylight there he was to be seen at the gate of the tribunal. Since then we let him go out no more, but he escaped us by the drains or by the skylights, so we stuffed up every opening with old rags and made all secure; then he drove short sticks into the wall and sprang from rung to rung like a magpie. Now we have stretched nets all round the court and we keep watch and ward. The old man's name is Philocleon,[29] 'tis the best name he could have, and the son is called Bdelycleon,[30] for he is a man very fit to cure an insolent fellow of his boasting.

BDELYCLEON. Xanthias! Sosias! Are you asleep?

XANTHIAS. Oh! oh!

SOSIAS. What is the matter?

XANTHIAS. Why, Bdelycleon is rising.

BDELYCLEON. Will neither of you come here? My father has got into the stove-chamber and is ferreting about like a rat in his hole. Take care he does not escape through the bath drain. You there, put all your weight against the door.

SOSIAS. Aye, aye, master.

BDELYCLEON. By Zeus! what is that noise in the chimney? Hullo! who are you?

PHILOCLEON. I am the smoke going up.

BDELYCLEON. Smoke? smoke of what wood?

PHILOCLEON. Of fig-wood.[31]

BDELYCLEON. Ah! 'this the most acrid of all. But you shall not get out. Where is the chimney cover?[32] Come down again. Now, up with another cross-bar. Now look out some fresh dodge. But am I not the most unfortunate of men? Henceforward, I shall only be called the son of the smoky old man. Slave, hold the door stoutly, throw your weight upon it, come, put heart into the work. I will come and help you. Watch both lock and bolt. Take care he does not gnaw through the peg.

PHILOCLEON. What are you dong, you wretches? Let me go out; it is imperative that I go and judge, or Dracontides will be acquitted.

BDELYCLEON. What a dreadful calamity for you!

PHILOCLEON. Once at Delphi, the god, whom I was consulting, foretold, that if an accused man escaped me, I should die of consumption.

BDELYCLEON. Apollo, the Saviour, what a prophecy!

PHILOCLEON. Ah! I beseech you, if you do not want my death, let me go.

BDELYCLEON. No, Philocleon, no never, by Posidon!

PHILOCLEON. Well then, I shall gnaw through the net[33] with my teeth.

BDELYCLEON. But you have no teeth.

PHILOCLEON. Oh! you rascal, how can I kill you? How? Give me a sword, quick, or a conviction tablet.

BDELYCLEON. Our friend is planning some great crime.

PHILOCLEON. No, by Zeus! but I want to go and sell my ass and its panniers, for 'this the first of the month.[34]

BDELYCLEON. Could I not sell it just as well?

PHILOCLEON. Not as well as I could.

BDELYCLEON. No, but better. Come, bring it here, bring it here by all means—if you can.

XANTHIAS. What a clever excuse he has found now! What cunning to get you to let him go out!

BDELYCLEON. Yes, but I have not swallowed the hook; I scented the trick. I will no in and fetch the ass, so that the old man may not point his weapons that way again....[35] Stupid old ass, are you weeping because you are going to be sold? Come, go a bit quicker. Why, what are you moaning and groaning for? You might be carrying another Odysseus.[36]

XANTHIAS. Why, certainly, so he is! someone has crept beneath his belly.

BDELYCLEON. Who, who? Let us see.

XANTHIAS. 'Tis he.

BDELYCLEON. What does this mean? Who are you? Come, speak!

PHILOCLEON. I am Nobody.

BDELYCLEON. Nobody? Of what country?

PHILOCLEON. Of Ithaca, son of Apodrasippides.[37]

BDELYCLEON. Ha! Mister Nobody, you will not laugh presently. Pull him out quick! Ah! the wretch, where has be crept to? Does he not resemble a she-ass to the life?

PHILOCLEON. If you do not leave me in peace, I shall commence proceedings.

BDELYCLEON. And what will the suit be about?

PHILOCLEON. The shade of an ass.[38]

BDELYCLEON. You are a poor man of very little wit, but thoroughly brazen.

PHILOCLEON. A poor man! Ah! by Zeus! you know not now what I am worth; but you will know when you disembowel the old Heliast's money bag.[39]

BDELYCLEON. Come, get back indoors, both you and your ass.

PHILOCLEON. Oh! my brethren of the tribunal! oh! Cleon! to the rescue!

BDELYCLEON. Go and bawl in there under lock and key. And you there, pile plenty of stones against the door, thrust the bolt home into the staple, and to keep this beam in its place roll that great mortar against it. Quick's the word.

SOSIAS. Oh! my god! whence did this brick fall on me?

XANTHIAS. Perhaps a rat loosened it.

SOSIAS. A rat? 'tis surely our gutter-judge,[40] who has crept beneath the tiles of the roof.

XANTHIAS. Ah! woe to us! there he is, he has turned into a sparrow; he will be flying off. Where is the net? where? pschit! pschit! get back!

BDELYCLEON. Ah! by Zeus! I would rather have to guard Scioné[41] than such a father.

SOSIAS. And how that we have driven him in thoroughly and he can no longer escape without our knowledge, can we not have a few winks of sleep, no matter how few?

BDELYCLEON. Why, wretch! the other jurymen will be here almost directly to summon my father!

SOSIAS. Why, 'tis scarcely dawn yet!

BDELYCLEON. Ah, they must have risen late to-day. Generally it is the middle of the night when they come to fetch him. They arrive here, carrying lanterns in their hands and singing the charming old verses of Phrynichus' "Sidonian Women";[42] 'tis their way of calling him.

SOSIAS. Well, if need be, we will chase them off with stones.

BDELYCLEON. What! you dare to speak so? Why, this class of old men, if irritated, becomes as terrible as a swarm of wasps. They carry below their loins the sharpest of stings, with which to sting their foe; they shout and leap and their stings burn like so many sparks.

SOSIAS. Have no fear! If I can find stones to throw into this nest of jurymen-wasps, I shall soon have them cleared off.

CHORUS. March on, advance boldly and bravely! Comias, your feet are dragging; once you were as tough as a dog-skin strap and now even Charinades walks better than you. Ha! Strymodorus of Conthylé, you best of mates, where is Euergides and where is Chales of Phyla? Ha, ha, bravo!

there you are, the last of the lads with whom we mounted guard together at Byzantium.[43] Do you remember how, one night, prowling round, we noiselessly stole the kneading-trough of a baker's-wife; we split it in two and cooked our green-stuff with it.—But let us hasten, for the case of the Laches[44] comes on to-day, and they all say he has embezzled a pot of money. Hence Cleon, our protector, advised us yesterday to come early and with a three days' stock of fiery rage so as to chastise him for his crimes. Let us hurry, comrades, before it is light; come, let us search every nook with our lanterns to see whether those who wish us ill have not set us some trap.

BOY. Ah! here is mud! Father, take care!

CHORUS. Pick up a blade of straw and trim the lamp of your lantern.

BOY. No, I can trim it quite well with my finger.

CHORUS. Why do you pull out the wick, you little dolt? Oil is scarce, and 'tis not you who suffer when it has to be paid for. (*Strikes him.*)

BOY. If you teach us again with your fists, we shall put out the lamps and go home; then you will have no light and will squatter about in the mud like ducks in the dark.

CHORUS. I know how to punish other offenders bigger than you. But I think I am treading in some mud. Oh! 'tis certain it will rain in torrents for four days at least; look, what thieves are in our lamps; that is always a sign of heavy rain; but the rain and the north wind will be good for the crops that are still standing.... Why, what can have happened to our mate, who lives here? Why does he not come to join our party? There used to be no need to haul him in our wake, for he would march at our head singing the verses of Phrynichus; he was a lover of singing. Should we not, friends, make a halt here and sign to call him out? The charm of my voice will fetch him out, if he hears it.

Why does the old man not show himself before the door? why does he not answer? Has he lost his shoes? has he stubbed his toe in the dark and thus got a swollen ankle? Perhaps he has a tumour in his groin. He was the hardest of us all; he alone *never* allowed himself to be moved. If anyone tried to move him, he would lower his head, saying, "You might just as well try to boil a stone." But I bethink me, an accused ma escaped us yesterday through his false pretence that he loved Athens and had been the first to unfold the Samian plot.[45] Perhaps his acquittal has so distressed Philocleon that he is abed with fever—he is quite capable of such a thing.— Friend, arise, do not thus vex your hear, but forget your wrath. Today we have to judge a man made wealthy by treason, one of those who set Thrace free;[46] we have to prepare him a funeral urn ... so march on, my boy, get a-going.

BOY. Father, would you give me something if I asked for it?

CHORUS. Assuredly, my child, but tell me what nice thing do you want me to buy you? A set of knuckle-bones, I suppose.

BOY. No, dad, I prefer figs; they are better.

CHORUS. No, by Zeus! even if you were to hang yourself with vexation.

BOY. Well then, I will lead you no father.

CHORUS. With my small pay, I am obliged to buy bread, wood, stew; and now you ask me for figs!

BOY. But, father, if the Archon[47] should not form a court to-day, how are we to buy our dinner? Have you some good hope to offer us or merely "Hellé's sacred waves"?[48]

CHORUS. Alas! alas! I have not a notion how we shall dine.

BOY. Oh! my poor mother! why did you let me see this day?

CHORUS. Oh! my little wallet! you seem like to be a mere useless ornament!

BOY. 'Tis our destiny to groan.

PHILOCLEON.[49] My friends, I have long been pining away while listening to you from my window, but I absolutely know not what do do. I am detained here, because I have long wanted to go with you to the law court and do all the harm I can. Oh! Zeus! cause the peals of they thunder to roll, change me quickly into smoke or make me into a Proxenides, a perfect braggart, like the son of Sellus. Oh, King of Heaven! hesitate not to grant me this favour, pity my misfortune or else may thy dazzling lightning instantly reduce me to ashes; then carry me hence, and may thy breath hurl me into some burning pickle[50] or turn me into one of the stones on which the votes are counted.

CHORUS. Who is it detains you and shuts you in? Speak, for you are talking to friends.

PHILOCLEON. 'Tis my son. But no bawling, he is there in front asleep; lower your voice.

CHORUS. But, poor fellow, what is his aim? what is his object?

PHILOCLEON. My friends, he will not have me judge nor do anyone any ill, but he wants me to stay at home and enjoy myself, and I will not.

CHORUS. This wretch, this Demolochocleon[51] dares to say such odious things, just because you tell the truth about our navy!

PHILOCLEON. He would not have dared, had he not been a conspirator.

CHORUS. Meanwhile, you must devise some new dodge. so that you can come down here without his knowledge.

PHILOCLEON. But what? Try to find some way. For myself, I am ready for anything, so much do I burn to run along the tiers of the tribunal with my voting-pebble in my hand.

CHORUS. There is surely some hole through which you could manage to squeeze from within, and escape dressed in rags, like the crafty Odysseus.[52]

PHILOCLEON. Everything is sealed fast; not so much as a gnat could get through. Think of some other plan; there is no possible hold of escape.

CHORUS. Do you recall how, when you were with the army at the taking of Naxos,[53] you descended so readily from the top of the wall by means of the spits you have stolen?

PHILOCLEON. I remember that well enough, but what connection is there with present circumstances? I was young, clever at thieving, I had all my strength, none watched over me, and I could run off without fear. But to-day men-at-arms are placed at every outlet to watch me, and two of them are lying in wait for me at this very door armed with spits, just as folk lie in wait for a cat that has stolen a piece of meat.

CHORUS. Come, discover some way as quick as possible. Here is the dawn come, my dear little friend.

PHILOCLEON. The best way is to gnaw through the net. Oh! goddess, who watches over the nets,[54] forgive me for making a hole in this one.

CHORUS. 'Tis acting like a man eager for his safety. Get your jaws to work!

PHILOCLEON. There! 'tis gnawed through! But no shouting! let Bdelycleon notice nothing!

CHORUS. Have no fear, have no fear! if he breathes a syllable, 'twill be to bruise his own knuckles; he will have to fight to defend his own head. We shall teach him not to insult the mysteries of the goddesses.[55] But fasten a rope to the window, tie it around your body and let yourself down to the ground, with your heart bursting with the fury of Diopithes.[56]

PHILOCLEON. But if these notice it and want to fish me up and drag me back into the house, what will you do? Tell me that.

CHORUS. We shall call up the full strength of out courage to your aid. That is what we will do.

PHILOCLEON. I trust myself to you and risk the danger. If misfortune overtakes me, take away my body, bathe it with your tears and bury it beneath the bar of the tribunal.

CHORUS. Nothing will happen to you, rest assured. Come friend, have courage and let yourself slide down while you invoke your country's gods.

PHILOCLEON. Oh! mighty Lycus![57] noble hero and my neighbour, thou, like myself, takest pleasure in the tears and the groans of the accused. If thou art come to live near the tribunal, 'tis with the express design of hearing them incessantly; thou alone of all the heroes hast wished to remain among those who weep. Have pity on me and save him, who lives close to thee; I swear I will never make water, never, nor relieve my belly with a fart against the railing of thy statue.

BDELYCLEON. Ho there! ho! get up!

SOSIAS. What's the matter?

BDELYCLEON. Methought I heard talking close to me.

SOSIAS. Is the old man at it again, escaping through some loophole?

BDELYCLEON. No, by Zeus! no, but he is letting himself down by a rope.

SOSIAS. Ha, rascal! what are you doing there? You shall not descend.

BDELYCLEON. Mount quick to the other window, strike him with the boughs that hang over the entrance; perchance he will turn back when he feels himself being thrashed.

PHILOCLEON. To the rescue! all you, who are going to have lawsuits this year—Smicythion, Tisiades, Chremon and Pheredipnus. 'Tis now or never, before they force me to return, that you must help.

CHORUS. Why do we delay to let loose that fury, that is so terrible, when our nests are attacked? I feel my angry sting is stiffening, that sharp sting, with which we punish our enemies. Come, children, cast your cloaks to the winds, run, shout, tell Cleon what is happening, that he may march against this foe to our city, who deserves death, since he proposes to prevent the trial of lawsuits.

BDELYCLEON. Friends, listen to the truth, instead of bawling.

CHORUS. By Zeus! we will shout to heaven and never forsake our friend. Why, this is intolerable, 'tis manifest tyranny. Oh! citizens, oh! Theorus,[58] the enemy of the gods! and all you flatterers, who rule us! come to our aid.

XANTHIAS. By Heracles! they have stings. Do you see them, master?

BDELYCLEON. 'Twas with these weapons that they killed Philippus the son of Gorgias[59] when he was put on trial.

CHORUS. And you too shall die. Turn yourselves this way, all, with your stings out for attack and throw yourselves upon him in good and serried order, and swelled up with wrath and rage. Let him learn to know the sort of foes he has dared to irritate.

XANTHIAS. The fight will be fast and furious, by great Zeus! I tremble at the sight of their stings.

CHORUS. Let this man go, unless you want to envy the tortoise his hard shell.

PHILOCLEON. Come, my dear companions, wasps with relentless hearts, fly against him, animated with your fury. Sting him in the back, in his eyes and on his fingers.

BDELYCLEON. Midas, Phryx, Masyntias, here! Come and help. Seize this man and hand him over to no one, otherwise you shall starve to death in chains. Fear nothing, I have often heard the crackling of fig-leaves in the fire.[60]

CHORUS. If you won't let him go, I shall bury this sting in your body.

PHILOCLEON. Oh, Cecrops, mighty hero with the tail of a dragon! Seest thou how these barbarians ill-use me—me, who have many a time made them weep a full bushel of tears?

CHORUS. Is not old age filled with cruel ills? What violence these two slaves offer to their old master! they have forgotten all bygones, the fur-coats and the jackets and the caps he bought for them; in winter he watched that their feet should not get frozen. And only see them now; there is no gentleness in their look nor any recollection of the slippers of other days.

PHILOCLEON. Will you let me go, you accursed animal? Don't you remember the day when I surprised you stealing the grapes; I tied you to an olive-tree and I cut open your bottom with such vigorous lashes that folks thought you had been pedicated. Get away, you are ungrateful. But let go of me, and you too, before my son comes up.

CHORUS. You shall repay us for all this and 'twill not be long first. Tremble at our ferocious glance; you shall taste our just anger.

BDELYCLEON. Strike! strike, Xanthias! Drive these wasps away from the house.

XANTHIAS. That's just what I am doing; but do you smoke them out thoroughly too.

SOSIAS. You will not go? The plague seize you! Will you not clear off? Xanthias, strike them with your stick!

XANTHIAS. And you, to smoke them out better, throw Aeschinus, the son of
Selartius, on the fire. Ah! we were bound to drive you off in the end.

BDELYCLEON. Eh! by Zeus! you would not have put them to flight so easily if they had fed on the verses of Philocles.

CHORUS. It is clear to all the poor that tyranny has attacked us sorely. Proud emulator of Amynias, you, who only take pleasure in doing ill, see how you are preventing us from obeying the laws of the city; you do not even seek a pretext or any plausible excuse, but claim to rule alone.

BDELYCLEON. Hold! A truce to all blows and brawling! Had we not better confer together and come to some understanding?

CHORUS. Confer with you, the people's foe! with you, a royalist, the accomplice of Brasidas![61] with you, who wear woollen fringes on your cloak and let your beard grow!

BDELYCLEON. Ah! it were better to separate altogether from my father than to steer my boat daily through such stormy seas!

CHORUS. Oh! you have but reached the parsley and the rue, to use the common saying.[62] What you are suffering is nothing! but welcome the hour when the advocate shall adduce all these same arguments against you and shall summon your accomplices to give witness.

BDELYCLEON. In the name of the gods! withdraw or we shall fight you the whole day long.

CHORUS. No, not as long as I retain an atom of breath. Ha! your desire is to tyrannize over us!

BDELYCLEON. Everything is now tyranny with us, no matter what is concerned, whether it be large or small. Tyranny! I have not heard the word mentioned once in fifty years, and now it is more common than salt-fish, the word is even current on the market. If you are buying gurnards and don't want anchovies, the huckster next door, who is selling the latter, at once exclaims, "That is a man, whose kitchen savours of tyranny!" If you ask for onions to season your fish, the green-stuff woman winks one eye and asks, "Ha! you ask for onions! are you seeking to tyrannize, or do you think that Athens must pay you your seasonings as a tribute?"

XANTHIAS. Yesterday I went to see a gay girl about noon and suggested she should mount and ride me; she flew into a rage, pretending I wanted to restore the tyranny of Hippias.[63]

BDELYCLEON. That's the talk that pleases the people! As for myself, I want my father to lead a joyous life like Morychus[64] instead of going away before dawn to basely calumniate and condemn; and for this I am accused of conspiracy and tyrannical practice!

PHILOCLEON. And quite right too, by Zeus! The most exquisite dishes do not make up to me for the life of which you deprive me. I scorn your red mullet and your eels, and would far rather eat a nice little law suitlet cooked in the pot.

BDELYCLEON. 'Tis because you have got used to seeking your pleasure in it; but if you will agree to keep silence and hear me, I think I could persuade you that you deceive yourself altogether.

PHILOCLEON. *I* deceive myself, when I am judging?

BDELYCLEON. You do not see that you are the laughing-stock of these men, whom you are ready to worship. You are their slave and do not know it.

PHILOCLEON. *I* a slave, I, who lord it over all!

BDELYCLEON. Not at all, you think you are ruling when you are only obeying. Tell me, father, what do you get out of the tribute paid by so many Greek towns?

PHILOCLEON. Much, and I appoint my colleagues jurymen.

23

BDELYCLEON. And I also. Release him, all of you, and bring me a sword. If my arguments do not prevail I will fall upon this blade. As for you, tell me whether you accept the verdict of the Court.

PHILOCLEON. May I never drink my Heliast's pay in honour of the good Genius, if I do not.

CHORUS. Tis now we have to draw upon our arsenal for some fresh weapon; above all do not side with this youth in his opinions. You see how serious the question has become; 'twill be all over with us, which the gods forfend, if he should prevail.

BDELYCLEON. Let someone bring me my tablets with all speed!

CHORUS. Your tablets? Ha, ha! what an importance you would fain assume!

BDELYCLEON. I merely wish to note down my father's points.

PHILOCLEON. But what will you say of it, if he should triumph in the debate?

CHORUS. That old men are no longer good for anything; we shall be perpetually laughed at in the streets, shall be called thallophores,[65] mere brief-bags. You are to be the champion of all our rights and sovereignty. Come, take courage! Bring into action all the resources of your wit.

PHILOCLEON. At the outset I will prove to you that there exists no king whose might is greater than ours. Is there a pleasure, a blessing comparable with that of a juryman? Is there a being who lives more in the midst of delights, who is more feared, aged though he be? From the moment I leave my bed, men of power, the most illustrious in the city, await me at the bar of the tribunal; the moment I am seen from the greatest distance, they come forward to offer me a gentle hand,—that has pilfered the public funds; they entreat me, bowing right low and with a piteous voice, "Oh! father," they say, "pity me, I adjure you by the profit *you* were able to make in the public service or in the army, when dealing with the victuals." Why, the man who thus speaks would not know of my existence, had I not let him off on some former occasion.

BDELYCLEON. Let us note this first point, the supplicants.

PHILOCLEON. These entreaties have appeased my wrath, and I enter—firmly resolved to do nothing that I have promised. Nevertheless I listen to the accused. Oh! what tricks to secure acquittal! Ah! there is no form of flattery that is not addressed to the heliast! Some groan over their poverty and they exaggerate the truth in order to make their troubles equal to my own. Others tell us anecdotes or some comic story from Aesop. Others, again, cut jokes; they fancy I shall be appeased if I laugh. If we are not even then won over, why, then they drag forward their young children by the hand, both boys and girls, who prostrate themselves and whine with one accord, and then the father, trembling as if before a god, beseeches me not to condemn him out of pity for them, "If you love the voice of the lamb, have pity on my son's"; and because I am fond of little sows,[66] I must yield to his daughter's prayers. Then we relax the heat of our wrath a little for him. Is not this great power indeed, which allows even wealth to be disdained?

BDELYCLEON. A second point to note, the disdain of wealth. And now recall to me what are the advantages you enjoy, you, who pretend to rule over Greece?

PHILOCLEON. Being entrusted with the inspection of the young men, we have a right to examine their organs. Is Aeagrus[67] accused, he is not acquitted before he has recited a passage from 'Niobe'[68] and he chooses the finest. If a flute-player gains his case, he adjusts his mouth-strap[69] in return and plays us the final air while we are leaving. A father on his death-bed names some husband for his daughter, who is his sole heir; but we care little for his will or for the shell so solemnly placed over the seal;[70] we give the young maiden to him who has best known how to secure our favour. Name me another duty that is so important and so irresponsible.

BDELYCLEON. Aye, 'tis a fine privilege, and the only one on which I can congratulate you; but surely to violate the will is to act badly towards the heiress.

PHILOCLEON. And if the Senate and the people have trouble in deciding some important case, it is decreed to send the culprits before the heliasts; then Euathlus[71] and the illustrious Colaconymus,[72] who cast away his shield, swear not to betray us and to fight for the people. Did ever an orator carry the day with his opinion if he had not first declared that the jury should be dismissed for the day as soon as they had given their first verdict? We are the only ones whom Cleon, the great bawler, does not badger. On the contrary, he protects and caresses us; he keeps off the flies, which is what you have never done for your father. Theorus, who is a man not less illustrious than Euphemius,[73] takes the sponge out of the pot and blacks our shoes. See then what good things you deprive and despoil me of. Pray, is this obeying or being a slave, as you pretended to be able to prove?

BDELYCLEON. Talk away to your heart's content; you must come to a stop at last and then you shall see that this grand power only resembles one of those things that, wash 'em as you will, remain as foul as ever.

PHILOCLEON. But I am forgetting the most pleasing thing of all. When I return home with my pay, everyone runs to greet me because of my money. First my daughter bathes me, anoints my feet, stoops to kiss me and, while she is calling me "her dearest father," fishes out my triobolus with her tongue;[74] then my little wife comes to wheedle me and brings a nice light cake; she sits beside me and entreats me in a thousand ways, "Do take this now; do have some more." All this delights me hugely, and I have no need to turn towards you or the steward to know when it shall please him to serve my dinner, all the while cursing and grumbling. But if he does not quickly knead my cake, I have this,[75] which is my defence, my shield against all ills. If you do not pour me out drink, I have brought this long-eared jar[76] full of wine. How it brays, when I bend back and bury its neck in my mouth! What terrible and noisy gurglings, and how I laugh at your wine-skins. As to power, am I not equal to the king of the gods? If our assembly is noisy, all say as they pass, "Great gods! the tribunal is rolling out its thunder!" If I let loose the lightning, the richest, aye, the noblest are half dead with fright and shit themselves with terror. You yourself are afraid of me, yea, by Demeter! you are afraid.

BDELYCLEON. May I die if you frighten me.

CHORUS. Never have I heard speech so elegant or so sensible.

PHILOCLEON. Ah! he thought he had only to turn me round his finger; he should, however, have known the vigour of my eloquence.

CHORUS. He has said everything without omission. I felt myself grow taller while I listened to him. Methought myself meting out justice in the Islands of the Blest, so much was I taken with the charm of his words.

BDELYCLEON. How overjoyed they are! What extravagant delight! Ah! ah! you are going to get a thrashing to-day.

CHORUS. Come, plot everything you can to beat him; 'tis not easy to soften me if you do not talk on my side, and if you have nothing but nonsense to spout, 'tis time to buy a good millstone, freshly cut withal, to crush my anger.

BDELYCLEON. The cure of a disease, so inveterate and so widespread in Athens, is a difficult task and of too great importance for the scope of Comedy. Nevertheless, my old father....

PHILOCLEON. Cease to call me by that name, for, if you do not prove me a slave and that quickly too, you must die by my hand, even if I must be deprived of my share in the sacred feasts.

BDELYCLEON. Listen to me, dear little father, unruffle that frowning brow and reckon, you can do so without trouble, not with pebbles, but on your fingers, what is the sum-total of the tribute paid by the allied towns; besides this we have the direct imposts, a mass of percentage dues, the fees of the courts of justice, the produce from the mines, the markets, the harbours, the public lands and the confiscations. All these together amount to close on two thousand talents. Take from this sum the annual pay of the dicasts; they number six thousand, and there have never been more in this town; so therefore it is one hundred and fifty talents that come to you.

PHILOCLEON. What! our pay is not even a tithe of the State revenue?

BDELYCLEON. Why no, certainly not.

PHILOCLEON. And where does the rest go then?

BDELYCLEON. To those who say: "I shall never betray the interests of the masses; I shall always fight for the people." And 'tis you, father, who let yourself be caught with their fine talk, who give them all power over yourself. They are the men who extort fifty talents at a time by threat and intimidation from the allies. "Pay tribute to me," they say, "or I shall loose the lightning on your town and destroy it." And you, you are content to gnaw the crumbs of your own might. What do the allies do? They see that the Athenian mob lives on the tribunal in niggard and miserable fashion, and they count you for nothing, for not more than the vote of Connus;[77] 'tis on those wretches that they lavish everything, dishes of salt fish, wine, tapestries, cheese, honey, sesame-fruit, cushions, flagons, rich clothing, chaplets, necklets, drinking-cups, all that yields pleasure and health. And you, their master, to you as a reward for all your toil both on land and sea, nothing is given, not even a clove of garlic to eat with your little fish.

PHILOCLEON. No, undoubtedly not; I have had to send and buy some from Eucharides. But you told me I was a slave. Prove it then, for I am dying with impatience.

BDELYCLEON. Is it not the worst of all slaveries to see all these wretches and their flatterers, whom they gorge with gold, at the head of affairs? As for you, you are content with the three obols they give you and which you have so painfully earned in the galleys, in battles and sieges. But what I stomach least is that you go to sit on the tribunal by order. Some lewd stripling, the son of Chereas, to wit, enters your house balancing his body, rotten with debauchery, on his straddling legs and charges you to come and judge at daybreak, and precisely to the minute. "He who only presents himself after the opening of the Court," says he, "will not get the triobolus." But he himself, though he arrives late, will nevertheless get his drachma as a public advocate. If an accused man makes him some present, he shares it with a colleague and the pair agree to arrange the matter like two sawyers, one of whom pulls and the other pushes. As for you, you have only eyes for the public pay-clerk, and you see nothing.

PHILOCLEON. Can it be I am treated thus? Oh! what is it you are saying? You stir me to the bottom of my heart! I am all ears! I cannot syllable what I feel.

BDELYCLEON. Consider then; you might be rich, both you and all the others; I know not why you let yourself be fooled by these folk who call themselves the people's friends. A myriad of towns obey you, from the Euxine to Sardis. What do you gain thereby? Nothing but this miserable pay, and even that is like the oil with which the flock of wool is impregnated and is doled to you drop by drop, just enough to keep you from dying of hunger. They want you to be poor, and I will tell you why. 'Tis so that you may know only those who nourish you, and so that, if it pleases them to loose you against one of their foes, you shall leap upon him with fury. If they wished to assure the well-being of the people, nothing would be easier for them. We have now a thousand towns that pay us tribute; let them command each of these to feed twenty Athenians; then twenty thousand of our citizens would be eating nothing but hare, would drink nothing but the purest of milk, and always crowned with garlands, would be enjoying the delights to which the great name of their country and the trophies of Marathon give them the right; whereas to-day you are like the hired labourers who gather the olives; you follow him who pays you.

PHILOCLEON. Alas! my hand is benumbed; I can no longer draw my sword.[78]
What has become of my strength?

BDELYCLEON. When they are afraid, they promise to divide Euboea[79] among you and to give each fifty bushels of wheat, but what have they given you? Nothing excepting, quite recently, five bushels of barley, and even these you have only obtained with great difficulty, on proving you were not aliens, and then choenix by choenix.[80] That is why I always kept you shut in; I wanted you to be fed by me and no longer at the beck of these blustering braggarts. Even now I am ready to let you have all you want, provided you no longer let yourself be suckled by the pay-clerk.

CHORUS. He was right who said, "Decide nothing till you have heard both sides," for it seems to me, that 'tis you who now gain the complete victory. My wrath is appeased, I throw away my sticks. Come, comrade, our contemporary, let yourself be gained over by his words; come, do not be too obstinate or too perverse. Why have I no relation, no ally to speak to me like this? Do not doubt it, 'tis a god who is now protecting you and loading you with his benefits. Accept them.

BDELYCLEON. I will feed him, I will give him everything that is suitable for an old man, oatmeal gruel, a cloak, soft furs and a maid to rub his loins and play with his tool. But he is silent and utters not a word; 'tis a bad sign.

CHORUS. He has thought the thing over and has recognized his folly; he reproaches himself for not having followed your advice always. But there he is, converted by your words, and has no doubt become wiser to alter his ways in future and to believe in none but you.

PHILOCLEON. Alas! alas!

BDELYCLEON. Now why this lamentation?

PHILOCLEON. A truce to your promises! What I love is down there, 'tis down there I want to be, there, where the herald cries, "Who has not yet voted? Let him rise!" I want to be the last to leave the urn of all. Oh, my soul, my soul! where art thou? come! oh! dark shadows, make way for me![81] By Heracles, may I reach the Court in time to convict Cleon of theft.

BDELYCLEON. Come, father, in the name of the gods, believe me!

PHILOCLEON. Believe you! Ask me anything, anything, except one.

BDELYCLEON. What is it? Let us hear.

PHILOCLEON. Not to judge any more! Before I consent, I shall have appeared before Pluto.

BDELYCLEON. Very well then, since you find so much pleasure in it, go down there no more, but stay here and deal out justice to your slaves.

PHILOCLEON. But what is there to judge? Are you mad?

BDELYCLEON. Everything as in a tribunal. If a servant opens a door secretly, you inflict upon him a simple fine; 'tis what you have repeatedly done down there. Everything can be arranged to suit you. If it is warm in the morning, you can judge in the sunlight; if it is snowing, then seated at your fire; if it rains, you go indoors; and if you only rise at noon, there will be no Thesmothetes[82] to exclude you from the precincts.

PHILOCLEON. The notion pleases me.

BDELYCLEON. Moreover, if a pleader is long-winded, you will not be fasting and chafing and seeking vengeance on the accused.

PHILOCLEON. But could I judge as well with my mouth full?

BDELYCLEON. Much better. Is it not said, that the dicasts, when deceived by lying witnesses, have need to ruminate well in order to arrive at the truth?

PHILOCLEON. Well said, but you have not told me yet who will pay salary.

BDELYCLEON. I will.

PHILOCLEON. So much the better; in this way I shall be paid by myself. Because that cursed jester, Lysistratus,[83] played me an infamous trick the other day. He received a drachma for the two of us[84] and went on the fish-market to get it changed and then brought me back three mullet scales. I took them for obols and crammed them into my mouth;[85] but the smell choked me and I quickly spat them out. So I dragged him before the Court.

BDELYCLEON. And what did he say to that?

PHILOCLEON. Well, he pretended I had the stomach of a cock. "You have soon digested the money," he said with a laugh.

BDELYCLEON. You see, that is yet another advantage.

PHILOCLEON. And no small one either. Come, do as you will.

BDELYCLEON. Wait! I will bring everything here.

PHILOCLEON. You see, the oracles are coming true; I have heard it foretold, that one day the Athenians would dispense justice in their own houses, that each citizen would have himself a little tribunal constructed in his porch similar to the altars of Hecaté,[86] and that there would be such before every door.

BDELYCLEON. Hold! what do you say? I have brought you everything needful and much more into the bargain. See, here is an *article,* should you want to piss; it shall be hung beside you on a nail.

PHILOCLEON. Good idea! Right useful at my age. You have found the true preventive of bladder troubles.

BDELYCLEON. Here is fire, and near to it are lentils, should you want to take a snack.

PHILOCLEON. 'Tis admirably arranged. For thus, even when feverish, I shall nevertheless receive my pay; and besides, I could eat my lentils without quitting my seat. But why this cock?

BDELYCLEON. So that, should you doze during some pleading, he may awaken you by crowing up there.

PHILOCLEON. I want only for one thing more; all the rest is as good as can be.

BDELYCLEON. What is that?

PHILOCLEON. If only they could bring me an image of the hero Lycus.[87]

BDELYCLEON. Here it is! Why, you might think it was the god himself!

PHILOCLEON. Oh! hero, my master! how repulsive you are to look at! 'Tis an exact portrait of Cleonymus!

SOSIAS. That is why, hero though he be, he has no weapon.

BDELYCLEON. The sooner you take your seat, the sooner I shall call a case.

PHILOCLEON. Call it, for I have been seated ever so long.

BDELYCLEON. Let us see. What case shall we bring up first? Is there a slave who has done something wrong? Ah! you Thracian there, who burnt the stew-pot t'other day.

PHILOCLEON. Hold, hold! Here is a fine state of things you had almost made me judge without a bar,[88] and that is the thing of all others most sacred among us.

BDELYCLEON. By Zeus! I had forgotten it, but I will run indoors and bring you one immediately. What is this after all, though, but mere force of habit!

XANTHIAS. Plague take the brute! Can anyone keep such a dog?

BDELYCLEON. Hullo! what's the matter?

33

XANTHIAS. Why, 'tis Labes,[89] who has just rushed into the kitchen and has seized a whole Sicilian cheese and gobbled it up.

BDELYCLEON. Good! this will be the first offence I shall make my father try. (*To Xanthias.*) Come along and lay your accusation.

XANTHIAS. No, not I; the other dog vows he will be accuser, if the matter is set down for trial.

BDELYCLEON. Well then, bring them both along.

XANTHIAS. I am coming.

PHILOCLEON. What is this?

BDELYCLEON. 'Tis the pig-trough[90] of the swine dedicated to Hestia.

PHILOCLEON. But it's sacrilege to bring it here.

BDELYCLEON. No, no, by addressing Hestia first,[91] I might, thanks to her, crush an adversary.

PHILOCLEON. Put an end to delay by calling up the case. My verdict is already settled.

BDELYCLEON. Wait! I must yet bring out the tablets[92] and the scrolls.[93]

PHILOCLEON. Oh! I am boiling, I am dying with impatience at your delays.
I could have traced the sentence in the dust.

BDELYCLEON. There you are.

PHILOCLEON. Then call the case.

BDELYCLEON. I am here.

PHILOCLEON. Firstly, who is this?

BDELYCLEON. Ah! my god! why, this is unbearable! I have forgotten the urns.

PHILOCLEON. Well now! where are you off to?

BDELYCLEON. To look for the urns.

PHILOCLEON. Unnecessary, I shall use these vases.[94]

BDELYCLEON. Very well, then we have all we need, except the clepsydra.

PHILOCLEON. Well then! and this? what is it if not a clepsydra?[95]

BDELYCLEON. True again! 'Tis calling things by their right name! Let fire be brought quickly from the house with myrtle boughs and incense, and let us invoke the gods before opening the sitting.

CHORUS. Offer them libations and your vows and we will thank them that a noble agreement has put an end to your bickerings and strife.

BDELYCLEON. And first let there be a sacred silence.

CHORUS. Oh! god of Delphi! oh! Phoebus Apollo! convert into the greatest blessing for us all what is now happening before this house, and cure us of our error, oh, Paean,[96] our helper!

BDELYCLEON. Oh! Powerful god, Apollo Aguieus,[97] who watchest at the door of my entrance hall, accept this fresh sacrifice; I offer it that you may deign to soften my father's excessive severity; he is as hard as iron, his heart is like sour wine; do thou pour into it a little honey. Let him become gentle like other men, let him take more interest in the accused than in the accusers, may he allow himself to be softened by entreaties; calm his acrid humour and deprive his irritable mind of all sting.

CHORUS. We unite our vows and chants to those of this new magistrate.[98] His words have won our favour and we are convinced that he loves the people more than any of the young men of the present day.

BDELYCLEON. If there be any judge near at hand, let him enter; once the proceedings have opened, we shall admit him no more.[99]

PHILOCLEON. Who is the defendant? Ha! what a sentence he will get!

XANTHIAS (*Prosecuting Council*). Listen to the indictment. A dog of Cydathenea doth hereby charge Labes of Aexonia with having devoured a Sicilian cheese by himself without accomplices. Penalty demanded, a collar of fig-tree wood.[100]

PHILOCLEON. Nay, a dog's death, if convicted.

BDELYCLEON. This is Labes, the defendant.

PHILOCLEON. Oh! what a wretched brute! how entirely he looks the rogue! He thinks to deceive me by keeping his jaws closed. Where is the plaintiff, the dog of Cydathenea?

DOG. Bow wow! bow wow!

BDELYCLEON. Here he is.

PHILOCLEON. Why, 'tis a second Labes, a great barker and a licker of dishes.

SOSIAS (*Herald*). Silence! Keep your seats! (*To Xanthias.*) And you, up on your feet and accuse him.

PHILOCLEON. Go on, and I will help myself and eat these lentils.

XANTHIAS. Men of the jury, listen to this indictment I have drawn up. He has committed the blackest of crimes, both against me and the seamen.[101] He sought refuge in a dark corner to glutton on a big Sicilian cheese, with which he sated his hunger.

PHILOCLEON. Why, the crime is clear; the foul brute this very moment belched forth a horrible odour of cheese right under my nose.

XANTHIAS. And he refused to share with me. And yet can anyone style himself your benefactor, when he does not cast a morsel to your poor dog?

PHILOCLEON. Then he has not shared?

XANTHIAS. Not with me, his comrade.

PHILOCLEON. Then his madness is as hot as my lentils.

BDELYCLEON. In the name of the gods, father! No hurried verdict without hearing the other side!

PHILOCLEON. But the evidence is plain; the fact speaks for itself.

XANTHIAS. Then beware of acquitting the most selfish of canine gluttons, who has devoured the whole cheese, rind and all, prowling round the platter.

PHILOCLEON. There is not even enough left for me to fill up the chinks in my pitcher.

XANTHIAS. Besides, you *must* punish him, because the same house cannot keep two thieves. Let me not have barked in vain, else I shall never bark again.

PHILOCLEON. Oh! the black deeds he has just denounced! What a shameless thief! Say, cock, is not that your opinion too? Ha, ha! He thinks as I do. Here, Thesmothetes![102] where are you? Hand me the vessel.

SOSIAS (*Thesmothetes*). Take it yourself. I go to call the witnesses; these are a plate, a pestle, a cheese knife, a brazier, a stew-pot and other half-burnt utensils. (*To Philocleon.*) But you have not finished? you are piddling away still! Have done and be seated.

PHILOCLEON. Ha, ha! I reckon I know somebody who will shit himself with fright today.

BDELYCLEON. Will you never cease showing yourself hard and intractable, and especially to the accused? You tear them to pieces tooth and nail.

PHILOCLEON. Come forward and defend yourself. What means this silence?
Answer.

SOSIAS. No doubt he has nothing to say.

BDELYCLEON. Not so, but I think he has got what happened once to Thucydides, when accused;[103] his jaws suddenly set fast. Get away! I will undertake your defence.—Gentlemen of the jury, 'tis a difficult thing to speak for a dog who has been calumniated, but nevertheless I will try. 'Tis a good dog, and he chivies the wolves finely.

PHILOCLEON. He! that thief and conspirator!

BDELYCLEON. But 'tis the best of all our dogs; he is capable of guarding a whole flock.

PHILOCLEON. And what good is that, if he eats the cheese?

BDELYCLEON. What? he fights for you, he guards your door; 'tis an excellent dog in every respect. Forgive him his larceny; he is wretchedly ignorant, he cannot play the lyre.

PHILOCLEON. I wish he did not know how to write either; then the rascal would not have drawn up his pleadings.

BDELYCLEON. Witnesses, I pray you, listen. Come forward, grafting-knife, and speak up; answer me clearly. You were paymaster at the time. Did you grate out to the soldiers what was given you?—He says he did so.

PHILOCLEON. But, by Zeus! he lies.

BDELYCLEON. Oh! have patience. Take pity on the unfortunate. Labes feeds only on fish-bones and fishes' heads and has not an instant of peace. The other is good only to guard the house; he never moves from here, but demands his share of all that is brought in and bites those who refuse.

PHILOCLEON. Oh! Heaven! have I fallen ill? I feel my anger cooling! Woe to me! I am softening!

BDELYCLEON. Have pity, father, pity, I adjure you; you would not have him dead. Where are his puppies? Come, poor little beasties, yap, up on your haunches, beg and whine!

PHILOCLEON. Descend, descend, descend, descend![104]

BDELYCLEON. I will descend, although that word, "descend," has too often raised false hope. None the less, I will descend.

PHILOCLEON. Plague seize it! Have I then done wrong to eat! What! I to be crying! Ah! I certainly should not be weeping, if I were not blown out with lentils.

BDELYCLEON. Then he is acquitted?

PHILOCLEON. I did not say so.

BDELYCLEON. Ah! my dear father, be good! be humane! Take this voting pebble and rush with your eyes closed to that second urn[105] and, father, acquit him.

PHILOCLEON. No, I know no more how to acquit than to play the lyre.

BDELYCLEON. Come quickly, I will show you the way.

PHILOCLEON. Is this the first urn?

BDELYCLEON. Yes.

PHILOCLEON. Then I have voted.

BDELYCLEON (*aside*). I have fooled him and he has acquitted in spite of himself.

PHILOCLEON. Come, I will turn out the urns. What is the result?

BDELYCLEON. We shall see.—Labes, you stand acquitted.—Eh! father, what's the matter, what is it?

PHILOCLEON. Ah me! ah me! water! water!

BDELYCLEON. Pull yourself together, sir!

PHILOCLEON. Tell me! Is he really acquitted?

BDELYCLEON. Yes, certainly.

PHILOCLEON. Then it's all over with me!

BDELYCLEON. Courage, dear father, don't let this afflict you so terribly.

PHILOCLEON. And so I have charged my conscience with the acquittal of an accused being! What will become of me? Sacred gods! forgive me. I did it despite myself; it is not in my character.

BDELYCLEON. Do not vex yourself, father; I will feed you well, will take you everywhere to eat and drink with me; you shall go to every feast; henceforth your life shall be nothing but pleasure, and Hyperbolus shall no longer have you for a tool. But come, let us go in.

PHILOCLEON. So be it; if you will, let us go in.

CHORUS (*Parabasis*). Go where it pleases you and may your happiness be great. You meanwhile, oh! countless myriads, listen to the sound counsels I am going to give you and take care they are not lost upon you. 'Twould be the fate of vulgar spectators, not that of such an audience. Hence, people, lend me your ear, if you love frank speaking. The poet has a reproach to make against his audience; he says you have ill-treated him in return for the many services he has rendered you. At first he kept himself in the background and lent help secretly to other poets,[106] and like the prophetic Genius, who hid himself in the belly of Eurycles,[107] slipped within the spirit of another and whispered to him many a comic hit. Later he ran the risks of the theatre on his own account, with his face uncovered, and dared to guide his Muse unaided. Though overladen with success and honours more than any of your poets, indeed despite all his glory, he does not yet believe he has attained his goal; his heart is not swollen with pride and he does not seek to seduce the young folk in the wrestling school.[108] If any lover runs up to him to complain because he is furious at seeing the object of his passion derided on the stage, he takes no heed of such reproaches, for he is only inspired with honest motives and his Muse is no go-between. From the very outset of his dramatic career he has disdained to assail those who were men, but with a courage worthy of Heracles himself he attacked the most formidable monsters, and at the beginning went straight for that beast[109] with the sharp teeth, with the terrible eyes that flashed lambent fire like those of Cynna,[110] surrounded by a hundred lewd flatterers who spittle-licked him to his heart's content; it had a voice like a roaring torrent, the stench of a seal, a foul Lamia's testicles,[111] and the rump of a camel. Our poet did not tremble at the sight of this horrible monster, nor did he dream of gaining him over; and again this very day he is fighting for your good. Last year besides, he attacked those pale, shivering and feverish beings[112] who strangled your fathers in the dark, throttled your grandfathers,[113] and who, lying in the beds of the most inoffensive, piled up against them lawsuits, summonses and witnesses to such an extent, that many of them flew in terror to the Polemarch for refuge.[114] Such is the champion you have found to purify your country of all its evil, and last year you betrayed him,[115] when he sowed the most novel ideas, which, however, did not strike root, because you did not understand their value; notwithstanding this, he swears by Bacchus, the while offering him libations, that none ever heard better comic verses. 'Tis a disgrace to you not to have caught their drift at once; as for the poet, he is none the less appreciated by the enlightened judges. He shivered his oars in rushing boldly forward to board his foe.[116] But in future, my dear fellow-citizens, love and honour more those of your poets who seek to imagine and express some new thought. Make their ideas your own, keep them in your caskets

41

like sweet-scented fruit.[117] If you do, your clothing will emit an odour of wisdom the whole year through.

Formerly we were untiring, especially in *other* exercises,[118] but 'tis over now; our brow is crowned with hair whiter than the swan. We must, however, rekindle a youthful ardour in these remnants of what was, and for myself, I prefer my old age to the curly hair and the finery of all these lewd striplings.

Should any among you spectators look upon me with wonder, because of this wasp waist, or not know the meaning of this sting, I will soon dispel his ignorance. We, who wear this appendage, are the true Attic men, who alone are noble and native to the soil, the bravest of all people. 'Tis we who, weapon in hand, have done so much for the country, when the Barbarian shed torrents of fire and smoke over our city in his relentless desire to seize our nests by force. At once we ran up, armed with lance and buckler, and, drunk with the bitter wine of anger, we gave them battle, man standing to man and rage distorting our lips.[119] A hail of arrows hid the sky. However, by the help of the gods, we drove off the foe towards evening. Before the battle an owl had flown over our army.[120] Then we pursued them with our lance point in their loins as one hunts the tunny-fish; they fled and we stung them in the jaw and in the eyes, so that even now the barbarians tell each other that there is nothing in the world more to be feared than the Attic wasp.

Oh! at that time I was terrible, I feared nothing; forth on my galleys I went in search of my foe and subjected him.[121] Then we never thought of rounding fine phrases, we never dreamt of calumny; 'twas who should prove the strongest rower. And thus we took many a town from the Medes,[122] and 'tis to us that Athens owes the tributes that our young men thieve to-day.

Look well at us, and you will see that we have all the character and habits of the wasp. Firstly, if roused, no beings are more irascible, more relentless than we are. In all other things, too, we act like wasps. We collect in swarms, in a kind of nests,[123] and some go a-judging with the Archon,[124] some with the Eleven,[125] others at the Odeon;[126] there are yet others, who hardly move at all, like the grubs in the cells, but remain glued to the walls[127] and bent double to the ground. We also pay full attention to the discovery of all sorts of means of existing and sting the first who comes, so as to live at his expense. Finally, we have among us drones,[128] who have no sting and who, without giving themselves the least trouble, seize on our revenues as they flow past them and devour them. 'Tis this that grieves us most of all, to see men who have never served or held either lance or oar in defence of their country, enriching themselves at our expense without ever raising a blister on their hands. In short, I give it as my deliberate opinion that in future every citizen not possessed of a sting shall not receive the triobolus.

PHILOCLEON. As long as I live, I will never give up this cloak; 'tis the one I wore in that battle[129] when Boreas delivered us from such fierce attacks,

BDELYCLEON. You do not know what is good for you.

PHILOCLEON. Ah! I know not how to use fine clothing! T'other day, when cramming myself with fried fish, I dropped so many grease spots that I had to pay three obols to the cleaner.

BDELYCLEON. At least have a try, since you have once for all handed the care for your well-being over to me.

PHILOCLEON. Very well then! what must I do?

BDELYCLEON. Take off your cloak, and put on this tunic in its stead.

PHILOCLEON. 'Twas well worth while to beget and bring up children, so that this one should now wish to choke me.

BDELYCLEON. Come, take this tunic and put it on without so much talk.

PHILOCLEON. Great gods! what sort of a cursed garment is this?

BDELYCLEON. Some call it a pelisse, others a Persian cloak.[130]

PHILOCLEON. Ah! I thought it was a wraprascal like those made at Thymaetia.[131]

BDELYCLEON. Pray, how should you know such garments? 'Tis only at Sardis you could have seen them, and you have never been there.

PHILOCLEON. I' faith, no! but it seems to me exactly like the mantle Morychus[132] sports.

BDELYCLEON. Not at all; I tell you they are woven at Ecbatana.

PHILOCLEON. What! are there woollen ox-guts[133] then at Ecbatana?

BDELYCLEON. Whatever are you talking about? These are woven by the Barbarians at great cost. I am certain this pelisse has consumed more than a talent of wool.[134]

PHILOCLEON. It should be called wool-waster then instead of pelisse.

BDELYCLEON. Come, father, just hold still for a moment and put it on.

PHILOCLEON. Oh! horrors! what a waft of heat the hussy wafts up my nose!

BDELYCLEON. Will you have done with this fooling?

PHILOCLEON. No, by Zeus! if need be, I prefer you should put me in the oven.

BDELYCLEON. Come! I will put it round you. There!

PHILOCLEON. At all events, bring out a crook.

BDELYCLEON. Why, whatever for?

PHILOCLEON. To drag me out of it before I am quite melted.

BDELYCLEON. Now take off those wretched clogs and put on these nice Laconian slippers.

PHILOCLEON. I put on odious slippers made by our foes! Never!

BDELYCLEON. Come! put your foot in and push hard. Quick!

PHILOCLEON. 'Tis ill done of you. You want me to put my foot on Laconian ground.

BDELYCLEON. Now the other.

PHILOCLEON. Ah! no, not that one; one of its toes holds the Laconians in horror.

BDELYCLEON. Positively you must.

PHILOCLEON. Alas! alas! Then I shall have no chilblains in my old age.[135]

BDELYCLEON. Now, hurry up and get them on; and now imitate the easy effeminate gait of the rich. See, like this.

PHILOCLEON. There!... Look at my get-up and tell me which rich man I most resemble in my walk.

BDELYCLEON. Why, you look like a garlic plaster on a boil.

PHILOCLEON. Ah! I am longing to swagger and sway my rump about.

BDELYCLEON. Now, will you know how to talk gravely with well-informed men of good class?

PHILOCLEON. Undoubtedly.

BDELYCLEON. What will you say to them?

PHILOCLEON. Oh, lots of things. First of all I shall say, that Lamia,[136] seeing herself caught, let fly a fart; then, that Cardopion and her mother....

BDELYCLEON. Come, no fabulous tales, pray! talk of realities, of domestic facts, as is usually done.

PHILOCLEON. Ah! I know something that is indeed most domestic. Once upon a time there was a rat and a cat....

BDELYCLEON. "Oh, you ignorant fool," as Theagenes said[137] to the scavenger in a rage. Are you going to talk of cats and rats among high-class people?

PHILOCLEON. Then what should I talk about?

BDELYCLEON. Tell some dignified story. Relate how you were sent on a solemn mission with Androcles and Clisthenes.

PHILOCLEON. On a mission! never in my life, except once to Paros,[138] a job which brought me in two obols a day.

BDELYCLEON. At least say, that you have just seen Ephudion making good play in the pancratium[139] with Ascondas and, that despite his age and his white hair, he is still robust in loin and arm and flank and that his chest is a very breastplate.

PHILOCLEON. Stop! stop! what nonsense! Who ever contested at the pancratium with a breast-plate on?

BDELYCLEON. That is how well-behaved folk like to talk. But another thing. When at wine, it would be fitting to relate some good story of your youthful days. What is your most brilliant feat?

PHILOCLEON. My best feat? Ah! 'twas when I stole Ergasion's vine-props.

BDELYCLEON. You and your vine-props! you'll be the death of me! Tell of one of your boar-hunts or of when you coursed the hare. Talk about some torch-race you were in; tell of some deed of daring.

PHILOCLEON. Ah! my most daring deed was when, quite a young man still, I prosecuted Phayllus, the runner, for defamation, and he was condemned by a majority of two votes.

BDELYCLEON. Enough of that! Now recline there, and practise the bearing that is fitting at table in society.

PHILOCLEON. How must I recline? Tell me quick!

BDELYCLEON. In an elegant style.

PHILOCLEON. Like this?

BDELYCLEON. Not at all.

PHILOCLEON. How then?

BDELYCLEON. Spread your knees on the tapestries and give your body the most easy curves, like those taught in the gymnasium. Then praise some bronze vase, survey the ceiling, admire the awning stretched over the court. Water is poured over our hands; the tables are spread; we sup and, after ablution, we now offer libations to the gods.

PHILOCLEON. But, by Zeus! this supper is but a dream, it appears!

BDELYCLEON. The flute-player has finished the prelude. The guests are Theorus, Aeschines, Phanus, Cleon, Acestor;[140] and beside this last, I don't know who else. You are with them. Shall you know exactly how to take up the songs that are started?

PHILOCLEON. Better than any born mountaineer of Attica.

BDELYCLEON. That we shall see. Suppose me to be Cleon. I am the first to begin the song of Harmodius, and you take it up: "There never was yet seen in Athens ...

PHILOCLEON. ... such a rogue or such a thief."[141]

BDELYCLEON. Why, you wretched man, 'twill be the end of you if you sing that. He will vow your ruin, your destruction, to chase you out of the country.

PHILOCLEON. Well! then I shall answer his threats with another song: "With your madness for supreme power, you will end by overthrowing the city, which even now totters towards ruin."

BDELYCLEON. And when Theorus, prone at Cleon's feet, takes his hand and sings, "Like Admetus, love those who are brave,"[142] what reply will you make him?

PHILOCLEON. I shall sing, "I know not how to play the fox, nor call myself the friend of both parties."

BDELYCLEON. Then comes the turn of Aeschines, the son of Sellus, and a well-trained and clever musician, who will sing, "Good things and riches for Clitagoras and me and eke for the Thessalians!"

PHILOCLEON. "The two of us have squandered a deal between us."

BDELYCLEON. At this game you seem at home. But come, we will go and dine with Philoctemon.—Slave! slave! place our dinner in a basket, and let us go for a good long drinking bout.

PHILOCLEON. By no means, it is too dangerous; for after drinking, one breaks in doors, one comes to blows, one batters everything. Anon, when the wine is slept off, one is forced to pay.

BDELYCLEON. Not if you are with decent people. Either they undertake to appease the offended person or, better still, you say something witty, you tell some comic story, perhaps one of those you have yourself heard at table, either in Aesop's style or in that of Sybaris; all laugh and the trouble is ended.

PHILOCLEON. Faith! 'tis worth while learning many stories then, if you are thus not punished for the ill you do. But come, no more delay!

CHORUS. More than once have I given proof of cunning and never of stupidity, but how much more clever is Amynias, the son of Sellus and of the race of forelock-wearers; him we saw one day coming to dine with Leogaras,[143] bringing as his share one apple and a pomegranate, and bear in mind he was as hungry as Antiphon.[144] He went on an embassy to Pharsalus,[145] and there he lived solely among the Thessalian mercenaries;[146] indeed, is he not the vilest of mercenaries himself?

Oh! blessed, oh! fortunate Automenes, how enviable is your fortune! You have three sons, the most industrious in the world; one is the friend of all, a very able man, the first among the lyre-players, the favourite of the Graces. The second is an actor, and his talent is beyond all praise. As for Ariphrades, he is by far the most gifted; his father would swear to me, that without any master whatever and solely through the spontaneous effort of his happy nature, he taught himself the use of his tongue in the lewd places[147] where he spends the whole of his time.

Some have said that I and Cleon were reconciled. This is the truth of the matter: Cleon was harassing me, persecuting and belabouring me in every way; and, when I was being fleeced, the public laughed at seeing me uttering such loud cries; not that they cared about me, but simply curious to know whether, when trodden down by my enemy, I would not hurl at him some taunt. Noticing this, I have played the wheedler a bit; but now, look! the prop is deceiving the vine![148]

XANTHIAS. Oh! tortoises! happy to have so hard a skin, thrice happy to carry this roof that protects your backs! Oh! creatures full of sense! what a happy thought to cover your bodies with this shell, which shields it from blows! As for me, I can no longer move; the stick has so belaboured my body.

CHORUS. Eh, what's the matter, child? for, old as he may be, one has the right to call anyone a child who has let himself be beaten.

XANTHIAS. Alas! my master is really the worst of all plagues. He was the most drunk of all the guests, and yet among them were Hippyllus, Antiphon, Lycon, Lysistratus, Theophrastus and Phrynichus. But he was a hundred times more insolent than any. As soon as he had stuffed himself with a host of good dishes, he began to leap and spring, to laugh and to let wind like a little ass well blown out with barley. Then he set to a-beating me with all his heart, shouting, "Slave! slave!" Lysistratus, as soon as he saw him, let fly this comparison at him. "Old fellow," said he, "you resemble one of the scum assuming the airs of a rich man or a stupid ass that has broken loose from its stable." "As for you," bawled the other at the top of his voice, "you are like a grasshopper,[149] whose cloak is worn to the thread, or like Sthenelus[150] after his clothes had been sold." All applauded excepting Theophrastus, who made a grimace as behoved a well-bred man like him. The old man called to him, "Hi! tell me then what you have to be proud of? Not so much mouthing, you, who so well know how to play the buffoon and to lick-spittle the rich!" 'Twas thus he insulted each in turn with the grossest of jests, and he reeled off a thousand of the most absurd and ridiculous speeches. At last, when he was thoroughly drunk, he started towards here, striking everyone he met. Hold, here he comes reeling along. I will be off for fear of his blows.

PHILOCLEON.[151] Halt! and let everyone begone, or I shall do an evil turn to some of those who insist on following me. Clear off, rascals, or I shall roast you with this torch!

BDELYCLEON. We shall all make you smart to-morrow for your youthful pranks. We shall come in a body to summon you to justice.

PHILOCLEON. Ho! ho! summon me! what old women's babble! Know that I can no longer bear to hear even the name of suits. Ha! ha! ha! this is what pleases *me*, "Down with the urns!" Won't you begone? Down with the dicasts! away with them, away with them! (*To the flute-girl.*) Mount up there, my little gilded cock-chafer; seize hold of this rope's end in your hand.[152] Hold it tight, but have a care; the rope's a bit old and worn, but it loves a nice rubbing still. Do you see how opportunely I get you away from the solicitations of those fellows, who wanted to make you work their tools in your mouth? You therefore owe me this return to gratify mine by masturbating it. But will you pay the debt? Oh! I know well you will not even try; you will play with me, you will laugh heartily at my poor old weapon as you have done at many another man's. And yet, if you would not be a naughty girl, I would redeem you, when my son is dead, and you should be my concubine, my little cuntling. At present I am not my own master; I am very young and am watched very closely. My dear son never lets me out of his sight; 'tis an unbearable creature, who would quarter a thread and skin a flint; he is afraid I should get lost, for I am his only father. But here he comes running towards us. But be quick, don't stir, hold these torches. I am going to play him a young man's trick, the same as he played me before I was initiated into the mysteries.

BDELYCLEON. Oh! oh! you debauched old dotard! you desire and, meseems, you love pretty baggages; but, by Apollo, it shall not be with impunity!

PHILOCLEON. Ah! you would be very glad to eat a lawsuit in vinegar, you would.

BDELYCLEON. 'Tis a rascally trick to steal the flute-girl away from the other guests.

PHILOCLEON. What flute-girl? Are you distraught, as if you had just returned from Pluto?

BDELYCLEON. By Zeus! But here is the Dardanian wench in person.[153]

PHILOCLEON. Nonsense. This is a torch that I have lit in the public square in honour of the gods.

BDELYCLEON. Is this a torch?

PHILOCLEON. A torch? Certainly. Do you not see it is of several different colours?

BDELYCLEON. And what is that black part in the middle?[154]

PHILOCLEON. 'Tis the pitch running out while it burns.

BDELYCLEON. And there, on the other side, surely that is a girl's bottom?

PHILOCLEON. No. 'Tis a small bit of the torch, that projects.

BDELYCLEON. What do you mean? what bit? Hi! you woman! come here!

PHILOCLEON. Ah! ah! What do you want to do?

BDELYCLEON. To take her from you and lead her away. You are too much worn out and can do nothing.

PHILOCLEON. Hear me! One day, at Olympia, I saw Euphudion boxing bravely against Ascondas;[155] he was already aged, and yet with a blow from his fist he knocked down his young opponent. So beware lest I blacken *your* eyes.

BDELYCLEON. By Zeus! you have Olympia at your finger-ends!

A BAKER'S WIFE (*to Bdelycleon*). Come to my help, I beg you, in the name of the gods! This cursed man, when striking out right and left with his torch, knocked over ten loaves worth an obolus apiece, and then, to cap the deal, four others.

BDELYCLEON. Do you see what lawsuits you are drawing upon yourself with your drunkenness? You will have to plead.

PHILOCLEON. Oh, no, no! a little pretty talk and pleasant tales will soon settle the matter and reconcile her with me.

BAKER'S WIFE. Not so, by the goddesses twain! It shall not be said that you have with impunity spoilt the wares of Myrtia,[156] the daughter of Ancylion and Sostraté.

PHILOCLEON. Listen, woman, I wish to tell you a lovely anecdote.

BAKER'S WIFE. Oh! friend, no anecdotes for me, thank you.

PHILOCLEON. One night Aesop was going out to supper. A drunken bitch had the impudence to bark near him. Aesop said to her, "Oh, bitch, bitch! you would do well to sell your wicked tongue and buy some wheat."

BAKER'S WIFE. You make a mock of me! Very well! Be you who you like, I shall summons you before the market inspectors[157] for damage done to my business. Chaerephon[158] here shall be my witness.

PHILOCLEON. But just listen, here's another will perhaps please you better. Lasus and Simonides[159] were contesting against each other for the singing prize. Lasus said, "Damn me if I care."

BAKER'S WIFE. Ah! really, did he now!

PHILOCLEON. As for you, Chaerephon, *can* you be witness to this woman, who looks as pale and tragic as Ino when she throws herself from her rock[160] … at the feet of Euripides?

BDELYCLEON. Here, methinks, comes another to summons you; *he* has his witness too. Ah! unhappy indeed we are!

ACCUSER. I summons you, old man, for outrage.

BDELYCLEON. For outrage? Oh! in the name of the gods, do not summons him! I will be answerable for him; name the penalty and I will be more grateful still.

PHILOCLEON. I ask for nothing better than to be reconciled with him; for I admit I struck him and threw stones at him. So, first come here. Will you leave it in my hands to name the indemnity I must pay, if I promise you my friendship as well, or will you fix it yourself?

ACCUSER. Fix it; I like neither lawsuits nor disputes.

PHILOCLEON. A man of Sybaris[161] fell from his chariot and wounded his head most severely; he was a very poor driver. One of his friends came up to him and said, "Every man to his trade." Well then, go you to Pittalus[162] to get mended.

BDELYCLEON. You are incorrigible.

ACCUSER (*to his witness*). At all events, make a note of his reply.

PHILOCLEON. Listen, instead of going off so abruptly. A woman at Sybaris broke a box.

ACCUSER (*to his witness*). I again ask you to witness this.

PHILOCLEON. The box therefore had the fact attested, but the woman said, "Never worry about witnessing the matter, but hurry off to buy a cord to tie it together with; 'twill be the more sensible course."

ACCUSER. Oh! go on with your ribaldry until the Archon calls the case.

BDELYCLEON (*to Philocleon*). No, by Demeter! you stay here no longer! I take you and carry you off.

PHILOCLEON. And what for?

BDELYCLEON. What for? I shall carry you to the house; else there would not be enough witnesses for the accusers.

PHILOCLEON. One day at Delphi, Aesop ...

BDELYCLEON. I don't care a fig for that.

PHILOCLEON. … was accused of having stolen a sacred vase. But he replied, that the horn beetle … (*Philocleon goes on with his fable while Bdelycleon is carrying him off the scene by main force.*)

BDELYCLEON. Oh, dear, dear! You drive me crazy with your horn-beetle.

CHORUS. I envy you your happiness, old man. What a contrast to his former frugal habits and his very hard life! Taught now in quite another school, he will know nothing but the pleasures of ease. Perhaps he will jib at it, for indeed 'tis difficult to renounce what has become one's second nature. However, many have done it, and adopting the ideas of others, have changed their use and wont. As for Philocleon's son, I, like all wise and judicious men, cannot sufficiently praise his filial tenderness and his tact. Never have I met a more amiable nature, and I have conceived the greatest fondness for him. How he triumphed on every point in his discussion with his father, when he wanted to bring him back to more worthy and honourable tastes!

XANTHIAS. By Bacchus! 'Tis some Evil Genius has brought this unbearable disorder into our house. The old man, full up with wine and excited by the sound of the flute, is so delighted, so enraptured, that he spends the night executing the old dances that Thespis first produced on the stage,[163] and just now he offered to prove to the modern tragedians, by disputing with them for the dancing prize, that they are nothing but a lot of old dotards.

PHILOCLEON. "Who loiters at the door of the vestibule?"[164]

XANTHIAS. Here comes our pest, our plague!

PHILOCLEON. Let down the barriers.[165] The dance is now to begin.

XANTHIAS. Or rather the madness.

PHILOCLEON. Impetuous movement already twists and racks my sides. How my nostrils wheeze! how my back cracks!

XANTHIAS. Go and fill yourself with hellebore.[166]

PHILOCLEON. Phrynichus is as bold as a cock and terrifies his rivals.

XANTHIAS. Oh! oh! have a care he does not kick you.

PHILOCLEON. His leg kicks out sky-high, and his arse gapes open.[167]

XANTHIAS. Do have a care.

PHILOCLEON. Look how easily my leg-joints move.

BDELYCLEON. Great gods! What does all this mean? Is it actual, downright madness?

PHILOCLEON. And now I summon and challenge my rivals. If there be a tragic poet who pretends to be a skilful dancer, let him come and contest the matter with me. Is there one? Is there *not* one?

BDELYCLEON. Here comes one, and one only.

PHILOCLEON. Who is the wretch?

BDELYCLEON. 'Tis the younger son of Carcinus.[168]

PHILOCLEON. I will crush him to nothing; in point of keeping time, I will knock him out, for he knows nothing of rhythm.

BDELYCLEON. Ah! ah! here comes his brother too, another tragedian, and another son of Carcinus.

PHILOCLEON. Him I will devour for my dinner.

BDELYCLEON. Oh! ye gods! I see nothing but crabs.[169] Here is yet another son of Carcinus.

PHILOCLEON. What is't comes here? A shrimp or a spider?[170]

BDELYCLEON. 'Tis a crab,[171]—a crabkin, the smallest of its kind; he writes tragedies.

PHILOCLEON. Oh! Carcinus, how proud you should be of your brood! What a crowd of kinglets have come swooping down here!

BDELYCLEON. Come, come, my poor father, you will have to measure yourself against them.

PHILOCLEON. Have pickle prepared for seasoning them, if I am bound to prove the victor.

CHORUS. Let us stand out of the way a little, so that they may twirl at their ease. Come, illustrious children of this inhabitant of the briny, brothers of the shrimps, skip on the sand and the shore of the barren sea; show us the lightning whirls and twirls of your nimble limbs. Glorious offspring of Phrynichus,[172] let fly your kicks, so that the spectators may be overjoyed at seeing your legs so high in air. Twist, twirl, tap your bellies, kick your legs to the sky. Here comes your famous father, the ruler of the sea,[173] delighted to see his three lecherous kinglets.[174] Go on with your dancing, if it pleases you, but as for us, we shall not join you. Lead us promptly off the stage, for never a Comedy yet was seen where the Chorus finished off with a dance.

* * * * *

FINIS OF "THE WASPS"

* * * * *

Footnotes:

[1] Meaning, Bdelycleon will thrash you if you do not keep a good watch on his father.

[2] The Corybantes, priests of Cybelé, comported themselves like madmen in the celebration of their mysteries and made the air resound with the the noise of their drums.

[3] Cleonymus had shown himself equally cowardly on all occasions; he is frequently referred to by Aristophanes, both in this and other comedies.

[4] The cloak and the staff were the insignia of the dicasts; the poet describes them as sheep, because they were Cleon's servile tools.

[5] An allusion to Cleon, who was a tanner.

[6] In Greek, [Greek: d_emos] ([Greek: d_emós], *fat*; [Greek: d_êmos], *people*) means both *fat* and *people*.

[7] A tool of Cleon's; he had been sent on an embassy to Persia (*vide* 'The Acharnians'). The crow is a thief and rapacious, just as Theorus was.

[8] In his life of Alcibiades, Plutarch mentions this defect in his speech; or it may have been a 'fine gentleman' affectation.

[9] Among the Greeks, *going to the crows* was equivalent to our *going to the devil*.

[10] No doubt the fee generally given to the street diviners who were wont to interpret dreams.

[11] Coarse buffoonery was welcomed at Megara, where, by the by, it is said that Comedy had its birth.

[12] To gain the favour of the audience, the Comic poets often caused fruit and cakes to be thrown to them.

[13] The gluttony of Heracles was a constant subject of jest with the Comic poets.

[14] The incident of Pylos (see 'The Knights').

[15] The Greek word for *friend of strangers* is [Greek: philoxenos], which happened also to be the name of one of the vilest debauchees in Athens.

[16] The tribunal of the Heliasts came next in dignity only to the Areopagus. The dicasts, or jurymen, generally numbered 500; at times it would call in the assistance of one or two other tribunals, and the number of judges would then rise to 1000 or even 1500.

[17] A water-clock, used in the courts for limiting the time of the pleaders.

[18] The pebble was held between the thumb and two fingers, in the same way as one would hold a pinch of incense.

[19] A young Athenian of great beauty, also mentioned by Plato in his 'Gorgias.' Lovers were font of writing the name of the object of their adoration on the walls (see 'The Acharnians').

[20] [Greek: K_emos], the Greek term for the funnel-shaped top of the voting urn, into which the judges dropped their voting pebbles.

[21] Racine has introduced this incident with some modification into his 'Plaideurs.'

[22] Although called *Heliasts* ([Greek: H_elios], the sun, the judges sat under cover. One of the columns that supported the roof is here referred to.

[23] The juryman gave his vote for condemnation by tracing a line horizontally across a waxed tablet. This was one method in use; another was by means of pebbles placed in one or other of two voting urns.

[24] Used for the purpose of voting. There were two urns, one for each of the two opinions, and each heliast placed a pebble in one of them.

[25] The Heliast's badge of office.

[26] To prepare him for initiation into the mysteries of the Corybantes.

[27] Who pretended to cure madness; they were priests of Cybelé.

[28] The sacred instrument of the Corybantes.

[29] *Friend of Cleon,* who had raised the daily salary of the Heliasts to three obols.

[30] *Enemy of Cleon.*

[31] The smoke of fig-wood is very acrid, like the character of the Heliasts.

[32] Used for closing the chimney, when needed.

[33] Which had been stretched all round the courtyard to prevent his escape.

[34] Market-day.

[35] He enters the courtyard, returning with the ass, under whose belly Philocleon is clinging.

[36] In the Odyssey (Bk. IX) Homer makes his hero, 'the wily' Odysseus, escape from the Cyclops' cave by clinging on under a ram's belly, which slips past its blinded master without noticing the trick played on him. Odysseus, when asked his name by the Cyclops, replies,*Outis*, Nobody.

[37] A name formed out of two Greek words, meaning, *running away on a horse.*

[38] The story goes that a traveller who had hired an ass, having placed himself in its shadow to escape the heat of the sun, was sued by the driver, who had pretended that he had let the ass, not but its shadow; hence the Greek proverb, *to quarrel about the shade of an ass*, i.e. about nothing at all.

[39] When you inherit from me.

[40] There is a similar incident in the 'Plaideurs.'

[41] A Macedonian town in the peninsula of Pallené; it had shaken off the Athenian yoke and was not retaken for two years.

[42] A disciple of Thespis, who even in his infancy devoted himself to the dramatic art. He was the first to introduce female characters on the stage. He flourished about 500 B.C., having won his first prize for Tragedy in 511 B.C., twelve years before Aeschylus.

[43] Originally subjected to Sparta by Pausanias in 478 B.C., it was retaken by Cimon in 471, or forty-eight years previous to the production of 'The Wasps.' The old Heliasts refer to this latter event.

[44] An Athenian general, who had been defeated when sent to Sicily with a fleet to the succour of Leontini; no doubt Cleon had charged him with treachery.

[45] The Samians were in league with the Persians, but a certain Carystion betrayed the plot, and thanks to this the Athenians were able to retake Samos before the island had obtained help from Asia.

[46] The towns of Thrace, up to that time the faithful allies of Athens, were beginning to throw off her yoke.

[47] Who fulfilled the office of president.

[48] Meaning, "Will it only remain for us to throw ourselves into the water?" Hellé, taken by a ram across the narrow strait, called the Hellespont after her name, fell into the waves and was drowned.

[49] He is a prisoner inside, and speaks through the closed doors.

[50] This boiling, acid pickle reminds him of the fiery, acrid temper of the heliasts.

[51] A name invented for the occasion; it really means, *Cleon who holds the people in his snares*.

[52] When he entered Troy as a spy.

[53] The island of Naxos was taken by Cimon, in consequence of sedition in the town of Naxos, about fifty years before the production of 'The Wasps.'

[54] One of the titles under which Artemis, the goddess of the chase, was worshipped.

[55] Demeter and Persephone. This was an accusation frequently brought against people in Athens.

[56] An orator of great violence of speech and gesture.

[57] For Philocleon, the titulary god was Lycus, the son of Pandion, the King of Athens, because a statue stood erected to him close to the spot where the tribunals sat, and because he recognized no other fatherland but the tribunals.

[58] A debauchee and an embezzler of public funds, already mentioned a little above.

[59] Aristophanes speaks of him in 'The Birds' as a traitor and as an alien who usurped the rights of the city.

[60] A Greek proverb signifying "Much ado about nothing."

[61] A Spartan general, who perished in the same battle as Cleon, before Amphipolis, in 422 B.C.

[62] Meaning, the mere beginnings of any matter.

[63] This 'figure of love'—woman atop of the man—is known in Greek as [Greek: hippos] (Latin *equus*, 'the horse'); note the play upon words with the name Hippias.

[64] A tragic poet, who was a great lover of good cheer, it appears.

[65] Old men, who carried olive branches in the processions of the Panathenaea. Those whose great age or infirmity forbade their being used for any other purpose were thus employed.

[66] An obscene pun. [Greek: Choiros] means both *a sow* and the female organ.

[67] A celebrated actor.

[68] There were two tragedies named 'Niobé,' one by Aeschylus and the other by Sophocles, both now lost.

[69] A double strap, which flute-players applied to their lips and was said to give softness to the tones.

[70] The shell was fixed over the seal to protect it.

[71] A calumniator and a traitor (see 'The Acharnians').

[72] Cleonymus, whose name the poet modifies, so as to introduce the idea of a flatterer ([Greek: kolax]).

[73] Another flatterer, a creature of Cleon's.

[74] Athenian poor, having no purse, would put small coins into mouth for safety. We know that the triobolus was the daily of the judges. Its value was about 4-1/2 d.

[75] A jar of wine, which he had bought with his pay.

[76] A jar with two long ears or handles, in this way resembling an ass.

[77] A well-known flute-player.

[78] We have already seen that when accepting his son's challenge he swore to fall upon his sword if defeated in the debate.

[79] Pericles had first introduced the custom of sending poor citizens, among whom the land was divided, into the conquered countries. The island of Aegina had been mainly divided in this way among Athenian colonists.

[80] The choenix was a measure corresponding to our quart.

[81] A verse borrowed from Euripides' 'Bellerophon.'

[82] i.e. a legislator. The name given in Athens to the last six of the nine Archons, because it was their special duty to see the laws respected.

[83] Mentioned both in 'The Acharnians' and 'The Knights.'

[84] The drachma was worth six obols, or twice the pay of a heliast.

[85] We have already seen that the Athenians sometimes kept their small money in their mouth.

[86] Which were placed in the courts; dogs were sacrificed on them.

[87] As already stated, the statue of Lycus stood close to the place where the tribunals sat.

[88] The barrier in the Heliaea, which separated the heliasts from the public.

[89] The whole of this comic trial of the dog Labes is an allusion to the general Laches, already mentioned, who had failed in Sicily. He was accused of taking bribes of money from the Sicilians.

[90] To serve for a bar.

[91] This was a customary formula, [Greek: aph' Estias archou], "begin from Hestia," first adore Vesta, the god of the family hearth. In similar fashion, the Romans said, *ab Jove principium.*

[92] For conviction and acquittal.

[93] On which the sentence was entered.

[94] No doubt the stew-pot and the wine-jar.

[95] The *article* Bdelycleon had brought.—The clepsydra was a kind of water-clock; the other vessel is compared to it, because of the liquid in it.

[96] A title of Apollo, worshipped as the god of healing.

[97] A title of Apollo, because of the sacrifices, which the Athenians offered him in the streets, from [Greek: aguia], a street.

[98] Bdelycleon.

[99] The formula used by the president before declaring the sitting of the Court opened.

[100] That is, by way of fine.

[101] A reference to the peculations Laches was supposed to have practised in keeping back part of the pay of the Athenian sailors engaged in the Sicilian Expedition.

[102] The [Greek: Thesmothetai] at Athens were the six junior Archons, who judged cases assigned to no special Court, presided at the allotment of magistrates, etc.

[103] Thucydides, son of Milesias, when accused by Pericles, could not say a word in his own defence. One would have said his tongue was paralysed. He was banished.—He must not be confounded with Thucydides the historian, whose exile took place after the production of 'The Wasps.'

[104] When the judges were touched by the pleading of the orator and were decided on acquittal, they said to the defending advocate, "*Cease speaking, descend from the rostrum.*"

[105] There were two urns, one called that of Conviction, the other of Acquittal.

[106] Meaning, that he had at first produced pieces under the name of other poets, such as Callistrates and Phidonides.

[107] Eurycles, an Athenian diviner, surnamed the Engastromythes ([Greek: muthos], speech, [Greek: en gastri], in the belly), because he was believed to

---

be inspired by a genius within him.—The same name was also given to the priestesses of Apollo, who spoke their oracles without moving their lips.

[108] Some poets misused their renown as a means of seduction among young men.

[109] Cleon, whom he attacked in 'The Knights,' the first Comedy that Aristophanes had produced in his own name.

[110] Cynna, like Salabaccha, was a shameless courtesan of the day.

[111] The lamiae were mysterious monsters, to whom the ancients ascribed the most varied forms. They were depicted most frequently with the face and bosom of a woman and the body of a serpent. Here Aristophanes endows them with organs of virility. It was said that the blood of young men had a special attraction for them. These lines, abusive of Cleon, occur again in the 'Peace,' II. 738-42.

[112] Socrates and the sophists, with whom the poet confounds him in his attacks.

[113] He likens them to vampires.

[114] The third Archon, whose duty was the protection of strangers. All cases involving the rights of citizenship were tried before him. These were a frequent cause of lawsuit at Athens.

[115] 'The Clouds' had not been well received.

[116] Aristophanes lets it be understood that the refusal to crown him arose from the fact that he had been too bold in his attack.

[117] To perfume their caskets, etc., the Ancients placed scented fruit, especially oranges, in them.

[118] The pastimes of love.

[119] At Marathon, where the Athenians defeated the Persian invaders, 490 B.C. The battle-field is a plain on the north-east coast of Attica, about twenty-seven miles from Athens.

[120] A favourable omen, of course. The owl was the bird of Athené.

[121] An allusion to Cimon's naval victories.

[122] The Cyclades islands and many towns on the coast of Asia Minor.

[123] The tribunals.

[124] The six last Archons presided over the civil courts and were styled Thesmothetae (see above).

[125] Magistrates, who had charge of criminal cases.

[126] Built by Pericles. Musical contests were held there. Here also took place distributions of flour, and the presence of the magistrates was no doubt necessary to decide on the spot any disputes that might arise regarding this.

[127] This, says the Scholiast, refers to magistrates appointed for the upkeep of the walls. They were selected by ballot from amongst the general body of Heliasts.

[128] The demagogues and their flatterers.

[129] The battle of Artemisium on the Euboean coast; a terrible storm arose and almost destroyed the barbarian fleet, while sparing that of the Athenians.

[130] A mantle trimmed with fur.

[131] A rural deme of Attica. Rough coats were made there, formed of skins sewn together.

[132] An effeminate poet.

[133] He compares the thick, shaggy stuff of the pelisse to the intestines of a bullock, which have a sort of crimped and curled look.

[134] An Attic talent was equal to about fifty-seven pounds avoirdupois.

[135] He grumbles over his own good fortune, as old men will.

[136] Lamia, the daughter of Belus and Libya, was loved by Zeus. Heré deprived her of her beauty and instilled her with a passion for blood; she is said to have plucked babes from their mothers' breast to devour them. Weary of her crimes, the gods turned her into a beast of prey.

[137] Theagenes, of the Acharnian deme, was afflicted with a weakness which caused him to be constantly letting off loud, stinking farts, even in public—the cause of many gibes on the part of the Comic poets and his contemporaries.

[138] He had been sent on a mission as an armed ambassador, i.e. as a common soldier, whose pay was two obols.

[139] The [Greek: pankration] was a combined exercise, including both wrestling and boxing.

[140] All these names have been already mentioned.

[141] Each time Philocleon takes up the song with words that are a satire on the guest who begins the strain.

[142] King Admetus (Euripides' 'Alcestis') had suffered his devoted wife Alcestis to die to save his life when ill to death. Heracles, however, to repay former benefits received, descended into Hades and rescued Alcestis from Pluto's clutches.

[143] A famous epicure, the Lucullus of Athens (see 'The Acharnians').

[144] A parasite renowned for his gluttony.

[145] A town in Thessaly.

[146] Because of his poverty.

[147] Four lines in 'The Knights' describe the infamous habits of Ariphrades in detail.

[148] That is, it ceases to support it; Aristophanes does the same to Cleon.

[149] Referring to Lysistratus' leanness.

[150] A tragic actor, whose wardrobe had been sold up, so the story went, by his creditors.

[151] He enters, followed closely by the persons he has ill-used, and leading a flute-girl by the hand.

[152] Meaning his penis.

[153] Dardanus, a district of Asia Minor, north of the Troad, supplied many flute-girls to the cities of Greece.

[154] Pointing to the flute-girl's *motte*.

[155] He tells his son the very story the latter had taught him.

[156] The name of the baker's wife.

[157] Or Agoranomi, who numbered ten at Athens.

[158] The disciple of Socrates.

[159] Lasus, a musician and dithyrambic poet, born about 500 B.C. in Argolis, was the rival of Simonides and thought himself his superior.

[160] Ino, the daughter of Cadmus and Harmonia. Being pursued by her husband, Athamas, whom the Fury Tisiphoné had driven mad, she threw herself into the sea with Melicerta, whereupon they were both changed into sea-goddesses.—This is the subject of one of Euripides' tragedies.

[161] A famous town in Magna Graecia, south coast of Italy.

[162] A celebrated physician.—Philocleon means, "Instead of starting an action, go and have yourself cared for; that is better worth your while."

[163] The dances that Thespis, the originator of Tragedy, interspersed with the speaking parts of his plays.

[164] A verse borrowed from an unknown Tragedy.

[165] As was done in the stadia when the races were to be started.

[166] The ancients considered it a specific against madness.

[167] Phrynichus, like all the ancient tragic writers, mingled many dances with his pieces.

[168] Tragic poet. His three sons had also written tragedies and were dancers into the bargain.

[169] Carcinus, by a mere transposition of the accent ([Greek: karkívos]), means *crab* in Greek; hence the pun.

[170] Carcinus' sons were small and thin.

[171] The third son of Carcinus.

[172] Meaning, the three sons of Carcinus, the dancers, because, as mentioned before, Phrynichus often introduced a chorus of dancers into his Tragedies.

[173] Carcinus himself.

[174] The Greek word is [Greek: triorchoi]—possessed of three testicles, of three-testicle power, inordinately lecherous; with the change of a letter ([Greek: triarchoi]) it means 'three rulers,' 'three kinglets.'

THE BIRDS

INTRODUCTION

The Birds' differs markedly from all the other Comedies of Aristophanes which have come down to us in subject and general conception. It is just an extravaganza pure and simple—a graceful, whimsical theme chosen expressly for the sake of the opportunities it afforded of bright, amusing dialogue, pleasing lyrical interludes, and charming displays of brilliant stage effects and pretty dresses. Unlike other plays of the same Author, there is here apparently no serious political *motif* underlying the surface burlesque and buffoonery.

Some critics, it is true, profess to find in it a reference to the unfortunate Sicilian Expedition, then in progress, and a prophecy of its failure and the political downfall of Alcibiades. But as a matter of fact, the whole thing seems rather an attempt on the dramatist's part to relieve the overwrought minds of his fellow-citizens, anxious and discouraged at the unsatisfactory reports from before Syracuse, by a work conceived in a lighter vein than usual and mainly unconnected with contemporary realities.

The play was produced in the year 414 B.C., just when success or failure in Sicily hung in the balance, though already the outlook was gloomy, and many circumstances pointed to impending disaster. Moreover, the public conscience was still shocked and perturbed over the mysterious affair of the mutilation of the Hermae, which had occurred immediately before the sailing of the fleet, and strongly suspicious of Alcibiades' participation in the outrage. In spite of the inherent charm of the subject, the splendid outbursts of lyrical poetry in some of the choruses and the beauty of the scenery and costumes, 'The Birds' failed to win the first prize. This was acclaimed to a play of Aristophanes' rival, Amipsias, the title of which, 'The Comastae,' *or* 'Revellers,' "seems to imply that the chief interest was derived from direct allusions to the outrage above mentioned and to the individuals suspected to have been engaged in it."

For this reason, which militated against its immediate success, viz. the absence of direct allusion to contemporary politics—there are, of course, incidental references here and there to topics and personages of the day—the play appeals perhaps more than any other of our Author's productions to the modern reader. Sparkling wit, whimsical fancy, poetic charm, are of all ages, and can be appreciated as readily by ourselves as by an Athenian audience of two thousand years ago, though, of course, much is inevitably lost "without the important adjuncts of music, scenery, dresses and what we may call 'spectacle' generally, which we know in this instance to have been on the most magnificent scale."

"The plot is this. Euelpides and Pisthetaerus, two old Athenians, disgusted with the litigiousness, wrangling and sycophancy of their countrymen, resolve upon quitting Attica. Having heard of the fame of Epops (the hoopoe), sometime called Tereus, and now King of the Birds, they determine, under the direction of a raven and a jackdaw, to seek from him and his subject birds a city free from all care and strife." Arrived at the Palace of Epops, they knock, and Trochilus (the wren), in a state of great flutter, as he mistakes them for fowlers, opens the door and informs them that his Majesty is asleep. When he awakes, the strangers appear before him, and after listening to a long and eloquent harangue on the superior attractions of a residence among the birds, they propose a notable scheme of their own to further enhance its advantages and definitely secure the sovereignty of the universe now exercised by the gods of Olympus.

The birds are summoned to meet in general council. They come flying up from all quarters of the heavens, and after a brief misunderstanding, during which they come near tearing the two human envoys to pieces, they listen to the exposition of the latters' plan. This is nothing less than the building of a new city, to be called Nephelococcygia, or 'Cloud-cuckoo-town,' between earth and heaven, to be garrisoned and guarded by the birds in such a way as to intercept all communication of the gods with their worshippers on earth. All steam of sacrifice will be prevented from rising to Olympus, and the Immortals will very soon be starved into an acceptance of any terms proposed.

The new Utopia is duly constructed, and the daring plan to secure the sovereignty is in a fair way to succeed. Meantime various quacks and charlatans, each with a special scheme for improving things, arrive from earth, and are one after the other exposed and dismissed. Presently arrives Prometheus, who informs Epops of the desperate straits to which the gods are by this time reduced, and advises him to push his claims and demand the hand of Basileia (Dominion), the handmaid of Zeus. Next an embassy from the Olympians appears on the scene, consisting of Heracles, Posidon and a god from the savage regions of the Triballians. After some disputation, it is agreed that all reasonable demands of the birds are to be granted, while Pisthetaerus is to have Basileia as his bride. The comedy winds up with the epithalamium in honour of the nuptials.

* * * * *

THE BIRDS

DRAMATIS PERSONAE

EUELPIDES.
PISTHETAERUS.
EPOPS (the Hoopoe).
TROCHILUS, Servant to Epops.
PHOENICOPTERUS.
HERALDS.
A PRIEST.
A POET.
A PROPHET.
METON, a Geometrician.
A COMMISSIONER.
A DEALER IN DECREES.
IRIS.
A PARRICIDE.
CINESIAS, a Dithyrambic Bard.
AN INFORMER.
PROMETHEUS.
POSIDON.
TRIBALLUS.
HERACLES.
SERVANT of PISTHETAERUS.
MESSENGERS.
CHORUS OF BIRDS.

SCENE: A wild, desolate tract of open country; broken rocks and brushwood occupy the centre of the stage.

* * * * *

THE BIRDS

EUELPIDES (*to his jay*).[175] Do you think I should walk straight for yon tree?

PISTHETAERUS (*to his crow*). Cursed beast, what are you croaking to me?... to retrace my steps?

EUELPIDES. Why, you wretch, we are wandering at random, we are exerting ourselves only to return to the same spot; 'tis labour lost.

PISTHETAERUS. To think that I should trust to this crow, which has made me cover more than a thousand furlongs!

EUELPIDES. And I to this jay, who has torn every nail from my fingers!

PISTHETAERUS. If only I knew where we were. . . .

EUELPIDES. Could you find your country again from here?

PISTHETAERUS. No, I feel quite sure I could not, any more than could Execestides[176] find his.

EUELPIDES. Oh dear! oh dear!

PISTHETAERUS. Aye, aye, my friend, 'tis indeed the road of "oh dears" we are following.

EUELPIDES. That Philocrates, the bird-seller, played us a scurvy trick, when he pretended these two guides could help us to find Tereus,[177] the Epops, who is a bird, without being born of one. He has indeed sold us this jay, a true son of Tharelides,[178] for an obolus, and this crow for three, but what can they do? Why, nothing whatever but bite and scratch!—What's the matter with you then, that you keep opening your beak? Do you want us to fling ourselves headlong down these rocks? There is no road that way.

PISTHETAERUS. Not even the vestige of a track in any direction.

EUELPIDES. And what does the crow say about the road to follow?

PISTHETAERUS. By Zeus, it no longer croaks the same thing it did.

EUELPIDES. And which way does it tell us to go now?

PISTHETAERUS. It says that, by dint of gnawing, it will devour my fingers.

EUELPIDES. What misfortune is ours! we strain every nerve to get to the birds,[179] do everything we can to that end, and we cannot find our way! Yes, spectators, our madness is quite different to that of Sacas. He is not a citizen, and would fain be one at any cost; we, on the contrary, born of an honourable tribe and family and living in the midst of our fellow-citizens, we have fled from our country as hard as ever we could go. 'Tis not that we hate it; we recognize it to be great and rich, likewise that everyone has the right to ruin himself; but the crickets only chirrup among the fig-trees for a month or two, whereas the Athenians spend their whole lives in chanting forth judgments from their law courts.[180] That is why we started off with a basket, a stew-pot and some myrtle boughs[181] and have come to seek a quiet country in which to settle. We are going to Tereus, the Epops, to learn from him, whether, in his aerial flights, he has noticed some town of this kind.

PISTHETAERUS. Here! look!

EUELPIDES. What's the matter?

PISTHETAERUS. Why, the crow has been pointing me to something up there for some time now.

EUELPIDES. And the jay is also opening its beak and craning its neck to show me I know not what. Clearly, there are some birds about here. We shall soon know, if we kick up a noise to start them.

PISTHETAERUS. Do you know what to do? Knock your leg against this rock.

EUELPIDES. And you your head to double the noise.

PISTHETAERUS. Well then use a stone instead; take one and hammer with it.

EUELPIDES. Good idea! Ho there, within! Slave! slave!

PISTHETAERUS. What's that, friend! You say, "slave," to summon Epops! 'Twould be much better to shout, "Epops, Epops!"

EUELPIDES. Well then, Epops! Must I knock again? Epops!

TROCHILUS. Who's there? Who calls my master?

EUELPIDES. Apollo the Deliverer! what an enormous beak![182]

TROCHILUS. Good god! they are bird-catchers.

EUELPIDES. The mere sight of him petrifies me with terror. What a horrible monster!

TROCHILUS. Woe to you!

EUELPIDES. But we are not men.

TROCHILUS. What are you, then?

EUELPIDES. I am the Fearling, an African bird.

TROCHILUS. You talk nonsense.

EUELPIDES. Well, then, just ask it of my feet.[183]

TROCHILUS. And this other one, what bird is it?

PISTHETAERUS. I? I am a Cackling,[184] from the land of the pheasants.

EUELPIDES. But you yourself, in the name of the gods! what animal are you?

TROCHILUS. Why, I am a slave-bird.

EUELPIDES. Why, have you been conquered by a cock?

TROCHILUS. No, but when my master was turned into a peewit, he begged me to become a bird too, to follow and to serve him.

EUELPIDES. Does a bird need a servant, then?

TROCHILUS. 'Tis no doubt because he was a man. At times he wants to eat a dish of loach from Phalerum; I seize my dish and fly to fetch him some. Again he wants some pea-soup; I seize a ladle and a pot and run to get it.

EUELPIDES. This is, then, truly a running-bird.[185] Come, Trochilus, do us the kindness to call your master.

TROCHILUS. Why, he has just fallen asleep after a feed of myrtle-berries and a few grubs.

EUELPIDES. Never mind; wake him up.

TROCHILUS. I am certain he will be angry. However, I will wake him to please you.

PISTHETAERUS. You cursed brute! why, I am almost dead with terror!

EUELPIDES. Oh! my god! 'twas sheer fear that made me lose my jay.

PISTHETAERUS. Ah! you great coward! were you so frightened that you let go your jay?

EUELPIDES. And did you not lose your crow, when you fell sprawling on the ground? Pray tell me that.

PISTHETAERUS. No, no.

EUELPIDES. Where is it, then?

PISTHETAERUS. It has flown away.

EUELPIDES. Then you did not let it go! Oh! you brave fellow!

EPOPS. Open the forest,[186] that I may go out!

EUELPIDES. By Heracles! what a creature! what plumage! What means this triple crest?

EPOPS. Who wants me?

EUELPIDES. The twelve great gods have used you ill, meseems.

EPOPS. Are you chaffing me about my feathers? I have been a man, strangers.

EUELPIDES. 'Tis not you we are jeering at.

EPOPS. At what, then?

EUELPIDES. Why, 'tis your beak that looks so odd to us.

EPOPS. This is how Sophocles outrages me in his tragedies. Know, I once was Tereus.[187]

EUELPIDES. You were Tereus, and what are you now? a bird or a peacock?[188]

EPOPS. I am a bird.

EUELPIDES. Then where are your feathers? For I don't see them.

EPOPS. They have fallen off.

EUELPIDES. Through illness.

EPOPS. No. All birds moult their feathers, you know, every winter, and others grow in their place. But tell me, who are you?

EUELPIDES. We? We are mortals.

EPOPS. From what country?

EUELPIDES. From the land of the beautiful galleys.[189]

EPOPS. Are you dicasts?[190]

EUELPIDES. No, if anything, we are anti-dicasts.

EPOPS. Is that kind of seed sown among you?[191]

EUELPIDES. You have to look hard to find even a little in our fields.

EPOPS. What brings you here?

EUELPIDES. We wish to pay you a visit.

EPOPS. What for?

EUELPIDES. Because you formerly were a man, like we are, formerly you had debts, as we have, formerly you did not want to pay them, like ourselves; furthermore, being turned into a bird, you have when flying seen all lands and seas. Thus you have all human knowledge as well as that of birds. And hence we have come to you to beg you to direct us to some cosy town, in which one can repose as if on thick coverlets.

EPOPS. And are you looking for a greater city than Athens?

EUELPIDES. No, not a greater, but one more pleasant to dwell in.

EPOPS. Then you are looking for an aristocratic country.

EUELPIDES. I? Not at all! I hold the son of Scellias in horror.[192]

EPOPS. But, after all, what sort of city would please you best?

EUELPIDES. A place where the following would be the most important business transacted.—Some friend would come knocking at the door quite early in the morning saying, "By Olympian Zeus, be at my house early, as soon as you have bathed, and bring your children too. I am giving a nuptial feast, so don't fail, or else don't cross my threshold when I am in distress."

EPOPS. Ah! that's what may be called being fond of hardships. And what say you?

PISTHETAERUS. My tastes are similar.

EPOPS. And they are?

PISTHETAERUS. I want a town where the father of a handsome lad will stop in the street and say to me reproachfully as if I had failed him, "Ah! Is this well done, Stilbonides! You met my son coming from the bath after the gymnasium and you neither spoke to him, nor embraced him, nor took him with you, nor ever once twitched his testicles. Would anyone call you an old friend of mine?"

EPOPS. Ah! wag, I see you are fond of suffering. But there is a city of delights, such as you want. 'Tis on the Red Sea.

EUELPIDES. Oh, no. Not a sea-port, where some fine morning the Salaminian[193] galley can appear, bringing a writ-server along. Have you no Greek town you can propose to us?

EPOPS. Why not choose Lepreum in Elis for your settlement?

EUELPIDES. By Zeus! I could not look at Lepreum without disgust, because of Melanthius.[194]

EPOPS. Then, again, there is the Opuntian, where you could live.

EUELPIDES. I would not be Opuntian[195] for a talent. But come, what is it like to live with the birds? You should know pretty well.

EPOPS. Why, 'tis not a disagreeable life. In the first place, one has no purse.

EUELPIDES. That does away with much roguery.

EPOPS. For food the gardens yield us white sesame, myrtle-berries, poppies and mint.

EUELPIDES. Why, 'tis the life of the newly-wed indeed.[196]

PISTHETAERUS. Ha! I am beginning to see a great plan, which will transfer the supreme power to the birds, if you will but take my advice.

EPOPS. Take your advice? In what way?

PISTHETAERUS. In what way? Well, firstly, do not fly in all directions with open beak; it is not dignified. Among us, when we see a thoughtless man, we ask, "What sort of bird is this?" and Teleas answers, "'Tis a man who has no brain, a bird that has lost his head, a creature you cannot catch, for it never remains in any one place."

EPOPS. By Zeus himself! your jest hits the mark. What then is to be done?

PISTHETAERUS. Found a city.

EPOPS. We birds? But what sort of city should we build?

PISTHETAERUS. Oh, really, really! 'tis spoken like a fool! Look down.

EPOPS. I am looking.

PISTHETAERUS. Now look upwards.

EPOPS. I am looking.

PISTHETAERUS. Turn your head round.

EPOPS. Ah! 'twill be pleasant for me, if I end in twisting my neck!

PISTHETAERUS. What have you seen?

EPOPS. The clouds and the sky.

PISTHETAERUS. Very well! is not this the pole of the birds then?

EPOPS. How their pole?

PISTHETAERUS. Or, if you like it, the land. And since it turns and passes through the whole universe, it is called, 'pole.'[197] If you build and fortify it, you will turn your pole into a fortified city.[198] In this way you will reign over mankind as you do over the grasshoppers and cause the gods to die of rabid hunger.

EPOPS. How so?

PISTHETAERUS. The air is 'twixt earth and heaven. When we want to go to Delphi, we ask the Boeotians[199] for leave of passage; in the same way, when men sacrifice to the gods, unless the latter pay you tribute, you exercise the right of every nation towards strangers and don't allow the smoke of the sacrifices to pass through your city and territory.

EPOPS. By earth! by snares! by network![200] I never heard of anything more cleverly conceived; and, if the other birds approve, I am going to build the city along with you.

PISTHETAERUS. Who will explain the matter to them?

EPOPS. You must yourself. Before I came they were quite ignorant, but since I have lived with them I have taught them to speak.

PISTHETAERUS. But how can they be gathered together?

EPOPS. Easily. I will hasten down to the coppice to waken my dear Procné;[201] as soon as they hear our voices, they will come to us hot wing.

PISTHETAERUS. My dear bird, lose no time, I beg. Fly at once into the coppice and awaken Procné.

EPOPS. Chase off drowsy sleep, dear companion. Let the sacred hymn gush from thy divine throat in melodious strains; roll forth in soft cadence your refreshing melodies to bewail the fate of Itys,[202] which has been the cause of so many tears to us both. Your pure notes rise through the thick leaves of the yew-tree right up to the throne of Zeus, where Phoebus listens to you, Phoebus with his golden hair. And his ivory lyre responds to your plaintive accents; he gathers the choir of the gods and from their immortal lips rushes a sacred chant of blessed voices. (*The flute is played behind the scene.*)

PISTHETAERUS. Oh! by Zeus! what a throat that little bird possesses. He has filled the whole coppice with honey-sweet melody!

EUELPIDES. Hush!

PISTHETAERUS. What's the matter?

EUELPIDES. Will you keep silence?

PISTHETAERUS. What for?

EUELPIDES. Epops is going to sing again.

EPOPS (*in the coppice*). Epopoi, poi, popoi, epopoi, popoi, here, here, quick, quick, quick, my comrades in the air; all you, who pillage the fertile lands of the husbandmen, the numberless tribes who gather and devour the barley seeds, the swift flying race who sing so sweetly. And you whose gentle twitter resounds through the fields with the little cry of tio, tio, tio, tio, tio, tio, tio, tio; and you who hop about the branches of the ivy in the gardens; the mountain birds, who feed on the wild olive berries or the arbutus, hurry to come at my call, trioto, trioto, totobrix; you also, who snap up the sharp-stinging gnats in the marshy vales, and you who dwell in the fine plain of Marathon, all damp with dew, and you, the francolin with speckled wings; you too, the halcyons, who flit over the swelling waves of the sea, come hither to hear the tidings; let all the tribes of long-necked birds assemble here; know that a clever old man has come to us, bringing an entirely new idea and proposing great reforms. Let all come to the debate here, here, here, here. Torotorotorotorotix, kikkobau, kikkobau, torotorotorotorolililix.

PISTHETAERUS. Can you see any bird?

EUELPIDES. By Phoebus, no! and yet I am straining my eyesight to scan the sky.

PISTHETAERUS. 'Twas really not worth Epops' while to go and bury himself in the thicket like a plover when a-hatching.

PHOENICOPTERUS. Torotina, torotina.

PISTHETAERUS. Hold, friend, here is another bird.

EUELPIDES. I' faith, yes! 'tis a bird, but of what kind? Isn't it a peacock?

PISTHETAERUS. Epops will tell us. What is this bird?

EPOPS. 'Tis not one of those you are used to seeing; 'tis a bird from the marshes.

PISTHETAERUS. Oh! oh! but he is very handsome with his wings as crimson as flame.

EPOPS. Undoubtedly; indeed he is called flamingo.[203]

EUELPIDES. Hi! I say! You!

PISTHETAERUS. What are you shouting for?

EUELPIDES. Why, here's another bird.

PISTHETAERUS. Aye, indeed; 'tis a foreign bird too. What is this bird from beyond the mountains with a look as solemn as it is stupid?

EPOPS. He is called the Mede.[204]

PISTHETAERUS. The Mede! But, by Heracles! how, if a Mede, has he flown here without a camel?

EUELPIDES. Here's another bird with a crest.

PISTHETAERUS. Ah! that's curious. I say, Epops, you are not the only one of your kind then?

EPOPS. This bird is the son of Philocles, who is the son of Epops;[205] so that, you see, I am his grandfather; just as one might say, Hipponicus,[206] the son of Callias, who is the son of Hipponicus.

PISTHETAERUS. Then this bird is Callias! Why, what a lot of his feathers he has lost![207]

EPOPS. That's because he is honest; so the informers set upon him and the women too pluck out his feathers.

PISTHETAERUS. By Posidon, do you see that many-coloured bird? What is his name?

EPOPS. This one? 'Tis the glutton.

PISTHETAERUS. Is there another glutton besides Cleonymus? But why, if he is Cleonymus, has he not thrown away his crest?[208] But what is the meaning of all these crests? Have these birds come to contend for the double stadium prize?[209]

EPOPS. They are like the Carians, who cling to the crests of their mountains for greater safety.[210]

PISTHETAERUS. Oh, Posidon! do you see what swarms of birds are gathering here?

EUELPIDES. By Phoebus! what a cloud! The entrance to the stage is no longer visible, so closely do they fly together.

PISTHETAERUS. Here is the partridge.

EUELPIDES. Faith! there is the francolin.

PISTHETAERUS. There is the poachard.

EUELPIDES. Here is the kingfisher. And over yonder?

EPOPS. 'Tis the barber.

EUELPIDES. What? a bird a barber?

PISTHETAERUS. Why, Sporgilus is one.[211] Here comes the owl.

EUELPIDES. And who is it brings an owl to Athens?[212]

PISTHETAERUS. Here is the magpie, the turtle-dove, the swallow, the horned owl, the buzzard, the pigeon, the falcon, the ring-dove, the cuckoo, the red-foot, the red-cap, the purple-cap, the kestrel, the diver, the ousel, the osprey, the wood-pecker.

EUELPIDES. Oh! oh! what a lot of birds! what a quantity of blackbirds! how they scold, how they come rushing up! What a noise! what a noise! Can they be bearing us ill-will? Oh! there! there! they are opening their beaks and staring at us.

PISTHETAERUS. Why, so they are.

CHORUS. Popopopopopopopoi. Where is he who called me? Where am I to find him?

EPOPS. I have been waiting for you this long while; I never fail in my word to my friends.

CHORUS. Tititititititiiti. What good thing have you to tell me?

EPOPS. Something that concerns our common safety, and that is just as pleasant as it is to the purpose. Two men, who are subtle reasoners, have come here to seek me.

CHORUS. Where? What? What are you saying?

EPOPS. I say, two old men have come from the abode of men to propose a vast and splendid scheme to us.

CHORUS. Oh! 'tis a horrible, unheard-of crime! What are you saying?

EPOPS. Nay! never let my words scare you.

CHORUS. What have you done then?

EPOPS. I have welcomed two men, who wish to live with us.

CHORUS. And you have dared to do that!

EPOPS. Aye, and am delighted at having done so.

CHORUS. Where are they?

EPOPS. In your midst, as I am.

CHORUS. Ah! ah! we are betrayed; 'tis sacrilege! Our friend, he who picked up corn-seeds in the same plains as ourselves, has violated our ancient laws; he has broken the oaths that bind all birds; he has laid a snare for me, he has handed us over to the attacks of that impious race which, throughout all time, has never ceased to war against us. As for this traitorous bird, we will decide his case later, but the two old men shall be punished forthwith; we are going to tear them to pieces.

PISTHETAERUS. 'Tis all over with us.

EUELPIDES. You are the sole cause of all our trouble. Why did you bring me from down yonder?

PISTHETAERUS. To have you with me.

EUELPIDES. Say rather to have me melt into tears.

PISTHETAERUS. Go to! you are talking nonsense.

EUELPIDES. How so?

PISTHETAERUS. How will you be able to cry when once your eyes are pecked out?

CHORUS. Io! io! forward to the attack, throw yourselves upon the foe, spill his blood; take to your wings and surround them on all sides. Woe to them! let us get to work with our beaks, let us devour them. Nothing can save them from our wrath, neither the mountain forests, nor the clouds that float in the sky, nor the foaming deep. Come, peck, tear to ribbons. Where is the chief of the cohort? Let him engage the right wing.

EUELPIDES. This is the fatal moment. Where shall I fly to, unfortunate wretch that I am?

PISTHETAERUS. Stay! stop here!

EUELPIDES. That they may tear me to pieces?

PISTHETAERUS. And how do you think to escape them?

EUELPIDES. I don't know at all.

PISTHETAERUS. Come, I will tell you. We must stop and fight them. Let us arm ourselves with these stew-pots.

EUELPIDES. Why with the stew-pots?

PISTHETAERUS. The owl will not attack us.[213]

EUELPIDES. But do you see all those hooked claws?

PISTHETAERUS. Seize the spit and pierce the foe on your side.

EUELPIDES. And how about my eyes?

PISTHETAERUS. Protect them with this dish or this vinegar-pot.

EUELPIDES. Oh! what cleverness! what inventive genius! You are a great general, even greater than Nicias,[214] where stratagem is concerned.

CHORUS. Forward, forward, charge with your beaks! Come, no delay. Tear, pluck, strike, flay them, and first of all smash the stew-pot.

EPOPS. Oh, most cruel of all animals, why tear these two men to pieces, why kill them? What have they done to you? They belong to the same tribe, to the same family as my wife.[215]

CHORUS. Are wolves to be spared? Are they not our most mortal foes? So let us punish them.

EPOPS. If they are your foes by nature, they are your friends in heart, and they come here to give you useful advice.

CHORUS. Advice or a useful word from their lips, from them, the enemies of my forbears!

EPOPS. The wise can often profit by the lessons of a foe, for caution is the mother of safety. 'Tis just such a thing as one will not learn from a friend and which an enemy compels you to know. To begin with, 'tis the foe and not the friend that taught cities to build high walls, to equip long vessels of war; and 'tis this knowledge that protects our children, our slaves and our wealth.

CHORUS. Well then, I agree, let us first hear them, for 'tis best; one can even learn something in an enemy's school.

PISTHETAERUS. Their wrath seems to cool. Draw back a little.

EPOPS. 'Tis only justice, and you will thank me later.

CHORUS. Never have we opposed your advice up to now.

PISTHETAERUS. They are in a more peaceful mood; put down your stew-pot and your two dishes; spit in hand, doing duty for a spear, let us mount guard inside the camp close to the pot and watch in our arsenal closely; for we must not fly.

EUELPIDES. You are right. But where shall we be buried, if we die?

PISTHETAERUS. In the Ceramicus;[216] for, to get a public funeral, we shall tell the Strategi that we fell at Orneae,[217] fighting the country's foes.

CHORUS. Return to your ranks and lay down your courage beside your wrath as the Hoplites do. Then let us ask these men who they are, whence they come, and with what intent. Here, Epops, answer me.

EPOPS. Are you calling me? What do you want of me?

CHORUS. Who are they? From what country?

EPOPS. Strangers, who have come from Greece, the land of the wise.

CHORUS. And what fate has led them hither to the land of the birds?

EPOPS. Their love for you and their wish to share your kind of life; to dwell and remain with you always.

CHORUS. Indeed, and what are their plans?

EPOPS. They are wonderful, incredible, unheard of.

CHORUS. Why, do they think to see some advantage that determines them to settle here? Are they hoping with our help to triumph over their foes or to be useful to their friends?

EPOPS. They speak of benefits so great it is impossible either to describe or conceive them; all shall be yours, all that we see here, there, above and below us; this they vouch for.

CHORUS. Are they mad?

EPOPS. They are the sanest people in the world.

CHORUS. Clever men?

EPOPS. The slyest of foxes, cleverness its very self, men of the world, cunning, the cream of knowing folk.

CHORUS. Tell them to speak and speak quickly; why, as I listen to you, I am beside myself with delight.

EPOPS. Here, you there, take all these weapons and hang them up inside close to the fire, near the figure of the god who presides there and under his protection;[218] as for you, address the birds, tell them why I have gathered them together.

PISTHETAERUS. Not I, by Apollo, unless they agree with me as the little ape of an armourer agreed with his wife, not to bite me, nor pull me by the testicles, nor shove things up my....

CHORUS. You mean the.... (*Puts finger to bottom.*) Oh! be quite at ease.

PISTHETAERUS. No, I mean my eyes.

CHORUS. Agreed.

PISTHETAERUS. Swear it.

CHORUS. I swear it and, if I keep my promise, let judges and spectators give me the victory unanimously.

PISTHETAERUS. It is a bargain.

CHORUS. And if I break my word, may I succeed by one vote only.

HERALD. Hearken, ye people! Hoplites, pick up your weapons and return to your firesides; do not fail to read the decrees of dismissal we have posted.

CHORUS. Man is a truly cunning creature, but nevertheless explain. Perhaps you are going to show me some good way to extend my power, some way that I have not had the wit to find out and which you have discovered. Speak! 'tis to your own interest as well as to mine, for if you secure me some advantage, I will surely share it with you. But what object can have induced you to come among us? Speak boldly, for I shall not break the truce,—until you have told us all.

PISTHETAERUS. I am bursting with desire to speak; I have already mixed the dough of my address and nothing prevents me from kneading it.... Slave! bring the chaplet and water, which you must pour over my hands. Be quick![219]

EUELPIDES. Is it a question of feasting? What does it all mean?

PISTHETAERUS. By Zeus, no! but I am hunting for fine, tasty words to break down the hardness of their hearts.—I grieve so much for you, who at one time were kings....

CHORUS. We kings! Over whom?

PISTHETAERUS. ... of all that exists, firstly of me and of this man, even of Zeus himself. Your race is older than Saturn, the Titans and the Earth.

CHORUS. What, older than the Earth!

PISTHETAERUS. By Phoebus, yes.

CHORUS. By Zeus, but I never knew that before!

PISTHETAERUS. 'Tis because you are ignorant and heedless, and have never read your Aesop. 'Tis he who tells us that the lark was born before all other creatures, indeed before the Earth; his father died of sickness, but the Earth did not exist then; he remained unburied for five days, when the bird in its dilemma decided, for want of a better place, to entomb its father in its own head.

EUELPIDES. So that the lark's father is buried at Cephalae.[220]

EPOPS. Hence, if we existed before the Earth, before the gods, the kingship belongs to us by right of priority.

EUELPIDES. Undoubtedly, but sharpen your beak well; Zeus won't be in a hurry to hand over his sceptre to the woodpecker.

PISTHETAERUS. It was not the gods, but the birds, who were formerly the masters and kings over men; of this I have a thousand proofs. First of all, I will point you to the cock, who governed the Persians before all other monarchs, before Darius and Megabyzus.[221] 'Tis in memory of his reign that he is called the Persian bird.

EUELPIDES. For this reason also, even to-day, he alone of all the birds wears his tiara straight on his head, like the Great King.[222]

PISTHETAERUS. He was so strong, so great, so feared, that even now, on account of his ancient power, everyone jumps out of bed as soon as ever he crows at daybreak. Blacksmiths, potters, tanners, shoemakers, bathmen, corn-dealers, lyre-makers and armourers, all put on their shoes and go to work before it is daylight.

EUELPIDES. I can tell you something anent that. 'Twas the cock's fault that I lost a splendid tunic of Phrygian wool. I was at a feast in town, given to celebrate the birth of a child; I had drunk pretty freely and had just fallen asleep, when a cock, I suppose in a greater hurry than the rest, began to crow. I thought it was dawn and set out for Alimos.[223] I had hardly got beyond the walls, when a footpad struck me in the back with his bludgeon; down I went and wanted to shout, but he had already made off with my mantle.

PISTHETAERUS. Formerly also the kite was ruler and king over the Greeks.

EPOPS. The Greeks?

PISTHETAERUS. And when he was king, 'twas he who first taught them to fall on their knees before the kites.[224]

EUELPIDES. By Zeus! 'tis what I did myself one day on seeing a kite; but at the moment I was on my knees, and leaning backwards[225] with mouth agape, I bolted an obolus and was forced to carry my bag home empty.[226]

PISTHETAERUS. The cuckoo was king of Egypt and of the whole of Phoenicia. When he called out "cuckoo," all the Phoenicians hurried to the fields to reap their wheat and their barley.[227]

EUELPIDES. Hence no doubt the proverb, "Cuckoo! cuckoo! go to the fields, ye circumcised."[228]

PISTHETAERUS. So powerful were the birds, that the kings of Grecian cities, Agamemnon, Menelaus, for instance, carried a bird on the tip of their sceptres, who had his share of all presents.[229]

EUELPIDES. That I didn't know and was much astonished when I saw Priam come upon the stage in the tragedies with a bird, which kept watching Lysicrates[230] to see if he got any present.

PISTHETAERUS. But the strongest proof of all is, that Zeus, who now reigns, is represented as standing with an eagle on his head as a symbol of his royalty;[231] his daughter has an owl, and Phoebus, as his servant, has a hawk.

EUELPIDES. By Demeter, 'tis well spoken. But what are all these birds doing in heaven?

PISTHETAERUS. When anyone sacrifices and, according to the rite, offers the entrails to the gods, these birds take their share before Zeus. Formerly the men always swore by birds and never by the gods; even now Lampon[232] swears by the goose, when he wants to lie.... Thus 'tis clear that you were great and sacred, but now you are looked upon as slaves, as fools, as Helots; stones are thrown at you as at raving madmen, even in holy places. A crowd of bird-catchers sets snares, traps, limed-twigs and nets of all sorts for you; you are caught, you are sold in heaps and the buyers finger you over to be certain you are fat. Again, if they would but serve you up simply roasted; but they rasp cheese into a mixture of oil, vinegar and laserwort, to which another sweet and greasy sauce is added, and the whole is poured scalding hot over your back, for all the world as if you were diseased meat.

CHORUS. Man, your words have made my heart bleed; I have groaned over the treachery of our fathers, who knew not how to transmit to us the high rank they held from their forefathers. But 'tis a benevolent Genius, a happy Fate, that sends you to us; you shall be our deliverer and I place the destiny of my little ones and my own in your hands with every confidence. But hasten to tell me what must be done; we should not be worthy to live, if we did not seek to regain our royalty by every possible means,

PISTHETAERUS. First I advise that the birds gather together in one city and that they build a wall of great bricks, like that at Babylon, round the plains of the air and the whole region of space that divides earth from heaven.

EPOPS. Oh, Cebriones! oh, Porphyrion![233] what a terribly strong place!

PISTHETAERUS. This, this being well done and completed, you demand back the empire from Zeus; if he will not agree, if he refuses and does not at once confess himself beaten, you declare a sacred war against him and forbid the gods henceforward to pass through your country with standing organ, as hitherto, for the purpose of fondling their Alcmenas, their Alopés, or their Semelés;[234] if they try to pass through, you infibulate them with rings so that they can fuck no longer. You send another messenger to mankind, who will proclaim to them that the birds are kings, that for the future they must first of all sacrifice to them, and only afterwards to the gods; that it is fitting to appoint to each deity the bird that has most in common with it. For instance, are they sacrificing to Aphrodité, let them at the same time offer barley to the coot;[235] are they immolating a sheep to Posidon, let them consecrate wheat in honour of the duck;[236] is a steer being offered to Heracles, let honey-cakes be dedicated to the gull;[237] is a goat being slain for King Zeus, there is a King-Bird, the wren,[238] to whom the sacrifice of a male gnat is due before Zeus himself even.

EUELPIDES. This notion of an immolated gnat delights me! And now let the great Zeus thunder!

EPOPS. But how will mankind recognize us as gods and not as jays? Us, who have wings and fly?

PISTHETAERUS. You talk rubbish! Hermes is a god and has wings and flies, and so do many other gods. First of all, Victory flies with golden wings, Eros is undoubtedly winged too, and Iris is compared by Homer to a timorous dove.[239] If men in their blindness do not recognize you as gods and continue to worship the dwellers in Olympus, then a cloud of sparrows greedy for corn must descend upon their fields and eat up all their seeds; we shall see then if Demeter will mete them out any wheat.

EUELPIDES. By Zeus, she'll take good care she does not, and you will see her inventing a thousand excuses.

PISTHETAERUS. The crows too will prove your divinity to them by pecking out the eyes of their flocks and of their draught-oxen; and then let Apollo cure them, since he is a physician and is paid for the purpose.[240]

EUELPIDES. Oh! don't do that! Wait first until I have sold my two young bullocks.

PISTHETAERUS. If on the other hand they recognize that you are God, the principle of life, that you are Earth, Saturn, Posidon, they shall be loaded with benefits.

EPOPS Name me one of these then.

PISTHETAERUS. Firstly, the locusts shall not eat up their vine-blossoms; a legion of owls and kestrels will devour them. Moreover, the gnats and the gall-bugs shall no longer ravage the figs; a flock of thrushes shall swallow the whole host down to the very last.

EPOPS. And how shall we give wealth to mankind? This is their strongest passion.

PISTHETAERUS. When they consult the omens, you will point them to the richest mines, you will reveal the paying ventures to the diviner, and not another shipwreck will happen or sailor perish.

EPOPS. No more shall perish? How is that?

PISTHETAERUS. When the auguries are examined before starting on a voyage, some bird will not fail to say, "Don't start! there will be a storm," or else, "Go! you will make a most profitable venture."

EUELPIDES. I shall buy a trading-vessel and go to sea. I will not stay with you.

PISTHETAERUS. You will discover treasures to them, which were buried in former times, for you know them. Do not all men say, "None know where my treasure lies, unless perchance it be some bird."[241]

EUELPIDES. I shall sell my boat and buy a spade to unearth the vessels.

EPOPS. And how are we to give them health, which belongs to the gods?

PISTHETAERUS. If they are happy, is not that the chief thing towards health? The miserable man is never well.

EPOPS. Old Age also dwells in Olympus. How will they get at it? Must they die in early youth?

PISTHETAERUS. Why, the birds, by Zeus, will add three hundred years to their life.

EPOPS. From whom will they take them?

PISTHETAERUS. From whom? Why, from themselves. Don't you know the cawing crow lives five times as long as a man?

EUELPIDES. Ah! ah! these are far better kings for us than Zeus!

PISTHETAERUS. Far better, are they not? And firstly, we shall not have to build them temples of hewn stone, closed with gates of gold; they will dwell amongst the bushes and in the thickets of green oak; the most venerated of birds will have no other temple than the foliage of the olive tree; we shall not go to Delphi or to Ammon to sacrifice;[242] but standing erect in the midst of arbutus and wild olives and holding forth our hands filled with wheat and barley, we shall pray them to admit us to a share of the blessings they enjoy and shall at once obtain them for a few grains of wheat.

CHORUS. Old man, whom I detested, you are now to me the dearest of all; never shall I, if I can help it, fail to follow your advice. Inspirited by your words, I threaten my rivals the gods, and I swear that if you march in alliance with me against the gods and are faithful to our just, loyal and sacred bond, we shall soon have shattered their sceptre. 'Tis our part to undertake the toil, 'tis yours to advise.

EPOPS. By Zeus! 'tis no longer the time to delay and loiter like Nicias;[243] let us act as promptly as possible.... In the first place, come, enter my nest built of brushwood and blades of straw, and tell me your names.

PISTHETAERUS. That is soon done; my name is Pisthetaerus.

EPOPS. And his?

PISTHETAERUS. Euelpides, of the deme of Thria.

EPOPS. Good! and good luck to you.

PISTHETAERUS. We accept the omen.

EPOPS. Come in here.

PISTHETAERUS. Very well, 'tis you who lead us and must introduce us.

EPOPS. Come then.

PISTHETAERUS. Oh! my god! do come back here. Hi! tell us how we are to follow you. You can fly, but we cannot.

EPOPS. Well, well.

PISTHETAERUS. Remember Aesop's fables. It is told there, that the fox fared very ill, because he had made an alliance with the eagle.

EPOPS. Be at ease. You shall eat a certain root and wings will grow on your shoulders.

PISTHETAERUS. Then let us enter. Xanthias and Manes,[244] pick up our baggage.

CHORUS. Hi! Epops! do you hear me?

EPOPS. What's the matter?

CHORUS. Take them off to dine well and call your mate, the melodious Procné, whose songs are worthy of the Muses; she will delight our leisure moments.

PISTHETAERUS. Oh! I conjure you, accede to their wish; for this delightful bird will leave her rushes at the sound of your voice; for the sake of the gods, let her come here, so that we may contemplate the nightingale.[245]

EPOPS. Let it be as you desire. Come forth, Procné, show yourself to these strangers.

PISTHETAERUS. Oh! great Zeus! what a beautiful little bird! what a dainty form! what brilliant plumage![246]

EUELPIDES. Do you know how dearly I should like to split her legs for her?

PISTHETAERUS. She is dazzling all over with gold, like a young girl.[247]

EUELPIDES. Oh! how I should like to kiss her!

PISTHETAERUS. Why, wretched man, she has two little sharp points on her beak.

EUELPIDES. I would treat her like an egg, the shell of which we remove before eating it; I would take off her mask and then kiss her pretty face.

EPOPS. Let us go in.

PISTHETAERUS. Lead the way, and may success attend us.

CHORUS. Lovable golden bird, whom I cherish above all others, you, whom I associate with all my songs, nightingale, you have come, you have come, to show yourself to me and to charm me with your notes. Come, you, who play spring melodies upon the harmonious flute,[248] lead off our anapaests.[249]

Weak mortals, chained to the earth, creatures of clay as frail as the foliage of the woods, you unfortunate race, whose life is but darkness, as unreal as a shadow, the illusion of a dream, hearken to us, who are immortal beings, ethereal, ever young and occupied with eternal thoughts, for we shall teach you about all celestial matters; you shall know thoroughly what is the nature of the birds, what the origin of the gods, of the rivers, of Erebus, and Chaos; thanks to us, Prodicus[250] will envy you your knowledge.

At the beginning there was only Chaos, Night, dark Erebus, and deep Tartarus. Earth, the air and heaven had no existence. Firstly, black-winged Night laid a germless egg in the bosom of the infinite deeps of Erebus, and from this, after the revolution of long ages, sprang the graceful Eros with his glittering golden wings, swift as the whirlwinds of the tempest. He mated in deep Tartarus with dark Chaos, winged like himself, and thus hatched forth our race, which was the first to see the light. That of the Immortals did not exist until Eros had brought together all the ingredients of the world, and from their marriage Heaven, Ocean, Earth and the imperishable race of blessed gods sprang into being. Thus our origin is very much older than that of the dwellers in Olympus. We are the offspring of Eros; there are a thousand proofs to show it. We have wings and we lend assistance to lovers. How many handsome youths, who had sworn to remain insensible, have not been vanquished by our power and have yielded themselves to their lovers when almost at the end of their youth, being led away by the gift of a quail, a waterfowl, a goose, or a cock.[251]

And what important services do not the birds render to mortals! First of all, they mark the seasons for them, springtime, winter, and autumn. Does the screaming crane migrate to Libya,—it warns the husbandman to sow, the pilot to take his ease beside his tiller hung up in his dwelling,[252] and Orestes[253] to weave a tunic, so that the rigorous cold may not drive him any more to strip other folk. When the kite reappears, he tells of the return of spring and of the period when the fleece of the sheep must be clipped. Is the swallow in sight? All hasten to sell their warm tunic and to buy some light clothing. We are your Ammon, Delphi, Dodona, your Phoebus Apollo.[254] Before undertaking anything, whether a business transaction, a marriage, or the purchase of food, you consult the birds by reading the omens, and you give this name of omen[255] to all signs that tell of the future. With you a word is an omen, you call a sneeze an omen, a meeting an omen, an unknown sound an omen, a slave or an ass an omen.[256] Is it not clear that we are a prophetic Apollo to you? If you recognize us as gods, we shall be your divining Muses, through us you will know the winds and the seasons, summer, winter, and the temperate months. We shall not withdraw ourselves to the highest clouds like Zeus, but shall be among you and shall give to you and to your children and the children of your children, health and wealth, long life, peace, youth, laughter, songs and feasts; in short, you will all be so well off, that you will be weary and satiated with enjoyment.

Oh, rustic Muse of such varied note, tio, tio, tio, tiotinx, I sing with you in the groves and on the mountain tops, tio, tio, tio, tio, tiotinx.[257] I pour forth sacred strains from my golden throat in honour of the god Pan,[258] tio, tio, tio, tiotinx, from the top of the thickly leaved ash, and my voice mingles with the mighty choirs who extol Cybelé on the mountain tops,[259] totototototototinx. 'Tis to our concerts that Phrynicus comes to pillage like a bee the ambrosia of his songs, the sweetness of which so charms the ear, tio, tio, tio, tio, tinx.

If there be one of you spectators who wishes to spend the rest of his life quietly among the birds, let him come to us. All that is disgraceful and forbidden by law on earth is on the contrary honourable among us, the birds. For instance, among you 'tis a crime to beat your father, but with us 'tis an estimable deed; it's considered fine to run straight at your father and hit him, saying, "Come, lift your spur if you want to fight."[260] The runaway slave, whom you brand, is only a spotted francolin with us.[261] Are you Phrygian like Spintharus?[262] Among us you would be the Phrygian bird, the goldfinch, of the race of Philemon.[263] Are you a slave and a Carian like Execestides? Among us you can create yourself forefathers;[264] you can always find relations. Does the son of Pisias want to betray the gates of the city to the foe? Let him become a partridge, the fitting offspring of his father; among us there is no shame in escaping as cleverly as a partridge.

So the swans on the banks of the Hebrus, tio, tio, tio, tio, tiotinx, mingle their voices to serenade Apollo, tio, tio, tio, tio, tiotinx, flapping their wings the while, tio, tio, tio, tio, tiotinx; their notes reach beyond the clouds of heaven; all the dwellers in the forests stand still with astonishment and delight; a calm rests upon the waters, and the Graces and the choirs in Olympus catch up the strain, tio, tio, tio, tio, tiotinx.

There is nothing more useful nor more pleasant than to have wings. To begin with, just let us suppose a spectator to be dying with hunger and to be weary of the choruses of the tragic poets; if he were winged, he would fly off, go home to dine and come back with his stomach filled. Some Patroclides in urgent need would not have to soil his cloak, but could fly off, satisfy his requirements, and, having recovered his breath, return. If one of you, it matters not who, had adulterous relations and saw the husband of his mistress in the seats of the senators, he might stretch his wings, fly thither, and, having appeased his craving, resume his place. Is it not the most priceless gift of all, to be winged? Look at Diitrephes![265] His wings were only wicker-work ones, and yet he got himself chosen Phylarch and then Hipparch; from being nobody, he has risen to be famous; 'tis now the finest gilded cock of his tribe.[266]

PISTHETAERUS. Halloa! What's this? By Zeus! I never saw anything so funny in all my life.[267]

EUELPIDES. What makes you laugh?

PISTHETAERUS. 'Tis your bits of wings. D'you know what you look like? Like a goose painted by some dauber-fellow.

EUELPIDES. And you look like a close-shaven blackbird.

PISTHETAERUS. 'Tis ourselves asked for this transformation, and, as Aeschylus has it, "These are no borrowed feathers, but truly our own."[268]

EPOPS. Come now, what must be done?

PISTHETAERUS. First give our city a great and famous name, then sacrifice to the gods.

EUELPIDES. I think so too.

EPOPS. Let's see. What shall our city be called?

PISTHETAERUS. Will you have a high-sounding Laconian name? Shall we call it Sparta?

EUELPIDES. What! call my town Sparta? Why, I would not use esparto for my bed,[269] even though I had nothing but bands of rushes.

PISTHETAERUS. Well then, what name can you suggest?

EUELPIDES. Some name borrowed from the clouds, from these lofty regions in which we dwell—in short, some well-known name.

PISTHETAERUS. Do you like Nephelococcygia?[270]

EPOPS. Oh! capital! truly 'tis a brilliant thought!

EUELPIDES. Is it in Nephelococcygia that all the wealth of Theogenes[271] and most of Aeschines'[272] is?

PISTHETAERUS. No, 'tis rather the plain of Phlegra,[273] where the gods withered the pride of the sons of the Earth with their shafts.

EUELPIDES. Oh! what a splendid city! But what god shall be its patron? for whom shall we weave the peplus?[274]

PISTHETAERUS. Why not choose Athené Polias?[275]

EUELPIDES. Oh! what a well-ordered town 'twould be to have a female deity armed from head to foot, while Clisthenes[276] was spinning!

PISTHETAERUS. Who then shall guard the Pelargicon?[277]

EPOPS. One of ourselves, a bird of Persian strain, who is everywhere proclaimed to be the bravest of all, a true chick of Ares.[278]

EUELPIDES. Oh! noble chick! what a well-chosen god for a rocky home!

PISTHETAERUS. Come! into the air with you to help the workers, who are building the wall; carry up rubble, strip yourself to mix the mortar, take up the hod, tumble down the ladder, an you like, post sentinels, keep the fire smouldering beneath the ashes, go round the walls, bell in hand,[279] and go to sleep up there yourself; then despatch two heralds, one to the gods above, the other to mankind on earth and come back here.

EUELPIDES. As for yourself, remain here, and may the plague take you for a troublesome fellow!

PISTHETAERUS. Go, friend, go where I send you, for without you my orders cannot be obeyed. For myself, I want to sacrifice to the new god, and I am going to summon the priest who must preside at the ceremony. Slaves! slaves! bring forward the basket and the lustral water.

CHORUS. I do as you do, and I wish as you wish, and I implore you to address powerful and solemn prayers to the gods, and in addition to immolate a sheep as a token of our gratitude. Let us sing the Pythian chant in honour of the god, and let Chaeris accompany our voices.

PISTHETAERUS (*to the flute-player*). Enough! but, by Heracles! what is this? Great gods! I have seen many prodigious things, but I never saw a muzzled raven.[280]

EPOPS. Priest! 'tis high time! Sacrifice to the new gods.

PRIEST. I begin, but where is he with the basket? Pray to the Vesta of the birds, to the kite, who presides over the hearth, and to all the god and goddess-birds who dwell in Olympus.

CHORUS. Oh! Hawk, the sacred guardian of Sunium, oh, god of the storks!

PRIEST. Pray to the swan of Delos, to Latona the mother of the quails, and to Artemis, the goldfinch.

PISTHETAERUS. 'Tis no longer Artemis Colaenis, but Artemis the goldfinch.[281]

PRIEST. And to Bacchus, the finch and Cybelé, the ostrich and mother of the gods and mankind.

CHORUS. Oh! sovereign ostrich, Cybelé, the mother of Cleocritus,[282] grant health and safety to the Nephelococcygians as well as to the dwellers in Chios....

PISTHETAERUS. The dwellers in Chios! Ah! I am delighted they should be thus mentioned on all occasions.[283]

CHORUS. ... to the heroes, the birds, to the sons of heroes, to the porphyrion, the pelican, the spoon-bill, the redbreast, the grouse, the peacock, the horned-owl, the teal, the bittern, the heron, the stormy petrel, the fig-pecker, the titmouse....

PISTHETAERUS. Stop! stop! you drive me crazy with your endless list. Why, wretch, to what sacred feast are you inviting the vultures and the sea-eagles? Don't you see that a single kite could easily carry off the lot at once? Begone, you and your fillets and all; I shall know how to complete the sacrifice by myself.

PRIEST. It is imperative that I sing another sacred chant for the rite of the lustral water, and that I invoke the immortals, or at least one of them, provided always that you have some suitable food to offer him; from what I see here, in the shape of gifts, there is naught whatever but horn and hair.

PISTHETAERUS. Let us address our sacrifices and our prayers to the winged gods.

A POET. Oh, Muse! celebrate happy Nephelococcygia in your hymns.

PISTHETAERUS. What have we here? Where do you come from, tell me? Who are you?

POET. I am he whose language is sweeter than honey, the zealous slave of the Muses, as Homer has it.

PISTHETAERUS. You a slave! and yet you wear your hair long?

POET. No, but the fact is all we poets are the assiduous slaves of the Muses according to Homer.

PISTHETAERUS. In truth your little cloak is quite holy too through zeal! But, poet, what ill wind drove you here?

POET. I have composed verses in honour of your Nephelococcygia, a host of splendid dithyrambs and parthenians,[284] worthy of Simonides himself.

PISTHETAERUS. And when did you compose them? How long since?

POET. Oh! 'tis long, aye, very long, that I have sung in honour of this city.

PISTHETAERUS. But I am only celebrating its foundation with this sacrifice;[285] I have only just named it, as is done with little babies.

POET. "Just as the chargers fly with the speed of the wind, so does the voice of the Muses take its flight. Oh! thou noble founder of the town of Aetna,[286] thou, whose name recalls the holy sacrifices,[287] make us such gift as thy generous heart shall suggest."

PISTHETAERUS. He will drive us silly if we do not get rid of him by some present. Here! you, who have a fur as well as your tunic, take it off and give it to this clever poet. Come, take this fur; you look to me to be shivering with cold.

POET. My Muse will gladly accept this gift; but engrave these verses of Pindar's on your mind.

PISTHETAERUS. Oh! what a pest! 'Tis impossible then to be rid of him.

POET. "Straton wanders among the Scythian nomads, but has no linen garment. He is sad at only wearing an animal's pelt and no tunic." Do you conceive my bent?

PISTHETAERUS. I understand that you want me to offer you a tunic. Hi! you (*to Euelpides*), take off yours; we must help the poet.... Come, you, take it and begone.

POET. I am going, and these are the verses that I address to this city: "Phoebus of the golden throne, celebrate this shivery, freezing city; I have travelled through fruitful and snow-covered plains. Tralala! Tralala!"[288]

PISTHETAERUS. What are you chanting us about frosts? Thanks to the tunic, you no longer fear them. Ah! by Zeus! I could not have believed this cursed fellow could so soon have learnt the way to our city. Come, priest, take the lustral water and circle the altar.

PRIEST. Let all keep silence!

A PROPHET. Let not the goat be sacrificed.[289]

PISTHETAERUS. Who are you?

PROPHET. Who am I? A prophet.

PISTHETAERUS. Get you gone.

PROPHET. Wretched man, insult not sacred things. For there is an oracle of Bacis, which exactly applies to Nephelococcygia.

PISTHETAERUS. Why did you not reveal it to me before I founded my city?

PROPHET. The divine spirit was against it.

PISTHETAERUS. Well, 'tis best to know the terms of the oracle.

PROPHET. "But when the wolves and the white crows shall dwell together between Corinth and Sicyon...."[290]

PISTHETAERUS. But how do the Corinthians concern me?

PROPHET. 'Tis the regions of the air that Bacis indicated in this manner. "They must first sacrifice a white-fleeced goat to Pandora, and give the prophet, who first reveals my words, a good cloak and new sandals."

PISTHETAERUS. Are the sandals there?

PROPHET.

Read. "And besides this a goblet of wine and a good share of the entrails of the victim."

PISTHETAERUS. Of the entrails—is it so written?

PROPHET. Read. "If you do as I command, divine youth, you shall be an eagle among the clouds; if not, you shall be neither turtle-dove, nor eagle, nor woodpecker."

PISTHETAERUS. Is all that there?

PROPHET. Read.

PISTHETAERUS. This oracle in no sort of way resembles the one Apollo dictated to me: "If an impostor comes without invitation to annoy you during the sacrifice and to demand a share of the victim, apply a stout stick to his ribs."

PROPHET. You are drivelling.

PISTHETAERUS. "And don't spare him, were he an eagle from out of the clouds, were it Lampon himself[291] or the great Diopithes."[292]

PROPHET. Is all that there?

PISTHETAERUS. Here, read it yourself, and go and hang yourself.

PROPHET. Oh! unfortunate wretch that I am.

PISTHETAERUS. Away with you, and take your prophecies elsewhere.

METON.[293] I have come to you.

PISTHETAERUS. Yet another pest. What have you come to do? What's your plan? What's the purpose of your journey? Why these splendid buskins?

METON. I want to survey the plains of the air for you and to parcel them into lots.

PISTHETAERUS. In the name of the gods, who are you?

METON. Who am I? Meton, known throughout Greece and at Colonus.[294]

PISTHETAERUS. What are these things?

METON. Tools for measuring the air. In truth, the spaces in the air have precisely the form of a furnace. With this bent ruler I draw a line from top to bottom; from one of its points I describe a circle with the compass. Do you understand?

PISTHETAERUS. Not the very least.

METON. With the straight ruler I set to work to inscribe a square within this circle; in its centre will be the marketplace, into which all the straight streets will lead, converging to this centre like a star, which, although only orbicular, sends forth its rays in a straight line from all sides.

PISTHETAERUS. Meton, you new Thales....[295]

METON. What d'you want with me?

PISTHETAERUS. I want to give you a proof of my friendship. Use your legs.

METON. Why, what have I to fear?

PISTHETAERUS. 'Tis the same here as in Sparta. Strangers are driven away, and blows rain down as thick as hail.

METON. Is there sedition in your city?

PISTHETAERUS. No, certainly not.

METON. What's wrong then?

PISTHETAERUS. We are agreed to sweep all quacks and impostors far from our borders.

METON. Then I'm off.

PISTHETAERUS. I fear me 'tis too late. The thunder growls already. (*Beats him.*)

METON. Oh, woe! oh, woe!

PISTHETAERUS. I warned you. Now, be off, and do your surveying somewhere else. (*Meton takes to his heels.*)

AN INSPECTOR. Where are the Proxeni?[296]

PISTHETAERUS. Who is this Sardanapalus?[297]

INSPECTOR. I have been appointed by lot to come to Nephelococcygia as inspector.[298]

PISTHETAERUS. An inspector! and who sends you here, you rascal?

INSPECTOR. A decree of Taleas.[299]

PISTHETAERUS. Will you just pocket your salary, do nothing, and be off?

INSPECTOR. I' faith! that I will; I am urgently needed to be at Athens to attend the assembly; for I am charged with the interests of Pharnaces.[300]

PISTHETAERUS. Take it then, and be off. See, here is your salary. (*Beats him.*)

INSPECTOR. What does this mean?

PISTHETAERUS. 'Tis the assembly where you have to defend Pharnaces.

INSPECTOR. You shall testify that they dare to strike me, the inspector.

PISTHETAERUS. Are you not going to clear out with your urns. 'Tis not to be believed; they send us inspectors before we have so much as paid sacrifice to the gods.

A DEALER IN DECREES. "If the Nephelococcygian does wrong to the Athenian...."

PISTHETAERUS. Now whatever are these cursed parchments?

DEALER IN DECREES. I am a dealer in decrees, and I have come here to sell you the new laws.

PISTHETAERUS. Which?

DEALER IN DECREES. "The Nephelococcygians shall adopt the same weights, measures and decrees as the Olophyxians."[301]

PISTHETAERUS. And you shall soon be imitating the Orotyxians. (*Beats him.*)

DEALER IN DECREES. Hullo! what are you doing?

PISTHETAERUS. Now will you be off with your decrees? For I am going to let *you* see some severe ones.

INSPECTOR (*returning*). I summon Pisthetaerus for outrage for the month of Munychion.[302]

PISTHETAERUS. Ha! my friend! are you still there?

DEALER IN DECREES. "Should anyone drive away the magistrates and not receive them, according to the decree duly posted..."

PISTHETAERUS. What! rascal! you are there too?

INSPECTOR. Woe to you! I'll have you condemned to a fine of ten thousand drachmae.

PISTHETAERUS. And I'll smash your urns.[303]

INSPECTOR. Do you recall that evening when you stooled against the column where the decrees are posted?

PISTHETAERUS. Here! here! let him be seized. (*The inspectors run off.*) Well! don't you want to stop any longer?

PRIEST. Let us get indoors as quick as possible; we will sacrifice the goat inside.[304]

CHORUS. Henceforth it is to me that mortals must address their sacrifices and their prayers. Nothing escapes my sight nor my might. My glance embraces the universe, I preserve the fruit in the flower by destroying the thousand kinds of voracious insects the soil produces, which attack the trees and feed on the germ when it has scarcely formed in the calyx; I destroy those who ravage the balmy terrace gardens like a deadly plague; all these gnawing crawling creatures perish beneath the lash of my wing. I hear it proclaimed everywhere: "A talent for him who shall kill Diagoras of Melos,[305] and a talent for him who destroys one of the dead tyrants."[306] We likewise wish to make our proclamation: "A talent to him among you who shall kill Philocrates, the Strouthian;[307] four, if he brings him to us alive. For this Philocrates skewers the finches together and sells them at the rate of an obolus for seven. He tortures the thrushes by blowing them out, so that they may look bigger, sticks their own feathers into the nostrils of blackbirds, and collects pigeons, which he shuts up and forces them, fastened in a net, to decoy others." That is what we wish to proclaim. And if anyone is keeping birds shut up in his yard, let him hasten to let them loose; those who disobey shall be seized by the birds and we shall put them in chains, so that in their turn they may decoy other men.

Happy indeed is the race of winged birds who need no cloak in winter! Neither do I fear the relentless rays of the fiery dog-days; when the divine grasshopper, intoxicated with the sunlight, when noon is burning the ground, is breaking out into shrill melody, my home is beneath the foliage in the flowery meadows. I winter in deep caverns, where I frolic with the mountain nymphs, while in spring I despoil the gardens of the Graces and gather the white, virgin berry on the myrtle bushes.

I want now to speak to the judges about the prize they are going to award; if they are favourable to us, we will load them with benefits far greater than those Paris[308] received. Firstly, the owls of Laurium,[309] which every judge desires above all things, shall never be wanting to you; you shall see them homing with you, building their nests in your money-bags and laying coins. Besides, you shall be housed like the gods, for we shall erect gables[310] over your dwellings; if you hold some public post and want to do a little pilfering, we will give you the sharp claws of a hawk. Are you dining in town, we will provide you with crops.[311] But, if your award is against us, don't fail to have metal covers fashioned for yourselves, like those they place over statues;[312] else, look out! for the day you wear a white tunic all the birds will soil it with their droppings.

PISTHETAERUS. Birds! the sacrifice is propitious. But I see no messenger coming from the wall to tell us what is happening. Ah! here comes one running himself out of breath as though he were running the Olympic stadium.

MESSENGER. Where, where is he? Where, where, where is he? Where, where, where is he? Where is Pisthetaerus, our leader?

PISTHETAERUS. Here am I.

MESSENGER. The wall is finished.

PISTHETAERUS. That's good news.

MESSENGER. 'Tis a most beautiful, a most magnificent work of art. The wall is so broad, that Proxenides, the Braggartian, and Theogenes could pass each other in their chariots, even if they were drawn by steeds as big as the Trojan horse.

PISTHETAERUS. 'Tis wonderful!

MESSENGER. Its length is one hundred stadia; I measured it myself.

PISTHETAERUS. A decent length, by Posidon! And who built such a wall?

MESSENGER. Birds—birds only; they had neither Egyptian brickmaker, nor stonemason, nor carpenter; the birds did it all themselves, I could hardly believe my eyes. Thirty thousand cranes came from Libya with a supply of stones,[313] intended for the foundations. The water-rails chiselled them with their beaks. Ten thousand storks were busy making bricks; plovers and other water fowl carried water into the air.

PISTHETAERUS. And who carried the mortar?

MESSENGER. Herons, in hods.

PISTHETAERUS. But how could they put the mortar into hods?

MESSENGER. Oh! 'twas a truly clever invention; the geese used their feet like spades; they buried them in the pile of mortar and then emptied them into the hods.

PISTHETAERUS. Ah! to what use cannot feet be put?[314]

MESSENGER. You should have seen how eagerly the ducks carried bricks. To complete the tale, the swallows came flying to the work, their beaks full of mortar and their trowel on their back, just the way little children are carried.

PISTHETAERUS. Who would want paid servants after this? But, tell me, who did the woodwork?

MESSENGER. Birds again, and clever carpenters too, the pelicans, for they squared up the gates with their beaks in such a fashion that one would have thought they were using axes; the noise was just like a dockyard. Now the whole wall is tight everywhere, securely bolted and well guarded; it is patrolled, bell in hand; the sentinels stand everywhere and beacons burn on the towers. But I must run off to clean myself; the rest is your business.

CHORUS. Well! what do you say to it? Are you not astonished at the wall being completed so quickly?

PISTHETAERUS. By the gods, yes, and with good reason 'Tis really not to be believed. But here comes another messenger from the wall to bring us some further news! What a fighting look he has!

SECOND MESSENGER. Oh! oh! oh! oh! oh! oh!

PISTHETAERUS. What's the matter?

SECOND MESSENGER. A horrible outrage has occurred; a god sent by Zeus has passed through our gates and has penetrated the realms of the air without the knowledge of the jays, who are on guard in the daytime.

PISTHETAERUS. Tis an unworthy and criminal deed. What god was it?

SECOND MESSENGER. We don't know that. All we know is, that he has got wings.

PISTHETAERUS. Why were not guards sent against him at once?

SECOND MESSENGER. We have despatched thirty thousand hawks of the legion of mounted archers.[315] All the hook-clawed birds are moving against him, the kestrel, the buzzard, the vulture, the great-horned owl; they cleave the air, so that it resounds with the flapping of their wings; they are looking everywhere for the god, who cannot be far away; indeed, if I mistake not, he is coming from yonder side.

PISTHETAERUS. All arm themselves with slings and bows! This way, all our soldiers; shoot and strike! Some one give me a sling!

CHORUS. War, a terrible war is breaking out between us and the gods! Come, let each one guard the Air, the son of Erebus,[316] in which the clouds float. Take care no immortal enters it without your knowledge. Scan all sides with your glance. Hark! methinks I can hear the rustle of the swift wings of a god from heaven.

PISTHETAERUS. Hi! you woman! where are you flying to? Halt, don't stir! keep motionless! not a beat of your wing!—Who are you and from what country? You must say whence you come.[317]

IRIS. I come from the abode of the Olympian gods.

PISTHETAERUS. What's your name, ship or cap?[318]

IRIS. I am swift Iris.

PISTHETAERUS. Paralus or Salaminia?[319]

IRIS. What do you mean?

PISTHETAERUS. Let a buzzard rush at her and seize her.[320]

IRIS. Seize me! But what do all these insults betoken?

PISTHETAERUS. Woe to you!

IRIS. 'Tis incomprehensible.

PISTHETAERUS. By which gate did you pass through the wall, wretched woman?

IRIS. By which gate? Why, great gods, I don't know.

PISTHETAERUS. You hear how she holds us in derision. Did you present yourself to the officers in command of the jays? You don't answer. Have you a permit, bearing the seal of the storks?

IRIS. Am I awake?

PISTHETAERUS. Did you get one?

IRIS. Are you mad?

PISTHETAERUS. No head-bird gave you a safe-conduct?

IRIS. A safe-conduct to me, you poor fool!

PISTHETAERUS. Ah! and so you slipped into this city on the sly and into these realms of air-land that don't belong to you.

IRIS. And what other road can the gods travel?

PISTHETAERUS. By Zeus! I know nothing about that, not I. But they won't pass this way. And you still dare to complain! Iris would ever have more justly suffered death.

IRIS. I am immortal.

PISTHETAERUS. You would have died nevertheless.—Oh! 'twould be truly intolerable! What! should the universe obey us and the gods alone continue their insolence and not understand that they must submit to the law of the strongest in their due turn? But tell me, where are you flying to?

IRIS. I? The messenger of Zeus to mankind, I am going to tell them to sacrifice sheep and oxen on the altars and to fill their streets with the rich smoke of burning fat.

PISTHETAERUS. Of which gods are you speaking?

IRIS. Of which? Why, of ourselves, the gods of heaven.

PISTHETAERUS. You, gods?

IRIS. Are there others then?

PISTHETAERUS. Men now adore the birds as gods, and 'tis to them, by Zeus, that they must offer sacrifices, and not to Zeus at all!

IRIS. Oh! fool! fool! Rouse not the wrath of the gods, for 'tis terrible indeed. Armed with the brand of Zeus, Justice would annihilate your race; the lightning would strike you as it did Lycimnius and consume both your body and the porticos of your palace.[321]

PISTHETAERUS. Here! that's enough tall talk. Just you listen and keep quiet! Do you take me for a Lydian or a Phrygian[322] and think to frighten me with your big words? Know, that if Zeus worries me again, I shall go at the head of my eagles, who are armed with lightning, and reduce his dwelling and that of Amphion to cinders.[323] I shall send more than six hundred porphyrions clothed in leopards' skins[324] up to heaven against him; and formerly a single Porphyrion gave him enough to do. As for you, his messenger, if you annoy me, I shall begin by stretching your legs asunder and so conduct myself, Iris though you be, that despite my age, you will be astonished. I will show you a fine long tool that will fuck you three times over.

IRIS. May you perish, you wretch, you and your infamous words!

PISTHETAERUS. Won't you be off quickly? Come, stretch your wings or look out for squalls!

IRIS. If my father does not punish you for your insults….

PISTHETAERUS. Ha!… but just you be off elsewhere to roast younger folk than us with your lightning.

CHORUS. We forbid the gods, the sons of Zeus, to pass through our city and the mortals to send them the smoke of their sacrifices by this road.

PISTHETAERUS. 'Tis odd that the messenger we sent to the mortals has never returned.

HERALD. Oh! blessed Pisthetaerus, very wise, very illustrious, very gracious, thrice happy, very…. Come, prompt me, somebody, do.

PISTHETAERUS. Get to your story!

HERALD. All peoples are filled with admiration for your wisdom, and they award you this golden crown.

PISTHETAERUS. I accept it. But tell me, why do the people admire me?

HERALD. Oh you, who have founded so illustrious a city in the air, you know not in what esteem men hold you and how many there are who burn with desire to dwell in it. Before your city was built, all men had a mania for Sparta; long hair and fasting were held in honour, men went dirty like Socrates and carried staves. Now all is changed. Firstly, as soon as 'tis dawn, they all spring out of bed together to go and seek their food, the same as you do; then they fly off towards the notices and finally devour the decrees. The bird-madness is so clear, that many actually bear the names of birds. There is a halting victualler, who styles himself the partridge; Menippus calls himself the swallow; Opontius the one-eyed crow; Philocles the lark; Theogenes the fox-goose; Lycurgus the ibis; Chaerephon the bat; Syracosius the magpie; Midias the quail;[325] indeed he looks like a quail that has been hit heavily over the head. Out of love for the birds they repeat all the songs which concern the swallow, the teal, the goose or the pigeon; in each verse you see wings, or at all events a few feathers. This is what is happening down there. Finally, there are more than ten thousand folk who are coming here from earth to ask you for feathers and hooked claws; so, mind you supply yourself with wings for the immigrants.

PISTHETAERUS. Ah! by Zeus, 'tis not the time for idling Go as quick as possible and fill every hamper, every basket you can find with wings. Manes[326] will bring them to me outside the walls, where I will welcome those who present themselves.

CHORUS. This town will soon be inhabited by a crowd of men.

PISTHETAERUS. If fortune favours us.

CHORUS. Folk are more and more delighted with it.

PISTHETAERUS. Come, hurry up and bring them along.

CHORUS. Will not man find here everything that can please him—wisdom, love, the divine Graces, the sweet face of gentle peace?

PISTHETAERUS. Oh! you lazy servant! won't you hurry yourself?

CHORUS. Let a basket of wings be brought speedily. Come, beat him as I do, and put some life into him; he is as lazy as an ass.

PISTHETAERUS. Aye, Manes is a great craven.

CHORUS. Begin by putting this heap of wings in order; divide them in three parts according to the birds from whom they came; the singing, the prophetic[327] and the aquatic birds; then you must take care to distribute them to the men according to their character.

PISTHETAERUS (to Manes). Oh! by the kestrels! I can keep my hands off you no longer; you are too slow and lazy altogether.

A PARRICIDE.[328] Oh! might I but become an eagle, who soars in the skies! Oh! might I fly above the azure waves of the barren sea![329]

PISTHETAERUS. Ha! 'twould seem the news was true; I hear someone coming who talks of wings.

PARRICIDE. Nothing is more charming than to fly; I burn with desire to live under the same laws as the birds; I am bird-mad and fly towards you, for I want to live with you and to obey your laws.

PISTHETAERUS. Which laws? The birds have many laws.

PARRICIDE. All of them; but the one that pleases me most is, that among the birds it is considered a fine thing to peck and strangle one's father.

PISTHETAERUS. Aye, by Zeus! according to us, he who dares to strike his father, while still a chick, is a brave fellow.

PARRICIDE. And therefore I want to dwell here, for I want to strangle my father and inherit his wealth.

PISTHETAERUS. But we have also an ancient law written in the code of the storks, which runs thus, "When the stork father has reared his young and has taught them to fly, the young must in their turn support the father."

PARRICIDE. 'Tis hardly worth while coming all this distance to be compelled to keep my father!

PISTHETAERUS. No, no, young friend, since you have come to us with such willingness, I am going to give you these black wings, as though you were an orphan bird; furthermore, some good advice, that I received myself in infancy. Don't strike your father, but take these wings in one hand and these spurs in the other; imagine you have a cock's crest on your head and go and mount guard and fight; live on your pay and respect your father's life. You're a gallant fellow! Very well, then! Fly to Thrace and fight.[330]

PARRICIDE. By Bacchus! 'Tis well spoken; I will follow your counsel.

PISTHETAERUS. 'Tis acting wisely, by Zeus.

CINESIAS.[331] "On my light pinions I soar off to Olympus; in its capricious flight my Muse flutters along the thousand paths of poetry in turn …"

PISTHETAERUS. This is a fellow will need a whole shipload of wings.

CINESIAS. … it is seeking fresh outlet."

PISTHETAERUS. Welcome, Cinesias, you lime-wood man![332] Why have you come here a-twisting your game leg in circles?

CINESIAS. "I want to become a bird, a tuneful nightingale."

PISTHETAERUS. Enough of that sort of ditty. Tell me what you want.

CINESIAS. Give me wings and I will fly into the topmost airs to gather fresh songs in the clouds, in the midst of the vapours and the fleecy snow.

PISTHETAERUS. Gather songs in the clouds?

CINESIAS. 'Tis on them the whole of our latter-day art depends. The most brilliant dithyrambs are those that flap their wings in void space and are clothed in mist and dense obscurity. To appreciate this, just listen.

PISTHETAERUS. Oh! no, no, no!

CINESIAS. By Hermes! but indeed you shall. "I shall travel through thine ethereal empire like a winged bird, who cleaveth space with his long neck...."

PISTHETAERUS. Stop! easy all, I say![333]

CINESIAS. ... as I soar over the seas, carried by the breath of the winds ...

PISTHETAERUS. By Zeus! but I'll cut your breath short.

CINESIAS. ... now rushing along the tracks of Notus, now nearing Boreas across the infinite wastes of the ether." (*Pisthetaerus beats him.*) Ah! old man, that's a pretty and clever idea truly!

PISTHETAERUS. What! are you not delighted to be cleaving the air?[334]

CINESIAS. To treat a dithyrambic poet, for whom the tribes dispute with each other, in this style![335]

PISTHETAERUS. Will you stay with us and form a chorus of winged birds as slender as Leotrophides[336] for the Cecropid tribe?

CINESIAS. You are making game of me, 'tis clear; but know that I shall never leave you in peace if I do not have wings wherewith to traverse the air.

AN INFORMER. What are these birds with downy feathers, who look so pitiable to me? Tell me, oh swallow with the long dappled wings.[337]

PISTHETAERUS. Oh! but 'tis a perfect invasion that threatens us. Here comes another of them, humming along.

INFORMER. Swallow with the long dappled wings, once more I summon you.

PISTHETAERUS. It's his cloak I believe he's addressing; faith, it stands in great need of the swallows' return.[338]

INFORMER. Where is he who gives out wings to all comers?

PISTHETAERUS. 'Tis I, but you must tell me for what purpose you want them.

INFORMER. Ask no questions. I want wings, and wings I must have.

PISTHETAERUS. Do you want to fly straight to Pellené?[339]

INFORMER. I? Why, I am an accuser of the islands,[340] an informer ...

PISTHETAERUS. A fine trade, truly!

INFORMER. ... a hatcher of lawsuits. Hence I have great need of wings to prowl round the cities and drag them before justice.

PISTHETAERUS. Would you do this better if you had wings?

INFORMER. No, but I should no longer fear the pirates; I should return with the cranes, loaded with a supply of lawsuits by way of ballast.

PISTHETAERUS. So it seems, despite all your youthful vigour, you make it your trade to denounce strangers?

INFORMER. Well, and why not? I don't know how to dig.

PISTHETAERUS. But, by Zeus! there are honest ways of gaining a living at your age without all this infamous trickery.

INFORMER. My friend, I am asking you for wings, not for words.

PISTHETAERUS. 'Tis just my words that give you wings.

INFORMER. And how can you give a man wings with your words?

PISTHETAERUS. 'Tis thus that all first start.

INFORMER. All?

PISTHETAERUS. Have you not often heard the father say to young men in the barbers' shops, "It's astonishing how Diitrephes' advice has made my son fly to horse-riding."—"Mine," says another, "has flown towards tragic poetry on the wings of his imagination."

INFORMER. So that words give wings?

PISTHETAERUS. Undoubtedly; words give wings to the mind and make a man soar to heaven. Thus I hope that my wise words will give you wings to fly to some less degrading trade.

INFORMER. But I do not want to.

PISTHETAERUS. What do you reckon on doing then?

INFORMER. I won't belie my breeding; from generation to generation we have lived by informing. Quick, therefore, give me quickly some light, swift hawk or kestrel wings, so that I may summon the islanders, sustain the accusation here, and haste back there again on flying pinions.

PISTHETAERUS. I see. In this way the stranger will be condemned even before he appears.

INFORMER. That's just it.

PISTHETAERUS. And while he is on his way here by sea, you will be flying to the islands to despoil him of his property.

INFORMER. You've hit it, precisely; I must whirl hither and thither like a perfect humming-top.

PISTHETAERUS. I catch the idea. Wait, i' faith, I've got some fine Corcyraean wings.[341] How do you like them?

INFORMER. Oh! woe is me! Why, 'tis a whip!

PISTHETAERUS. No, no; these are the wings, I tell you, that set the top a-spinning.

INFORMER. Oh! oh! oh!

PISTHETAERUS. Take your flight, clear off, you miserable cur, or you will soon see what comes of quibbling and lying. Come, let us gather up our wings and withdraw.

CHORUS. In my ethereal nights I have seen many things new and strange and wondrous beyond belief. There is a tree called Cleonymus belonging to an unknown species; it has no heart, is good for nothing and is as tall as it is cowardly. In springtime it shoots forth calumnies instead of buds and in autumn it strews the ground with bucklers in place of leaves.[342]

Far away in the regions of darkness, where no ray of light ever enters, there is a country, where men sit at the table of the heroes and dwell with them always—save always in the evening. Should any mortal meet the hero Orestes at night, he would soon be stripped and covered with blows from head to foot.[343]

PROMETHEUS. Ah! by the gods! if only Zeus does not espy me! Where is Pisthetaerus?

PISTHETAERUS. Ha! what is this? A masked man!

PROMETHEUS. Can you see any god behind me?

PISTHETAERUS. No, none. But who are you, pray?

PROMETHEUS. What's the time, please?

PISTHETAERUS. The time? Why, it's past noon. Who are you?

PROMETHEUS. Is it the fall of day? Is it no later than that?[344]

PISTHETAERUS. Oh! 'pon my word! but you grow tiresome!

PROMETHEUS. What is Zeus doing? Is he dispersing the clouds or gathering them?[345]

PISTHETAERUS. Take care, lest I lose all patience.

PROMETHEUS. Come, I will raise my mask.

PISTHETAERUS. Ah! my dear Prometheus!

PROMETHEUS. Stop! stop! speak lower!

PISTHETAERUS. Why, what's the matter, Prometheus?

PROMETHEUS. H'sh, h'sh! Don't call me by my name; you will be my ruin, if Zeus should see me here. But, if you want me to tell you how things are going in heaven, take this umbrella and shield me, so that the gods don't see me.

PISTHETAERUS. I can recognize Prometheus in this cunning trick. Come, quick then, and fear nothing; speak on.

PROMETHEUS. Then listen.

PISTHETAERUS. I am listening, proceed!

PROMETHEUS. It's all over with Zeus.

PISTHETAERUS. Ah! and since when, pray?

PROMETHEUS. Since you founded this city in the air. There is not a man who now sacrifices to the gods; the smoke of the victims no longer reaches us. Not the smallest offering comes! We fast as though it were the festival of Demeter.[346] The barbarian gods, who are dying of hunger, are bawling like Illyrians[347] and threaten to make an armed descent upon Zeus, if he does not open markets where joints of the victims are sold.

PISTHETAERUS. What! there are other gods besides you, barbarian gods who dwell above Olympus?

PROMETHEUS. If there were no barbarian gods, who would be the patron of
Execestides?[348]

PISTHETAERUS. And what is the name of these gods?

PROMETHEUS. Their name? Why, the Triballi.[349]

PISTHETAERUS. Ah, indeed! 'tis from that no doubt that we derive the word 'tribulation.'[350]

PROMETHEUS. Most likely. But one thing I can tell you for certain, namely, that Zeus and the celestial Triballi are going to send deputies here to sue for peace. Now don't you treat, unless Zeus restores the sceptre to the birds and gives you Basileia[351] in marriage.

PISTHETAERUS. Who is this Basileia?

PROMETHEUS. A very fine young damsel, who makes the lightning for Zeus; all things come from her, wisdom, good laws, virtue, the fleet, calumnies, the public paymaster and the triobolus.

PISTHETAERUS. Ah! then she is a sort of general manageress to the god.

PROMETHEUS. Yes, precisely. If he gives you her for your wife, yours will be the almighty power. That is what I have come to tell you; for you know my constant and habitual goodwill towards men.

PISTHETAERUS. Oh, yes! 'tis thanks to you that we roast our meat.[352]

PROMETHEUS. I hate the gods, as you know.

PISTHETAERUS. Aye, by Zeus, you have always detested them.

PROMETHEUS. Towards them I am a veritable Timon;[353] but I must return in all haste, so give me the umbrella; if Zeus should see me from up there, he would think I was escorting one of the Canephori.[354]

PISTHETAERUS. Wait, take this stool as well.

CHORUS. Near by the land of the Sciapodes[355] there is a marsh, from the borders whereof the odious Socrates evokes the souls of men. Pisander[356] came one day to see his soul, which he had left there when still alive. He offered a little victim, a camel,[357] slit his throat and, following the example of Ulysses, stepped one pace backwards.[358] Then that bat of a Chaerephon[359] came up from hell to drink the camel's blood.

POSIDON.[360] This is the city of Nephelococcygia, Cloud-cuckoo-town, whither we come as ambassadors. (*To Triballus*.) Hi! what are you up to? you are throwing your cloak over the left shoulder. Come, fling it quick over the right! And why, pray, does it draggle this fashion? Have you ulcers to hide like Laespodias?[361] Oh! democracy![362] whither, oh! whither are you leading us? Is it possible that the gods have chosen such an envoy?

TRIBALLUS. Leave me alone.

POSIDON. Ugh! the cursed savage! you are by far the most barbarous of all the gods.—Tell me, Heracles, what are we going to do?

HERACLES. I have already told you that I want to strangle the fellow who has dared to block us in.

POSIDON. But, my friend, we are envoys of peace.

HERACLES. All the more reason why I wish to strangle him.

PISTHETAERUS. Hand me the cheese-grater; bring me the silphium for sauce; pass me the cheese and watch the coals.[363]

HERACLES. Mortal! we who greet you are three gods.

PISTHETAERUS. Wait a bit till I have prepared my silphium pickle.

HERACLES. What are these meats?[364]

PISTHETAERUS. These are birds that have been punished with death for attacking the people's friends.

HERACLES. And you are seasoning them before answering us?

PISTHETAERUS. Ah! Heracles! welcome, welcome! What's the matter?[365]

HERACLES. The gods have sent us here as ambassadors to treat for peace.

A SERVANT. There's no more oil in the flask.

PISTHETAERUS. And yet the birds must be thoroughly basted with it.[366]

HERACLES. We have no interest to serve in fighting you; as for you, be friends and we promise that you shall always have rain-water in your pools and the warmest of warm weather. So far as these points go we are armed with plenary authority.

PISTHETAERUS. We have never been the aggressors, and even now we are as well disposed for peace as yourselves, provided you agree to one equitable condition, namely, that Zeus yield his sceptre to the birds. If only this is agreed to, I invite the ambassadors to dinner.

HERACLES. That's good enough for me. I vote for peace.

POSIDON. You wretch! you are nothing but a fool and a glutton. Do you want to dethrone your own father?

PISTHETAERUS. What an error! Why, the gods will be much more powerful if the birds govern the earth. At present the mortals are hidden beneath the clouds, escape your observation, and commit perjury in your name; but if you had the birds for your allies, and a man, after having sworn by the crow and Zeus, should fail to keep his oath, the crow would dive down upon him unawares and pluck out his eye.

POSIDON. Well thought of, by Posidon![367]

HERACLES. My notion too.

PISTHETAERUS. (*to the Triballian*). And you, what's your opinion?

TRIBALLUS. Nabaisatreu.[368]

PISTHETAERUS. D'you see? he also approves. But hear another thing in which we can serve you. If a man vows to offer a sacrifice to some god and then procrastinates, pretending that the gods can wait, and thus does not keep his word, we shall punish his stinginess.

POSIDON. Ah! ah! and how?

PISTHETAERUS. While he is counting his money or is in the bath, a kite will relieve him, before he knows it, either in coin or in clothes, of the value of a couple of sheep, and carry it to the god.

HERACLES. I vote for restoring them the sceptre.

POSIDON. Ask the Triballian.

HERACLES. Hi! Triballian, do you want a thrashing?

TRIBALLUS. Saunaka baktarikrousa.[368]

HERACLES. He says, "Right willingly."

POSIDON. If that be the opinion of both of you, why, I consent too.

HERACLES. Very well! we accord the sceptre.

PISTHETAERUS. Ah! I was nearly forgetting another condition. I will leave
Heré to Zeus, but only if the young Basileia is given me in marriage.

POSIDON. Then you don't want peace. Let us withdraw.

PISTHETAERUS. It matters mighty little to me. Cook, look to the gravy.

HERACLES. What an odd fellow this Posidon is! Where are you off to? Are we going to war about a woman?

POSIDON. What else is there to do?

HERACLES. What else? Why, conclude peace.

POSIDON. Oh! the ninny! do you always want to be fooled? Why, you are seeking your own downfall. If Zeus were to die, after having yielded them the sovereignty, you would be ruined, for you are the heir of all the wealth he will leave behind.

PISTHETAERUS. Oh! by the gods! how he is cajoling you. Step aside, that I may have a word with you. Your uncle is getting the better of you, my poor friend.[369] The law will not allow you an obolus of the paternal property, for you are a bastard and not a legitimate child.

HERACLES. I a bastard! What's that you tell me?

PISTHETAERUS. Why, certainly; are you not born of a stranger woman?[370] Besides, is not Athené recognized as Zeus' sole heiress? And no daughter would be that, if she had a legitimate brother.

HERACLES. But what if my father wished to give me his property on his death-bed, even though I be a bastard?

PISTHETAERUS. The law forbids it, and this same Posidon would be the first to lay claim to his wealth, in virtue of being his legitimate brother. Listen; thus runs Solon's law: "A bastard shall not inherit, if there are legitimate children; and if there are no legitimate children, the property shall pass to the nearest kin."

HERACLES. And I get nothing whatever of the paternal property?

PISTHETAERUS. Absolutely nothing. But tell me, has your father had you entered on the registers of his phratria?[371]

HERACLES. No, and I have long been surprised at the omission.

PISTHETAERUS. What ails you, that you should shake your fist at heaven? Do you want to fight it? Why, be on my side, I will make you a king and will feed you on bird's milk and honey.

HERACLES. Your further condition seems fair to me. I cede you the young damsel.

POSIDON. But I, I vote against this opinion.

PISTHETAERUS. Then all depends on the Triballian. (*To the Triballian.*) What do you say?

TRIBALLUS. Big bird give daughter pretty and queen.

HERACLES. You say that you give her?

POSIDON. Why no, he does not say anything of the sort, that he gives her; else I cannot understand any better than the swallows.

PISTHETAERUS. Exactly so. Does he not say she must be given to the swallows?

POSIDON. Very well! you two arrange the matter; make peace, since you wish it so; I'll hold my tongue.

HERACLES. We are of a mind to grant you all that you ask. But come up there with us to receive Basileia and the celestial bounty.

PISTHETAERUS. Here are birds already cut up, and very suitable for a nuptial feast.

HERACLES. You go and, if you like, I will stay here to roast them.

PISTHETAERUS. You to roast them! you are too much the glutton; come along with us.

HERACLES. Ah! how well I would have treated myself!

PISTHETAERUS. Let some bring me a beautiful and magnificent tunic for the wedding.

CHORUS.[372] At Phanae,[373] near the Clepsydra,[374] there dwells a people who have neither faith nor law, the Englottogastors,[375] who reap, sow, pluck the vines and the figs[376] with their tongues; they belong to a barbaric race, and among them the Philippi and the Gorgiases[377] are to be found; 'tis these Englottogastorian Phillippi who introduced the custom all over Attica of cutting out the tongue separately at sacrifices.[378]

A MESSENGER. Oh, you, whose unbounded happiness I cannot express in words, thrice happy race of airy birds, receive your king in your fortunate dwellings. More brilliant than the brightest star that illumes the earth, he is approaching his glittering golden palace; the sun itself does not shine with more dazzling glory. He is entering with his bride at his side[379] whose beauty no human tongue can express; in his hand he brandishes the lightning, the winged shaft of Zeus; perfumes of unspeakable sweetness pervade the ethereal realms. 'Tis a glorious spectacle to see the clouds of incense wafting in light whirlwinds before the breath of the Zephyr! But here he is himself. Divine Muse! let thy sacred lips begin with songs of happy omen.

CHORUS. Fall back! to the right! to the left! advance![380] Fly around this happy mortal, whom Fortune loads with her blessings. Oh! oh! what grace! what beauty! Oh, marriage so auspicious for our city! All honour to this man! 'tis through him that the birds are called to such glorious destinies. Let your nuptial hymns, your nuptial songs, greet him and his Basileia! 'Twas in the midst of such festivities that the Fates formerly united Olympian Here to the King who governs the gods from the summit of his inaccessible throne. Oh! Hymen! oh! Hymenaeus! Rosy Eros with the golden wings held the reins and guided the chariot; 'twas he, who presided over the union of Zeus and the fortunate Heré. Oh! Hymen! oh! Hymenaeus!

PISTHETAERUS. I am delighted with your songs, I applaud your verses. Now celebrate the thunder that shakes the earth, the flaming lightning of Zeus and the terrible flashing thunderbolt.

CHORUS. Oh, thou golden flash of the lightning! oh, ye divine shafts of flame, that Zeus has hitherto shot forth! Oh, ye rolling thunders, that bring down the rain! 'Tis by the order of our king that ye shall now stagger the earth! Oh, Hymen! 'tis through thee that he commands the universe and that he makes Basileia, whom he has robbed from Zeus, take her seat at his side. Oh! Hymen! oh! Hymenaeus!

PISTHETAERUS. Let all the winged tribes of our fellow-citizens follow the bridal couple to the palace of Zeus[381] and to the nuptial couch! Stretch forth your hands, my dear wife! Take hold of me by my wings and let us dance; I am going to lift you up and carry you through the air.

CHORUS. Oh, joy! Io Paean! Tralala! victory is thine, oh, thou greatest of the gods!

* * * * *

FINIS OF "THE BIRDS"

* * * * *

Footnotes:

[175] Euelpides is holding a jay and Pisthetaerus a crow; they are the guides who are to lead them to the kingdom of the birds.

[176] A stranger, who wanted to pass as an Athenian, although coming originally from a far-away barbarian country.

[177] A king of Thrace, a son of Ares, who married Procné, the daughter of Pandion, King of Athens, whom he had assisted against the Megarians. He violated his sister-in-law, Philomela, and then cut out her tongue; she nevertheless managed to convey to her sister how she had been treated. They both agreed to kill Itys, whom Procné had born to Tereus, and dished up the limbs of his own son to the father; at the end of the meal Philomela appeared and threw the child's head upon the table. Tereus rushed with drawn sword upon the princesses, but all the actors in this terrible scene were metamorphised. Tereus became an Epops (hoopoe), Procné a swallow, Philomela a nightingale, and Itys a goldfinch. According to Anacreon and Apollodorus it was Procné who became the nightingale and Philomela the swallow, and this is the version of the tradition followed by Aristophanes.

[178] An Athenian who had some resemblance to a jay—so says the Scholiast, at any rate.

[179] Literally, *to go to the crows*, a proverbial expression equivalent to our *going to the devil*.

[180] They leave Athens because of their hatred of lawsuits and informers; this is the especial failing of the Athenians satirized in 'The Wasps.'

[181] Myrtle boughs were used in sacrifices, and the founding of every colony was started by a sacrifice.

[182] The actors wore masks made to resemble the birds they were supposed to represent.

[183] Fear had had disastrous effects upon Euelpides' internal economy, this his feet evidenced.

[184] The same mishap had occurred to Pisthetaerus.

[185] The Greek word for a wren, [Greek: trochilos], is derived from the same root as [Greek: trechein], to run.

[186] No doubt there was some scenery to represent a forest. Besides, there is a pun intended. The words answering for *forest* and *door* ([Greek: hul_e and thura]) in Greek only differ slightly in sound.

[187] Sophocles had written a tragedy about Tereus, in which, no doubt, the king finally appears as a hoopoe.

[188] A [Greek: para prosdokian]; one would expect the question to be "bird or man."—Are you a peacock? The hoopoe resembles the peacock inasmuch as both have crests.

[189] Athens.

[190] The Athenians were madly addicted to lawsuits. (*Vide* 'The Wasps.')

[191] As much as to say, *Then you have such things as anti-dicasts?* And Euelpides practically replies, *Very few.*

[192] His name was Aristocrates; he was a general and commanded a fleet sent in aid of Corcyra.

[193] The State galley, which carried the officials of the Athenian republic to their several departments and brought back those whose time had expired; it was this galley that was sent to Sicily to fetch back Alcibiades, who was accused of sacrilege.

[194] A tragic poet, who was a leper; there is a play, of course, on the Lepreum.

[195] An allusion to Opuntius, who was one-eyed.

[196] The newly-married ate a sesame cake, decorated with garlands of myrtle, poppies, and mint.

[197] From [Greek: polein], to turn.

[198] The Greek words for *pole* and *city* ([Greek: polos] and [Greek: polis]) only differ by a single letter.

[199] Boeotia separated Attica from Phocis.

[200] He swears by the powers that are to him dreadful.

[201] As already stated, according to the legend, accepted by Aristophanes, it was Procné who was turned into the nightingale.

[202] The son of Tereus and Procné.

[203] An African bird, that comes to the southern countries of Europe, to Greece, Italy, and Spain; it is even seen in Provence.

[204] Aristophanes amusingly mixes up real birds with people and individuals, whom he represents in the form of birds; he is personifying the Medians here.

[205] Philocles, a tragic poet, had written a tragedy on Tereus, which was simply a plagiarism of the play of the same name by Sophocles. Philocles is the son of Epops, because he got his inspiration from Sophocles' Tereus, and at the same time is father to Epops, since he himself produced another Tereus.

[206] This Hipponicus is probably the orator whose ears Alcibiades boxed to gain a bet; he was a descendant of Callias, who was famous for his hatred of Pisistratus.

[207] This Callias, who must not be confounded with the foe of Pisistratus, had ruined himself.

[208] Cleonymus had cast away his shield; he was as great a glutton as he was a coward.

[209] A race in which the track had to be circled twice.

[210] A people of Asia Minor; when pursued by the Ionians they took refuge in the mountains.

[211] An Athenian barber.

[212] The owl was dedicated to Athené, and being respected at Athens, it had greatly multiplied. Hence the proverb, *taking owls to Athens*, similar to our English *taking coals to Newcastle*.

[213] An allusion to the Feast of Pots; it was kept at Athens on the third day of the Anthesteria, when all sorts of vegetables were stewed together and offered for the dead to Bacchus and Athené. This Feast was peculiar to Athens.—Hence Pisthetaerus thinks that the owl will recognize they are Athenians by seeing the stew-pots, and as he is an Athenian bird, he will not attack them.

[214] Nicias, the famous Athenian general.—The siege of Melos in 417 B.C., or two years previous to the production of 'The Birds,' had especially done him great credit. He was joint commander of the Sicilian expedition.

[215] Procné, the daughter of Pandion, King of Athens.

[216] A space beyond the walls of Athens which contained the gardens of the Academy and the graves of citizens who had died for their country.

[217] A town in Western Argolis, where the Athenians had been recently defeated. The somewhat similar word in Greek, [Greek: ornithes], signifies *birds*.

[218] Epops is addressing the two slaves, no doubt Xanthias and Manes, who are mentioned later on.

[219] It was customary, when speaking in public and also at feasts, to wear a chaplet; hence the question Euelpides puts. The guests wore chaplets of flowers, herbs, and leaves, which had the property of being refreshing.

[220] A deme of Attica. In Greek the word ([Greek: kephalai]) also means *heads*, and hence the pun.

[221] One of Darius' best generals. After his expedition against the Scythians, this prince gave him the command of the army which he left in

Europe. Megabyzus took Perinthos (afterwards called Heraclea) and conquered Thrace.

[222] All Persians wore the tiara, but always on one side; the Great King alone wore it straight on his head.

[223] Noted as the birthplace of Thucydides, a deme of Attica of the tribe of Leontis. Demosthenes tells us it was thirty-five stadia from Athens.

[224] The appearance of the kite in Greece betokened the return of springtime; it was therefore worshipped as a symbol of that season.

[225] To look at the kite, who no doubt was flying high in the sky.

[226] As already shown, the Athenians were addicted to carrying small coins in their mouths.—This obolus was for the purpose of buying flour to fill the bag he was carrying.

[227] In Phoenicia and Egypt the cuckoo makes its appearance about harvest-time.

[228] This was an Egyptian proverb, meaning, *When the cuckoo sings we go harvesting*. Both the Phoenicians and the Egyptians practised circumcision.

[229] The staff, called a sceptre, generally terminated in a piece of carved work, representing a flower, a fruit, and most often a bird.

[230] A general accused of treachery. The bird watches Lysicrates, because, according to Pisthetaerus, he had a right to a share of the presents.

[231] It is thus that Phidias represents his Olympian Zeus.

[232] One of the diviners sent to Sybaris (in Magna Graecia, S. Italy) with the Athenian colonists, who rebuilt the town under the new name of Thurium.

[233] As if he were saying, "Oh, gods!" Like Lampon, he swears by the birds, instead of swearing by the gods.—The names of these birds are those of two of the Titans.

[234] Alcmena, wife of Amphitryon, King of Thebes and mother of Heracles.—Semelé, the daughter of Cadmus and Hermioné and mother of Bacchus; both seduced by Zeus.—Alopé, daughter of Cercyon, a robber, who reigned at Eleusis and was conquered by Perseus. Alopé was honoured with Posidon's caresses; by him she had a son named Hippothous, at first brought up by shepherds but who afterwards was restored to the throne of his grandfather by Theseus.

[235] Because the bald patch on the coot's head resembles the shaven and depilated 'motte.'

[236] Because water is the duck's domain, as it is that of Posidon.

[237] Because the gull, like Heracles, is voracious.

[238] The Germans still call it *Zaunkönig* and the French *roitelet*, both names thus containing the idea of *king*.

[239] The Scholiast draws our attention to the fact that Homer says this of Heré and not of Iris (Iliad, V. 778); it is only another proof that the text of Homer has reached us in a corrupted form, or it may be that Aristophanes was liable, like other people, to occasional mistakes of quotation.

[240] In sacrifices.

[241] An Athenian proverb.

[242] A celebrated temple to Zeus in an oasis of Libya.

[243] Nicias was commander, along with Demosthenes, and later on Alcibiades, of the Athenian forces before Syracuse, in the ill-fated Sicilian Expedition, 415-413 B.C. He was much blamed for dilatoriness and indecision.

[244] Servants of Pisthetaerus and Euelpides.

[245] It has already been mentioned that, according to the legend followed by Aristophanes, Procné had been changed into a nightingale and Philomela into a swallow.

[246] The actor, representing Procné, was dressed out as a courtesan, but wore the mask of a bird.

[247] Young unmarried girls wore golden ornaments; the apparel of married women was much simpler.

[248] The actor, representing Procné, was a flute-player.

[249] The parabasis.

[250] A sophist of the island of Ceos, a disciple of Protagoras, as celebrated for his knowledge as for his eloquence. The Athenians condemned him to death as a corrupter of youth in 396 B.C.

[251] Lovers were wont to make each other presents of birds. The cock and the goose are mentioned, of course, in jest.

[252] i.e. that it gave notice of the approach of winter, during which season the Ancients did not venture to sea.

[253] A notorious robber.

[254] Meaning, "*We are your oracles.*"—Dodona was an oracle in Epirus.—The temple of Zeus there was surrounded by a dense forest, all the trees of which were endowed with the gift of prophecy; both the sacred oaks and the pigeons that lived in them answered the questions of those who came to consult the oracle in pure Greek.

[255] The Greek word for *omen* is the same as that for *bird*—[Greek: ornis].

[256] A satire on the passion of the Greeks for seeing an omen in everything.

[257] An imitation of the nightingale's song.

[258] God of the groves and wilds.

[259] The 'Mother of the Gods'; roaming the mountains, she held dances, always attended by Pan and his accompanying rout of Fauns and Satyrs.

[260] An allusion to cock-fighting; the birds are armed with brazen spurs.

[261] An allusion to the spots on this bird, which resemble the scars left by a branding iron.

[262] He was of Asiatic origin, but wished to pass for an Athenian.

[263] Or Philamnon, King of Thrace; the Scholiast remarks that the Phrygians and the Thracians had a common origin.

[264] The Greek word here, [Greek: pappos], is also the name of a little bird.

[265] A basket-maker who had become rich.—The Phylarchs were the headmen of the tribes, [Greek: Phulai]. They presided at the private assemblies and were charged with the management of the treasury.—The Hipparchs, as the name implies, were the leaders of the cavalry; there were only two of these in the Athenian army.

[266] He had now become a senator, member of the [Greek: Boul_e].

[267] Pisthetaerus and Euelpides now both return with wings.

[268] Meaning, 'tis we who wanted to have these wings.—The verse from Aeschylus, quoted here, is taken from 'The Myrmidons,' a tragedy of which only a few fragments remain.

[269] The Greek word signified the city of Sparta, and also a kind of broom used for weaving rough matting, which served for the beds of the very poor.

[270] A fanciful name constructed from [Greek: nephel_e], a cloud, and [Greek: kokkux], a cuckoo; thus a city of clouds and cuckoos.— *Wolkenkukelheim*[*] is a clever approximation in German. Cloud-cuckoo-town, perhaps, is the best English equivalent.

[* Transcriber's note: So in original. The correct German word is *Wolkenkuckucksheim*.]

[271] He was a boaster nicknamed [Greek: Kapnos], *smoke*, because he promised a great deal and never kept his word.

[272] Also mentioned in 'The Wasps.'

[273] Because the war of the Titans against the gods was only a fiction of the poets.

[274] A sacred cloth, with which the statue of Athené in the Acropolis was draped.

[275] Meaning, to be patron-goddess of the city. Athené had a temple of this name.

[276] An Athenian effeminate, frequently ridiculed by Aristophanes.

[277] This was the name of the wall surrounding the Acropolis.

[278] i.e. the fighting-cock.

[279] To waken the sentinels, who might else have fallen asleep.—There are several merry contradictions in the various parts of this list of injunctions.

[280] In allusion to the leather strap which flute-players wore to constrict the cheeks and add to the power of the breath. The performer here no doubt wore a raven's mask.

[281] Hellanicus, the Mitylenian historian, tells that this surname of Artemis is derived from Colaenus, King of Athens before Cecrops and a descendant

of Hermes. In obedience to an oracle he erected a temple to the goddess, invoking her as Artemis Colaenis (the Artemis of Colaenus).

[282] This Cleocritus, says the Scholiast, was long-necked and strutted like an ostrich.

[283] The Chians were the most faithful allies of Athens, and hence their name was always mentioned in prayers, decrees, etc.

[284] Verses sung by maidens.

[285] This ceremony took place on the tenth day after birth, and may be styled the pagan baptism.

[286] Hiero, tyrant of Syracuse.—This passage is borrowed from Pindar.

[287] [Greek: Hierón] in Greek means sacrifice.

[288] A parody of poetic pathos, not to say bathos.

[289] Which the priest was preparing to sacrifice.

[290] Orneae, a city in Argolis ([Greek: ornis] in Greek means a bird). It was because of this similarity in sound that the prophet alludes to Orneae.

[291] Noted Athenian diviner, who, when the power was still shared between Thucydides and Pericles, predicted that it would soon be centred in the hands of the latter; his ground for this prophecy was the sight of a ram with a single horn.

[292] No doubt another Athenian diviner, and possibly the same person whom Aristophanes names in 'The Knights' and 'The Wasps' as being a thief.

[293] A celebrated geometrician and astronomer.

[294] A deme contiguous to Athens. It is as though he said, "Well known throughout all England and at Croydon."

[295] Thales was no less famous as a geometrician than he was as a sage.

[296] Officers of Athens, whose duty was to protect strangers who came on political or other business, and see to their interests generally.

[297] He addresses the inspector thus because of the royal and magnificent manners he assumes.

[298] Magistrates appointed to inspect the tributary towns.

[299] A much-despised citizen, already mentioned. He ironically supposes him invested with the powers of an Archon, which ordinarily were entrusted only to men of good repute.

[300] A Persian satrap.—An allusion to certain orators, who, bribed with Asiatic gold, had often defended the interests of the foe in the Public Assembly.

[301] A Macedonian people in the peninsula of Chalcidice. This name is chosen because of its similarity to the Greek word [Greek: o_ophuresthai], *to groan*. It is from another verb, [Greek: ototuzein], meaning the same thing, that Pisthetaerus coins the name of Ototyxians, i.e. groaners, because he is about to beat the dealer.—The mother-country had the right to impose any law it chose upon its colonies.

[302] Corresponding to our month of April.

[303] Which the inspector had brought with him for the purpose of inaugurating the assemblies of the people or some tribunal.

[304] So that the sacrifices might no longer be interrupted.

[305] A disciple of Democrites; he passed over from superstition to atheism. The injustice and perversity of mankind led him to deny the existence of the gods, to lay bare the mysteries and to break the idols. The Athenians had put a price on his head, so he left Greece and perished soon afterwards in a storm at sea.

[306] By this jest Aristophanes means to imply that tyranny is dead, and that no one aspires to despotic power, though this silly accusation was constantly being raised by the demagogues and always favourably received by the populace.

[307] A poulterer.—Strouthian, used in joke to designate him, as if from the name of his 'deme,' is derived from [Greek: strouthos], *a sparrow*. The birds' foe is thus grotesquely furnished with an ornithological surname.

[308] From Aphrodité (Venus), to whom he had awarded the apple, prize of beauty, in the contest of the "goddesses three."

[309] Laurium was an Athenian deme at the extremity of the Attic peninsula containing valuable silver mines, the revenues of which were largely employed in the maintenance of the fleet and payment of the crews. The "owls of Laurium," of course, mean pieces of money; the Athenian coinage was stamped with a representation of an owl, the bird of Athené.

[310] A pun impossible to keep in English, on the two meanings of the word [Greek: aetos], which signifies both an eagle and the gable of a house or pediment of a temple.

[311] That is, birds' crops, into which they could stow away plenty of good things.

[312] The Ancients appear to have placed metal discs over statues standing in the open air, to save them from injury from the weather, etc.

[313] So as not to be carried away by the wind when crossing the sea, cranes are popularly supposed to ballast themselves with stones, which they carry in their beaks.

[314] Pisthetaerus modifies the Greek proverbial saying, "To what use cannot hands be put?"

[315] A corps of Athenian cavalry was so named.

[316] Chaos, Night, Tartarus, and Erebus alone existed in the beginning; Eros was born from Night and Erebus, and he wedded Chaos and begot Earth, Air, and Heaven; so runs the fable.

[317] Iris appears from the top of the stage and arrests her flight in mid-career.

[318] Ship, because of her wings, which resemble oars; cap, because she no doubt wore the head-dress (as a messenger of the gods) with which Hermes is generally depicted.

[319] The names of the two sacred galleys which carried Athenian officials on State business.

[320] A buzzard is named in order to raise a laugh, the Greek name [Greek: triorchos] also meaning, etymologically, provided with three testicles, vigorous in love.

[321] Iris' reply is a parody of the tragic style.—'Lycimnius' is, according to the Scholiast, the title of a tragedy by Euripides, which is about a ship that is struck by lightning.

[322] i.e. for a poltroon, like the slaves, most of whom came to Athens from these countries.

[323] A parody of a passage in the lost tragedy of 'Niobe' of Aeschylus.

[324] Because this bird has a spotted plumage.—Porphyrion is also the name of one of the Titans who tried to storm heaven.

[325] All these surnames bore some relation to the character or the build of the individual to whom the poet applies them.—Chaerephon, Socrates' disciple, was of white and ashen hue.—Opontius was one-eyed.—Syracosius was a braggart.—Midias had a passion for quail-fights, and, besides, resembled that bird physically.

[326] Pisthetaerus' servant, already mentioned.

[327] From the inspection of which auguries were taken, e.g. the eagles, the vultures, the crows.

[328] Or rather, a young man who contemplated parricide.

[329] A parody of verses in Sophocles' 'Oenomaus.'

[330] The Athenians were then besieging Amphipolis in the Thracian Chalcidicé.

[331] There was a real Cinesias—a dithyrambic poet, born at Thebes.

[332] The Scholiast thinks that Cinesias, who was tall and slight of build, wore a kind of corset of lime-wood to support his waist—surely rather a far-fetched interpretation!

[333] The Greek word used here was the word of command employed to stop the rowers.

[334] Cinesias makes a bound each time that Pisthetaerus struck him.

[335] The tribes of Athens, or rather the rich citizens belonging to them, were wont on feast-days to give representations of dithyrambic choruses as well as of tragedies and comedies.

[336] Another dithyrambic poet, a man of extreme leanness.

[337] A parody of a hemistich from 'Alcaeus.'—The informer is dissatisfied at only seeing birds of sombre plumage and poor appearance. He would have preferred to denounce the rich.

[338] The informer, says the Scholiast, was clothed with a ragged cloak, the tatters of which hung down like wings, in fact, a cloak that could not protect him from the cold and must have made him long for the swallows' return, i.e. the spring.

[339] A town in Achaia, where woollen cloaks were made.

[340] His trade was to accuse the rich citizens of the subject islands, and drag them before the Athenian courts; he explains later the special advantages of this branch of the informer's business.

[341] That is, whips—Corcyra being famous for these articles.

[342] Cleonymus is a standing butt of Aristophanes' wit, both as an informer and a notorious poltroon.

[343] In allusion to the cave of the bandit Orestes; the poet terms him a hero only because of his heroic name Orestes.

[344] Prometheus wants night to come and so reduce the risk of being seen from Olympus.

[345] The clouds would prevent Zeus seeing what was happening below him.

[346] The third day of the festival of Demeter was a fast.

[347] A semi-savage people, addicted to violence and brigandage.

[348] Who, being reputed a stranger despite his pretension to the title of a citizen, could only have a strange god for his patron or tutelary deity.

[349] The Triballi were a Thracian people; it was a term commonly used in Athens to describe coarse men, obscene debauchees and greedy parasites.

[350] There is a similar pun in the Greek.

[351] i.e. the *supremacy* of Greece, the real object of the war

[352] Prometheus had stolen the fire from the gods to gratify mankind.

[353] A celebrated misanthrope, contemporary to Aristophanes. Hating the society of men, he had only a single friend, Apimantus, to whom he was attached, because of their similarity of character; he also liked Alcibiades, because he foresaw that this young man would be the ruin of his country.

[354] The Canephori were young maidens, chosen from the first families of the city, who carried baskets wreathed with myrtle at the feast of Athené, while at those of Bacchus and Demeter they appeared with gilded baskets.—The daughters of 'Metics,' or resident aliens, walked behind them, carrying an umbrella and a stool.

[355] According to Ctesias, the Sciapodes were a people who dwelt on the borders of the Atlantic. Their feet were larger than the rest of their bodies, and to shield themselves from the sun's rays they held up one of their feet as an umbrella.—By giving the Socratic philosophers the name of Sciapodes here ([Greek: *podes*], feet, and [Greek: *skia*], shadow) Aristophanes wishes to convey that they are walking in the dark and busying themselves with the greatest nonsense.

[356] This Pisander was a notorious coward; for this reason the poet jestingly supposes that he had lost his soul, the seat of courage.

[357] A [Greek: para prosdokian], considering the shape and height of the camel, which can certainly not be included in the list of *small* victims, e.g. the sheep and the goat.

[358] In the evocation of the dead, Book XI of the Odyssey.

[359] Chaerephon was given this same title by the Herald earlier in this comedy.—Aristophanes supposes him to have come from hell because he is lean and pallid.

[360] Posidon appears on the stage accompanied by Heracles and a Triballian god.

[361] An Athenian general.—Neptune is trying to give Triballus some notions of elegance and good behaviour.

[362] Aristophanes supposes that democracy is in the ascendant in Olympus as it is in Athens.

[363] He is addressing his servant, Manes.

[364] Heracles softens at sight of the food.—Heracles is the glutton of the comic poets.

[365] He pretends not to have seen them at first, being so much engaged with his cookery.

[366] He pretends to forget the presence of the ambassadors.

[367] Posidon jestingly swears by himself.

[368] The barbarian god utters some gibberish which Pisthetaerus interprets into consent.

[369] Heracles, the god of strength, was far from being remarkable in the way of cleverness.

[370] This was Athenian law.

[371] The poet attributes to the gods the same customs as those which governed Athens, and according to which no child was looked upon as legitimate unless his father had entered him on the registers of his phratria. The phratria was a division of the tribe and consisted of thirty families.

[372] The chorus continues to tell what it has seen on its flights.

[373] The harbour of the island of Chios; but this name is here used in the sense of being the land of informers ([Greek: phainein], to denounce).

[374] i.e. near the orators' platform, or [Greek: B_ema], in the Public Assembly, or [Greek: Ekkl_esia], because there stood the [Greek: klepsudra], or water-clock, by which speeches were limited.

[375] A coined name, made up of [Greek: gl_otta], the tongue, and [Greek: gast_er], the stomach, and meaning those who fill their stomach with what they gain with their tongues, to wit, the orators.

[376] [Greek: Sukon] a fig, forms part of the word, [Greek: sukophant_es], which in Greek means an informer.

---

[377] Both rhetoricians.

[378] Because they consecrated it specially to the god of eloquence.

[379] Basileia, whom he brings back from heaven.

[380] Terms used in regulating a dance.

[381] Where Pisthetaerus is henceforth to reign.

THE FROGS

INTRODUCTION

Like 'The Birds' this play rather avoids politics than otherwise, its leading *motif*, over and above the pure fun and farce for their own sake of the burlesque descent into the infernal regions, being a literary one, an onslaught on Euripides the Tragedian and all his works and ways.

It was produced in the year 405 B.C., the year after 'The Birds,' and only one year before the Peloponnesian War ended disastrously for the Athenian cause in the capture of the city by Lysander. First brought out at the Lenaean festival in January, it was played a second time at the Dionysia in March of the same year—a far from common honour. The drama was not staged in the Author's own name, we do not know for what reasons. but it won the first prize, Phrynichus' 'Muses' being second.

The plot is as follows. The God Dionysus, patron of the Drama, is dissatisfied with the condition of the Art of Tragedy at Athens, and resolves to descend to Hades in order to bring back again to earth one of the old tragedians—Euripides, he thinks, for choice. Dressing himself up, lion's skin and club complete, as Heracles, who has performed the same perilous journey before, and accompanied by his slave Xanthias (a sort of classical Sancho Panza) with the baggage, he starts on the fearful expedition.

Coming to the shores of Acheron, he is ferried over in Charon's boat—Xanthias has to walk round—the First Chorus of Marsh Frogs (from which the play takes its title) greeting him with prolonged croakings. Approaching Pluto's Palace in fear and trembling, he knocks timidly at the gate. Being presently admitted, he finds a contest on the point of being held before the King of Hades and the Initiates of the Eleusinian Mysteries, who form the Second Chorus, between Aeschylus, the present occupant of the throne of tragic excellence in hell, and the pushing, self-satisfied, upstart Euripides, who is for ousting him from his pride of place.

Each poet quotes in turn from his Dramas, and the indignant Aeschylus makes fine fun of his rival's verses, and shows him up in the usual Aristophanic style as a corrupter of morals, a contemptible casuist, and a professor of the dangerous new learning of the Sophists, so justly held in suspicion by true-blue Athenian Conservatives. Eventually a pair of scales is brought in, and verses alternately spouted by the two candidates are weighed against each other, the mighty lines of the Father of Tragedy making his flippant, finickin little rival's scale kick the beam every time.

Dionysus becomes a convert to the superior merits of the old school of tragedy, and contemptuously dismisses Euripides, to take Aeschylus back with him to the upper world instead, leaving Sophocles meantime in occupation of the coveted throne of tragedy in the nether regions.

Needless to say, the various scenes of the journey to Hades, the crossing of Acheron, the Frogs' choric songs, and the trial before Pluto, afford opportunities for much excellent fooling in our Author's very finest vein of drollery, and "seem to have supplied the original idea for those modern burlesques upon the Olympian and Tartarian deities which were at one time so popular."

* * * * *

THE FROGS

DRAMATIS PERSONAE

DIONYSUS.
XANTHIAS, his Servant.
HERACLES.
A DEAD MAN.
CHARON.
AEACUS.
FEMALE ATTENDANT OF PERSEPHONÉ.
INKEEPERS' WIVES.
EURIPIDES.
AESCHYLUS.
PLUTO.
CHORUS OF FROGS.
CHORUS OF INITIATES.

SCENE: In front of the temple of Heracles, and on the banks of Acheron in the Infernal Regions.

* * * * *

THE FROGS

XANTHIAS. Now am I to make one of those jokes that have the knack of always making the spectators laugh?

DIONYSUS. Aye, certainly, any one you like, excepting "I am worn out." Take care you don't say that, for it gets on my nerves.

XANTHIAS. Do you want some other drollery?

DIONYSUS. Yes, only not, "I am quite broken up."

XANTHIAS. Then what witty thing shall I say?

DIONYSUS. Come, take courage; only ...

XANTHIAS. Only what?

DIONYSUS. ... don't start saying as you shift your package from shoulder to shoulder, "Ah! that's a relief!"

XANTHIAS. May I not at least say, that unless I am relieved of this cursed load I shall let wind?

DIONYSUS. Oh! for pity's sake, no! you don't want to make me spew.

XANTHIAS. What need then had I to take this luggage, if I must not copy the porters that Phrynichus, Lycis and Amipsias[382] never fail to put on the stage?

DIONYSUS. Do nothing of the kind. Whenever I chance to see one of these stage tricks, I always leave the theatre feeling a good year older.

XANTHIAS. Oh! my poor back! you are broken and I am not allowed to make a single joke.

DIONYSUS. Just mark the insolence of this Sybarite! I, Dionysus, the son of a … wine-jar,[383] I walk, I tire myself, and I set yonder rascal upon an ass, that he may not have the burden of carrying his load.

XANTHIAS. But am I not carrying it?

DIONYSUS. No, since you are on your beast.

XANTHIAS. Nevertheless I am carrying this….

DIONYSUS. What?

XANTHIAS. … and it is very heavy.

DIONYSUS. But this burden you carry is borne by the ass.

XANTHIAS. What I have here, 'tis certainly I who bear it, and not the ass, no, by all the gods, most certainly not!

DIONYSUS. How can you claim to be carrying it, when you are carried?

XANTHIAS. That I can't say; but this shoulder is broken, anyhow.

DIONYSUS. Well then, since you say that the ass is no good to you, pick her up in your turn and carry her.

XANTHIAS. What a pity I did not fight at sea;[384] I would baste your ribs for that joke.

DIONYSUS. Dismount, you clown! Here is a door,[385] at which I want to make my first stop. Hi! slave! hi! hi! slave!

HERACLES (*from inside the Temple*). Do you want to beat in the door? He knocks like a Centaur.[386] Why, what's the matter?

DIONYSUS. Xanthias!

XANTHIAS. Well?

DIONYSUS. Did you notice?

XANTHIAS. What?

DIONYSUS. How I frightened him?

XANTHIAS. Bah! you're mad!

HERACLES. Ho, by Demeter! I cannot help laughing; it's no use biting my lips, I must laugh.

DIONYSUS. Come out, friend; I have need of you.

HERACLES. Oh! 'tis enough to make a fellow hold his sides to see this lion's-skin over a saffron robe![387] What does this mean? Buskins[388] and a bludgeon! What connection have they? Where are you off to in this rig?

DIONYSUS. When I went aboard Clisthenes[389]....

HERACLES. Did you fight?

DIONYSUS. We sank twelve or thirteen ships of the enemy.

HERACLES. You?

DIONYSUS. Aye, by Apollo!

HERACLES. You have dreamt it.[390]

DIONYSUS. As I was reading the 'Andromeda'[391] on the ship, I suddenly felt my heart afire with a wish so violent....

HERACLES. A wish! of what nature?

DIONYSUS. Oh, quite small, like Molon.[392]

HERACLES. You wished for a woman?

DIONYSUS. No.

HERACLES. A young boy, then?

DIONYSUS. Nothing of the kind.

HERACLES. A man?

DIONYSUS. Faugh!

HERACLES. Might you then have had dealings with Clisthenes?

DIONYSUS. Have mercy, brother; no mockery! I am quite ill, so greatly does my desire torment me!

HERACLES. And what desire is it, little brother?

DIONYSUS. I cannot disclose it, but I will convey it to you by hints. Have you ever been suddenly seized with a desire for pea-soup?

HERACLES. For pea-soup! oh! oh! yes, a thousand times in my life.[393]

DIONYSUS. Do you take me or shall I explain myself in some other way?

HERACLES. Oh! as far as the pea-soup is concerned, I understand marvellously well.

DIONYSUS. So great is the desire, which devours me, for Euripides.

HERACLES. But he is dead.[394]

DIONYSUS. There is no human power can prevent my going to him.

HERACLES. To the bottom of Hades?

DIONYSUS. Aye, and further than the bottom, an it need.

HERACLES. And what do you want with him?

DIONYSUS. I want a master poet; "some are dead and gone, and others are good for nothing."[395]

HERACLES. Is Iophon[396] dead then?

DIONYSUS. He is the only good one left me, and even of him I don't know quite what to think.

HERACLES. Then there's Sophocles, who is greater than Euripides; if you must absolutely bring someone back from Hades, why not make him live again?

DIONYSUS. No, not until I have taken Iophon by himself and tested him for what he is worth. Besides, Euripides is very artful and won't leave a stone unturned to get away with me, whereas Sophocles is as easy-going with Pluto as he was when on earth.

HERACLES. And Agathon? Where is he?[397]

DIONYSUS. He has left me; 'twas a good poet and his friends regret him.

HERACLES. And whither has the poor fellow gone?

DIONYSUS. To the banquet of the blest.

HERACLES. And Xenocles?[398]

DIONYSUS. May the plague seize him!

HERACLES. And Pythangelus?[399]

XANTHIAS. They don't say ever a word of poor me, whose shoulder is quite shattered.

HERACLES. Is there not a crowd of other little lads, who produce tragedies by the thousand and are a thousand times more loquacious than Euripides?

DIONYSUS. They are little sapless twigs, chatterboxes, who twitter like the swallows, destroyers of the art, whose aptitude is withered with a single piece and who sputter forth all their talent to the tragic Muse at their first attempt. But look where you will, you will not find a creative poet who gives vent to a noble thought.

HERACLES. How creative?

DIONYSUS. Aye, creative, who dares to risk "the ethereal dwellings of Zeus," or "the wing of Time," or "a heart that is above swearing by the sacred emblems," and "a tongue that takes an oath, while yet the soul is unpledged."[400]

HERACLES. Is that the kind of thing that pleases you?

DIONYSUS. I'm more than madly fond of it.

HERACLES. But such things are simply idiotic. you feel it yourself.

DIONYSUS. "Don't come trespassing on my mind; you have a brain of your own to keep thoughts in."[401]

HERACLES. But nothing could be more detestable.

DIONYSUS. Where cookery is concerned, you can be my master.[402]

XANTHIAS. They don't say a thing about me!

DIONYSUS. If I have decked myself out according to your pattern, 'tis that you may tell me, in case I should need them, all about the hosts who received you, when you journeyed to Cerberus; tell me of them as well as of the harbours, the bakeries, the brothels, the drinking-shops, the fountains, the roads, the eating-houses and of the hostels where there are the fewest bugs.

XANTHIAS. They never speak of me.[403]

HERACLES. Go down to hell? Will you be ready to dare that, you madman?

DIONYSUS. Enough of that; but tell me the shortest road, that is neither too hot nor too cold, to get down to Pluto.

HERACLES. Let me see, what is the best road to show you? Aye, which? Ah! there's the road of the gibbet and the rope. Go and hang yourself.

DIONYSUS. Be silent! your road is choking me.

HERACLES. There is another path, both very short and well-trodden; the one that goes through the mortar.[404]

DIONYSUS. 'Tis hemlock you mean to say.

HERACLES. Precisely so.

DIONYSUS. That road is both cold and icy. Your legs get frozen at once.[405]

HERACLES. Do you want me to tell you a very steep road, one that descends very quickly?

DIONYSUS. Ah! with all my heart; I don't like long walks.

HERACLES. Go to the Ceramicus.[406]

DIONYSUS. And then?

HERACLES. Mount to the top of the highest tower ...

DIONYSUS. To do what?

HERACLES. ... and there keep your eye on the torch, which is to be the signal. When the spectators demand it to be flung, fling yourself ...

DIONYSUS. Where?

HERACLES. … down.

DIONYSUS. But I should break the two hemispheres of my brain. Thanks for your road, but I don't want it.

HERACLES. But which one then?

DIONYSUS. The one you once travelled yourself.

HERACLES. Ah! that's a long journey. First you will reach the edge of the vast, deep mere of Acheron.

DIONYSUS. And how is that to be crossed?

HERACLES. There is an ancient ferryman, Charon by name, who will pass you over in his little boat for a diobolus.

DIONYSUS. Oh! what might the diobolus has everywhere! But however has it got as far as that?

HERACLES. 'Twas Theseus who introduced its vogue.[407] After that you will see snakes and all sorts of fearful monsters …

DIONYSUS. Oh! don't try to frighten me and make me afraid, for I am quite decided.

HERACLES. … then a great slough with an eternal stench, a veritable cesspool, into which those are plunged who have wronged a guest, cheated a young boy out of the fee for his complaisance, beaten their mother, boxed their father's ears, taken a false oath or transcribed some tirade of Morsimus.[408]

DIONYSUS. For mercy's sake, add likewise—or learnt the Pyrrhic dance of Cinesias.[409]

HERACLES. Further on 'twill be a gentle concert of flutes on every side, a brilliant light, just as there is here, myrtle groves, bands of happy men and women and noisy plaudits.

DIONYSUS. Who are these happy folk?

HERACLES. The initiate.[410]

XANTHIAS. And I am the ass that carries the Mysteries;[411] but I've had enough of it.

HERACLES. They will give you all the information you will need, for they live close to Pluto's palace, indeed on the road that leads to it. Farewell, brother, and an agreeable journey to you. (*He returns into his Temple.*)

DIONYSUS. And you, good health. Slave! take up your load again.

XANTHIAS. Before having laid it down?

DIONYSUS. And be quick about it too.

XANTHIAS. Oh, no, I adjure you! Rather hire one of the dead, who is going to Hades.

DIONYSUS. And should I not find one....

XANTHIAS. Then you can take me.

DIONYSUS. You talk sense. Ah! here they are just bringing a dead man along. Hi! man, 'tis you I'm addressing, you, dead fellow there! Will you carry a package to Pluto for me?

DEAD MAN. Is't very heavy?

DIONYSUS. This. (*He shows him the baggage, which Xanthias has laid on the ground.*)

DEAD MAN. You will pay me two drachmae.

DIONYSUS. Oh! that's too dear.

DEAD MAN. Well then, bearers, move on.

DIONYSUS. Stay, friend, so that I may bargain with you.

DEAD MAN. Give me two drachmae, or it's no deal.

DIONYSUS. Hold! here are nine obols.

DEAD MAN. I would sooner go back to earth again.

XANTHIAS. Is that cursed rascal putting on airs? Come, then, I'll go.

DIONYSUS. You're a good and noble fellow. Let us make the best of our way to the boat.

CHARON. Ahoy, ahoy! put ashore.

XANTHIAS. What's that?

DIONYSUS. Why, by Zeus, 'tis the mere of which Heracles spoke, and I see the boat.

XANTHIAS. Ah! there's Charon.

DIONYSUS. Hail! Charon.

DEAD MAN. Hail! Charon.

CHARON. Who comes hither from the home of cares and misfortunes to rest on the banks of Lethé? Who comes to the ass's fleece, who is for the land of the Cerberians, or the crows, or Taenarus?

DIONYSUS. I am.

CHARON. Get aboard quick then.

DIONYSUS. Where will you ferry me to? Where are you going to land me?

CHARON. In hell, if you wish. But step in, do.

DIONYSUS. Come here, slave.

CHARON. I carry no slave, unless he has fought at sea to save his skin.

XANTHIAS. But I could not, for my eyes were bad.

CHARON. Well then! be off and walk round the mere.

XANTHIAS. Where shall I come to a halt?

CHARON. At the stone of Auaenus, near the drinking-shop.

DIONYSUS. Do you understand?

XANTHIAS. Perfectly. Oh! unhappy wretch that I am, surely, surely I must have met something of evil omen as I came out of the house?[412]

CHARON. Come, sit to your oar. If there be anyone else who wants to cross, let him hurry. Hullo! what are you doing?

DIONYSUS. What am I doing? I am sitting on the oar[413] as you told me.

CHARON. Will you please have the goodness to place yourself there, pot-belly?

DIONYSUS. There.

CHARON. Put out your hands, stretch your arms.

DIONYSUS. There.

CHARON. No tomfoolery! row hard, and put some heart into the work!

DIONYSUS. Row! and how can I? I, who have never set foot on a ship?

CHARON. There's nothing easier; and once you're at work, you will hear some enchanting singers.

DIONYSUS. Who are they?

CHARON. Frogs with the voices of swans; 'tis most delightful.

DIONYSUS. Come, set the stroke.

CHARON. Yo ho! yo ho!

FROGS. Brekekekex, coax, coax, brekekekekex, coax. Slimy offspring of the marshland, let our harmonious voices mingle with the sounds of the flute, coax, coax! let us repeat the songs that we sing in honour of the Nysaean Dionysus[414] on the day of the feast of pots,[415] when the drunken throng reels towards our temple in the Limnae.[416] Brekekekex, coax, coax.

DIONYSUS. I am beginning to feel my bottom getting very sore, my dear little coax, coax.

FROGS. Brekekekex, coax, coax.

DIONYSUS. But doubtless you don't care.

FROGS. Brekekekex, coax, coax.

DIONYSUS. May you perish with your coax, your endless coax!

FROGS. And why change it, you great fool? I am beloved by the Muses with the melodious lyre, by the goat-footed Pan, who draws soft tones out of his reed; I am the delight of Apollo, the god of the lyre, because I make the rushes, which are used for the bridge of the lyre, grow in my marshes. Brekekekex, coax, coax.

DIONYSUS. I have got blisters and my behind is all of a sweat; by dint of constant movement, it will soon be saying....

FROGS. Brekekekex, coax, coax.

DIONYSUS. Come, race of croakers, be quiet.

FROGS. Not we; we shall only cry the louder. On fine sunny days, it pleases us to hop through galingale and sedge and to sing while we swim; and when Zeus is pouring down his rain, we join our lively voices to the rustle of the drops. Brekekekex, coax, coax.

DIONYSUS. I forbid you to do it.

FROGS. Oh! that would be too hard!

DIONYSUS. And is it not harder for me to wear myself out with rowing?

FROGS. Brekekekex, coax, coax.

DIONYSUS. May you perish! I don't care.

FROGS. And from morning till night we will shriek with the whole width of our gullets, "Brekekekex, coax, coax."

DIONYSUS. I will cry louder than you all.

FROGS. Oh! don't do that!

DIONYSUS. Oh, yes, I will. I shall cry the whole day, if necessary, until I no longer hear your coax. (*He begins to cry against the frogs, who finally stop.*) Ah! I knew I would soon put an end to your coax.

CHARON. Enough, enough, a last pull, ship oars, step ashore and pay your passage money.

DIONYSUS. Look! here are my two obols…. Xanthias! where is Xanthias? Hi! Xanthias!

XANTHIAS (*from a distance*). Hullo!

DIONYSUS. Come here.

XANTHIAS. I greet you, master.

DIONYSUS. What is there that way?

XANTHIAS. Darkness and mud!

DIONYSUS. Did you see the parricides and the perjured he told us of?

XANTHIAS. Did you?

DIONYSUS. Ha! by Posidon! I see some of them now.[417] Well, what are we going to do?

XANTHIAS. The best is to go on, for 'tis here that the horrible monsters are, Heracles told us of.

DIONYSUS. Ah! the wag! He spun yarns to frighten me, but I am a brave fellow and he is jealous of me. There exists no greater braggart than Heracles. Ah! I wish I might meet some monster, so as to distinguish myself by some deed of daring worthy of my daring journey.

XANTHIAS. Ah! hark! I hear a noise.

DIONYSUS (*all of a tremble*). Where then, where?

XANTHIAS. Behind you.

DIONYSUS. Place yourself behind me.

XANTHIAS. Ah! 'tis in front now.

DIONYSUS. Then pass to the front.

XANTHIAS. Oh! what a monster I can see!

DIONYSUS. What's it like?

XANTHIAS. Dreadful, terrible! it assumes every shape; now 'tis a bull, then a mule; again it is a most beautiful woman.

DIONYSUS. Where is she that I may run toward her?

XANTHIAS. The monster is no longer a woman; 'tis now a dog.

DIONYSUS. Then it is the Empusa.[418]

XANTHIAS. Its whole face is ablaze.

DIONYSUS. And it has a brazen leg?

XANTHIAS. Aye, i' faith! and the other is an ass's leg,[419] rest well assured of that.

DIONYSUS. Where shall I fly to?

XANTHIAS. And I?

DIONYSUS. Priest,[420] save me, that I may drink with you.

XANTHIAS. Oh! mighty Heracles! we are dead men.

DIONYSUS. Silence! I adjure you. Don't utter that name.

XANTHIAS. Well then, we are dead men, Dionysus!

DIONYSUS. That still less than the other.

XANTHIAS. Keep straight on, master, here, here, this way.

DIONYSUS. Well?

XANTHIAS. Be at ease, all goes well and we can say with Hegelochus, "After the storm, I see the return of the *cat*."[421] The Empusa has gone.

DIONYSUS. Swear it to me.

XANTHIAS. By Zeus!

DIONYSUS. Swear it again.

XANTHIAS. By Zeus!

DIONYSUS. Once more.

XANTHIAS. By Zeus!

DIONYSUS. Oh! my god! how white I went at the sight of the Empusa! But yonder fellow got red instead, so horribly afraid was he![422] Alas! to whom do I owe this terrible meeting? What god shall I accuse of having sought my death? Might it be "the Aether, the dwelling of Zeus," or "the wing of Time"?[423]

XANTHIAS. Hist!

DIONYSUS. What's the matter?

XANTHIAS. Don't you hear?

DIONYSUS. What then?

XANTHIAS. The sound of flutes.

DIONYSUS. Aye, certainly, and the wind wafts a smell of torches hither, which bespeaks the Mysteries a league away. But make no noise; let us hide ourselves and listen.

CHORUS.[424] Iacchus, oh! Iacchus! Iacchus, oh! Iacchus!

XANTHIAS. Master, these are the initiates, of whom Heracles spoke and who are here at their sports; they are incessantly singing of Iacchus, just like Diagoras.[425]

DIONYSUS. I believe you are right, but 'tis best to keep ourselves quiet till we get better information.

CHORUS. Iacchus, venerated god, hasten at our call. Iacchus, oh! Iacchus! come into this meadow, thy favourite resting-place; come to direct the sacred choirs of the Initiate; may a thick crown of fruit-laden myrtle branches rest on thy head and may thy bold foot step this free and joyful dance, taught us by the Graces—this pure, religious measure, that our sacred choirs rehearse.

XANTHIAS. Oh! thou daughter of Demeter, both mighty and revered, what a delicious odour of pork!

DIONYSUS. Cannot you keep still then, fellow, once you get a whiff of a bit of tripe?

CHORUS. Brandish the flaming torches and so revive their brilliancy. Iacchus, oh! Iacchus! bright luminary of our nocturnal Mysteries. The meadow sparkles with a thousand fires; the aged shake off the weight of cares and years; they have once more found limbs of steel, wherewith to take part in thy sacred measures; and do thou, blessed deity, lead the dances of youth upon this dewy carpet of flowers with a torch in thine hand.

Silence, make way for our choirs, you profane and impure souls, who have neither been present at the festivals of the noble Muses, nor ever footed a dance in their honour, and who are not initiated into the mysterious language of the dithyrambs of the voracious Cratinus;[426] away from here he who applauds misplaced buffoonery. Away from here the bad citizen, who for his private ends fans and nurses the flame of sedition, the chief who sells himself, when his country is weathering the storms, and surrenders either fortresses or ships; who, like Thorycion,[427] the wretched collector of tolls, sends prohibited goods from Aegina to Epidaurus, such as oar-leathers, sailcloth and pitch, and who secures a subsidy for a hostile fleet,[428] or soils the statues of Hecaté,[429] while he is humming some dithyramb. Away from here, the orator who nibbles at the salary of the poets, because he has been scouted in the ancient solemnities of Dionysus; to all such I say, and I repeat, and I say it again for the third time, "Make way for the choruses of the Initiate." But you, raise you your voice anew; resume your nocturnal hymns as it is meet to do at this festival.

Let each one advance boldly into the retreats of our flowery meads, let him mingle in our dances, let him give vent to jesting, to wit and to satire. Enough of junketing, lead forward! let our voices praise the divine protectress[430] with ardent love, yea! praise her, who promises to assure the welfare of this country for ever, in spite of Thorycion.

Let our hymns now be addressed to Demeter, the Queen of Harvest, the goddess crowned with ears of corn; to her be dedicated the strains of our divine concerts. Oh! Demeter, who presidest over the pure mysteries, help us and protect thy choruses; far from all danger, may I continually yield myself to sports and dancing, mingle laughter with seriousness, as is fitting at thy festivals, and as the reward for my biting sarcasms may I wreathe my head with the triumphal fillets. And now let our songs summon hither the lovable goddess, who so often joins in our dances.

Oh, venerated Dionysus, who hast created such soft melodies for this festival, come to accompany us to the goddess, show that you can traverse a long journey without wearying.[431] Dionysus, the king of the dance, guide my steps. 'Tis thou who, to raise a laugh and for the sake of economy,[432] hast torn our sandals and our garments; let us bound, let us dance at our pleasure, for we have nothing to spoil. Dionysus, king of the dance, guide my steps. Just now I saw through a corner of my eye a ravishing young girl, the companion of our sports; I saw the nipple of her bosom peeping through a rent in her tunic. Dionysus, king of the dance, guide my steps.

DIONYSUS. Aye, I like to mingle with these choruses; I would fain dance and sport with that young girl.

XANTHIAS. And I too.

CHORUS. Would you like us to mock together at Archidemus? He is still awaiting his seven-year teeth to have himself entered as a citizen;[433] but he is none the less a chief of the people among the Athenians and the greatest rascal of 'em all. I am told that Clisthenes is tearing the hair out of his rump and lacerating his cheeks on the tomb of Sebinus, the Anaphlystian;[434] with his forehead against the ground, he is beating his bosom and groaning and calling him by name. As for Callias,[435] the illustrious son of Hippobinus, the new Heracles, he is fighting a terrible battle of love on his galleys; dressed up in a lion's skin, he fights a fierce naval battle—with the girls' cunts.

DIONYSUS. Could you tell us where Pluto dwells? We are strangers and have just arrived.

CHORUS. Go no farther, and know without further question that you are at his gates.

DIONYSUS. Slave, pick up your baggage.

XANTHIAS. This wretched baggage, 'tis like Corinth, the daughter of Zeus, for it's always in his mouth.[436]

CHORUS. And now do ye, who take part in this religious festival, dance a gladsome round in the flowery grove in honour of the goddess.[437]

DIONYSUS. As for myself, I will go with the young girls and the women into the enclosure, where the nocturnal ceremonies are held; 'tis I will bear the sacred torch.

CHORUS. Let us go into the meadows, that are sprinkled with roses, to form, according to our rites, the graceful choirs, over which the blessed Fates preside. 'Tis for us alone that the sun doth shine; his glorious rays illumine the Initiate, who have led the pious life, that is equally dear to strangers and citizens.

DIONYSUS. Come now! how should we knock at this door? How do the dwellers in these parts knock?

XANTHIAS. Lose no time and attack the door with vigour, if you have the courage of Heracles as well as his costume.

DIONYSUS. Ho! there! Slave!

AEACUS. Who's there?

DIONYSUS. Heracles, the bold.

AEACUS. Ah! wretched, impudent, shameless, threefold rascal, the most rascally of rascals. Ah! 'tis you who hunted out our dog Cerberus, whose keeper I was! But I have got you to-day; and the black stones of Styx, the rocks of Acheron, from which the blood is dripping, and the roaming dogs of Cocytus shall account to me for you; the hundred-headed Hydra shall tear your sides to pieces; the Tartessian Muraena[438] shall fasten itself on your lungs and the Tithrasian[439] Gorgons shall tear your kidneys and your gory entrails to shreds; I will go and fetch them as quickly as possible.

XANTHIAS. Eh! what are you doing there?

DIONYSUS (*stooping down*). I have just shit myself! Invoke the god.[440]

XANTHIAS. Get up at once. How a stranger would laugh, if he saw you.

DIONYSUS. Ah! I'm fainting. Place a sponge on my heart.

XANTHIAS. Here, take it.

DIONYSUS. Place it yourself.

XANTHIAS. But where? Good gods, where *is* your heart?

DIONYSUS. It has sunk into my shoes with fear. (*Takes his slave's hand holding the sponge, and applies it to his bottom.*)

XANTHIAS. Oh! you most cowardly of gods and men!

DIONYSUS. What! I cowardly? I, who have asked you for a sponge! 'Tis what no one else would have done.

XANTHIAS. How so?

DIONYSUS. A poltroon would have fallen backwards, being overcome with the fumes; as for me, I got up and moreover I wiped myself clean.

XANTHIAS. Ah! by Posidon! a wonderful feat of intrepidity!

DIONYSUS. Aye, certainly. And you did not tremble at the sound of his threatening words?

XANTHIAS. They never troubled me.

DIONYSUS. Well then, since you are so brave and fearless, become what I am, take this bludgeon and this lion's hide, you, whose heart has no knowledge of fear; I, in return, will carry the baggage.

XANTHIAS. Here, take it, take it quick! 'this my duty to obey you, and behold, Heracles-Xanthias! Do I look like a coward of your kidney?

DIONYSUS. No. You are the exact image of the god of Melité,[441] dressed up as a rascal. Come, I will take the baggage.

FEMALE ATTENDANT OF PERSEPHONÉ. Ah! is it you then, beloved Heracles? Come in. As soon as ever the goddess, my mistress Persephoné, knew of your arrival, she quickly had the bread into the oven and clapped two or three pots of bruised peas upon the fire; she has had a whole bullock roasted and both cakes and rolled backed. Come in quick!

XANTHIAS. No, thank you.

ATTENDANT. Oh! by Apollo! I shall not let you off. She has also had poultry boiled for you, sweetmeats makes, and has prepared you some delicious wine. Come then, enter with me.

XANTHIAS. I am much obliged.

ATTENDANT. Are you mad? I will not let you go. There is likewise and enchanted flute-girl specially for you, and two or three dancing wenches.

XANTHIAS. What do you say? Dancing wenches?

ATTENDANT. In the prime of their life and all freshly depilated. Come, enter, for the cook was going to take the fish off the fire and the table was being spread.

XANTHIAS. Very well then! Run in quickly and tell the dancing-girls I am coming. Slave! pick up the baggage and follow me.

DIONYSUS. Not so fast! Oh! indeed! I disguise you as Heracles for a joke and you take the thing seriously! None of your nonsense, Xanthias! Take back the baggage.

XANTHIAS. What? You are not thinking of taking back what you gave me yourself?

DIONYSUS. No, I don't think about it; I do it. Off with that skin!

XANTHIAS. Witness how i am treated, ye great dogs, and be my judges!

DIONYSUS. What gods? Are you so stupid, such a fool? How can you, a slave and a mortal, be the son of Alcmena?

XANTHIAS. Come then! 'tis well! take them. But perhaps you will be needing me one day, an it please the gods.

CHORUS. 'Tis the act of a wise and sensible man, who has done much sailing, always to trim his sail towards the quarter whence the fair wind wafts, rather than stand stiff and motionless like a god Terminus.[442] To change your part to serve your own interest is to act like a clever man, a true Theramenes.[443]

DIONYSUS. Faith! 'twould be funny indeed if Xanthias, a slave, were indolently stretched out on purple cushions and fucking the dancing-girl; if he were then to ask me for a pot, while I, looking on, would be rubbing my tool, and this master rogue, on seeing it, were to know out my front teeth with a blow of his fist.

FIRST INKEEPER'S WIFE. Here! Plathané, Plathané! do come! here is the rascal who once came into our shop and ate up sixteen loaves for us.

SECOND INKEEPER'S WIFE. Aye, truly, 'tis he himself!

XANTHIAS. This is turning out rough for somebody.

FIRST WIFE. And besides that, twenty pieces of boiled meat at half an obolus apiece.

XANTHIAS. There's someone going to get punished.

FIRST WIFE. And I don't know how many cloves of garlic.

DIONYSUS. You are rambling, my dear, you don't know what you are saying.

FIRST WIFE. Hah! you thought I should not know you, because of your buskins! And then all the salt fish, I had forgotten that!

SECOND WIFE. And then, alas! the fresh cheese that he devoured, osier baskets and all! Ten, when I asked for my money, he started to roar and shoot terrible looks at me.

XANTHIAS. As! I recognize him well by that token; 'tis just his way.

SECOND WIFE. And he drew out his sword like a madman.

FIRST WIFE. By the gods, yes.

SECOND WIFE. Terrified to death, we clambered up to the upper storey, and he fled at top speed, carrying off our baskets with him.

XANTHIAS. Ah! this is again his style! But you ought to take action.

FIRST WIFE. Run quick and call Cleon, my patron.

SECOND WIFE. And you, should you run against Hyperbolus,[444] bring him to me; we will knock the life out of our robber.

FIRST WIFE. Oh! you miserable glutton! how I should delight in breaking those grinders of yours, which devoured my goods!

SECOND WIFE. And I in hurling you into the malefactor's pit.

FIRST WIFE. And I in slitting with one stroke of the sickle that gullet that bolted down the tripe. But I am going to fetch Cleon; he shall summon you before the court this very day and force you to disgorge.

DIONYSUS. May I die, if Xanthias is not my dearest friend.

XANTHIAS. Can I be the son of Alcmena, I, a slave and a mortal?

DIONYSUS. I know, I know, that you are in a fury and you have the right to be; you can even beat me and I will not reply. But if I ever take this costume from you again, may I die of the most fearful torture—I, my wife, my children, all those who belong to me, down to the very last, and blear-eyed Archidemus[445] into the bargain.

XANTHIAS. I accept your oath, and on those terms I agree.

CHORUS. 'Tis now your cue, since you have resumed the dress, to act the brave and to throw terror into your glance, thus recalling the god whom you represent. But if you play your part badly, if you yield to any weakness, you will again have to load your shoulders with the baggage.

XANTHIAS. Friends, your advice is good, but I was thinking the same myself; if there is any good to be got, my master will again want to despoil me of this costume, of that I am quite certain. Ne'ertheless, I am going to show a fearless heart and shoot forth ferocious looks. And lo! the time for it has come, for I hear a noise at the door.

AEACUS (*to his slaves*). Bind me this dog-thief,[446] that he may be punished. Hurry yourselves, hurry!

DIONYSUS. This is going to turn out badly for someone.

XANTHIAS. Look to yourselves and don't come near me.

AEACUS. Hah! you would show fight! Ditylas, Sceblyas, Pardocas,[447] come here and have at him!

DIONYSUS. Ah! you would strike him because he has stolen!

XANTHIAS. 'Tis horrible!

DIONYSUS. 'Tis a revolting cruelty!

XANTHIAS. By Zeus! may I die, if I ever came here or stole from you the value of a pin! But I will act nobly; take this slave, put him to the question, and if you obtain the proof of my guilt, put me to death.

AEACUS. In what manner shall I put him to the question?

XANTHIAS. In every manner; you may lash him to the wooden horse, hang him, cut him open with scourging, flay him, twist his limbs, pour vinegar down his nostrils, load him with bricks, anything you like; only don't beat him with leeks or fresh garlic.[448]

AEACUS. 'Tis well conceived; but if the blows maim your slave, you will be claiming damages from me.

XANTHIAS. No, certainly not! set about putting him to the question.

AEACUS. It shall be done here, for I wish him to speak in your presence. Come, put down your pack, and be careful not to lie.

DIONYSUS. I forbid you to torture me, for I am immortal; if you dare it, woe to you!

AEACUS. What say you?

DIONYSUS. I say that I am an immortal, Dionysus, the son of Zeus, and that this fellow is only a slave.

AEACUS (*to Xanthias*). D'you hear him?

XANTHIAS. Yes. 'Tis all the better reason for beating him with rods, for, if he is a god, he will not feel the blows.

DIONYSUS (*to Xanthias*).

But why, pray, since you also claim to be a god, should you not be beaten like myself?

XANTHIAS (*to Aeacus*).

That's fair. Very well then, whichever of us two you first see crying and caring for the blows, him believe not to be a god.

AEACUS. 'Tis spoken like a brave fellow; you don't refuse what is right. Strip yourselves.

XANTHIAS. To do the thing fairly, how do you propose to act?

AEACUS. Oh! that's easy. I shall hit you one after the other.

XANTHIAS. Well thought of.

AEACUS. There! (*He strikes Xanthias.*)

XANTHIAS. Watch if you see me flinch.

AEACUS. I have already struck you.

XANTHIAS. No, you haven't.

AEACUS. Why, you have not felt it at all, I think. Now for t'other one.

DIONYSUS. Be quick about it.

AEACUS. But I have struck you.

DIONYSUS. Ah! I did not even sneeze. How is that?

AEACUS. I don't know; come, I will return to the first one.

XANTHIAS. Get it over. Oh, oh!

AEACUS. What does that "oh, oh!" mean? Did it hurt you?

XANTHIAS. Oh, no! but I was thinking of the feasts of Heracles, which are being held at Diomeia.[449]

AEACUS. Oh! what a pious fellow! I pass on to the other again.

DIONYSUS. Oh! oh!

AEACUS. What's wrong?

DIONYSUS. I see some knights.[450]

AEACUS. Why are you weeping?

DIONYSUS. Because I can smell onions.

AEACUS. Ha! so you don't care a fig for the blows?

DIONYSUS. Not the least bit in the world.

AEACUS. Well, let us proceed. Your turn now.

XANTHIAS. Oh, I say!

AEACUS. What's the matter?

XANTHIAS. Pull out this thorn.[451]

AEACUS. What? Now the other one again.

DIONYSUS. "Oh, Apollo!... King of Delos and Delphi!"

XANTHIAS. He felt that. Do you hear?

DIONYSUS. Why, no! I was quoting an iambic of Hipponax.

XANTHIAS. 'Tis labour in vain. Come, smite his flanks.

AEACUS. No, present your belly.

DIONYSUS. Oh, Posidon …

XANTHIAS. Ah! here's someone who's feeling it.

DIONYSUS. … who reignest on the Aegean headland and in the depths of the azure sea.[452]

AEACUS. By Demeter, I cannot find out which of you is the god. But come in; the master and Persephoné will soon tell you, for they are gods themselves.

DIONYSUS. You are quite right; but you should have thought of that before you beat us.

CHORUS. Oh! Muse, take part in our sacred choruses; our songs will enchant you and you shall see a people of wise men, eager for a nobler glory than that of Cleophon,[453] the braggart, the swallow, who deafens us with his hoarse cries, while perched upon a Thracian tree. He whines in his barbarian tongue and repeats the lament of Philomela with good reason, for even if the votes were equally divided, he would have to perish.[454]

The sacred chorus owes the city its opinion and its wise lessons. First I demand that equality be restored among the citizens, so that none may be disquieted. If there be any whom the artifices of Phrynichus have drawn into any error,[455] let us allow them to offer their excuses and let us forget these old mistakes. Furthermore, that there be not a single citizen in Athens who is deprived of his rights; otherwise would it not be shameful to see slaves become masters and treated as honourably as Plataeans, because they helped in a single naval fight?[456] Not that I censure this step, for, on the contrary I approve it; 'tis the sole thing you have done that is sensible. But those citizens, both they and their fathers, have so often fought with you and are allied to you by ties of blood, so ought you not to listen to their prayers and pardon them their single fault? Nature has given you wisdom, therefore let your anger cool and let all those who have fought together on Athenian galleys live in brotherhood and as fellow-citizens, enjoying the same equal rights; to show ourselves proud and intractable about granting the rights of the city, especially at a time when we are riding at the mercy of the waves,[457] is a folly, of which we shall later repent.

If I am adept at reading the destiny or the soul of a man, the fatal hour for little Cligenes[458] is near, that unbearable ape, the greatest rogue of all the washermen, who use a mixture of ashes and Cimolian earth and call it potash.[458] He knows it; hence he is always armed for war; for he fears, if he ventures forth without his bludgeon, he would be stripped of his clothes when he is drunk.

I have often noticed that there are good and honest citizens in Athens, who are as old gold is to new money. The ancient coins are excellent in point of standard; they are assuredly the best of all moneys; they alone are well struck and give a pure ring; everywhere they obtain currency, both in Greece and in strange lands; yet we make no use of them and prefer those bad copper pieces quite recently issued and so wretchedly struck. Exactly in the same way do we deal with our citizens. If we know them to be well-born, sober, brave, honest, adepts in the exercises of the gymnasium and in the liberal arts, they are the butts of our contumely and we have only a use for the petty rubbish, consisting of strangers, slaves and low-born folk not worth a whit more, mushrooms of yesterday, whom formerly Athens would not have even wanted as scapegoats. Madmen, do change your ways at last; employ the honest men afresh; if you are fortunate through doing this, 'twill be but right, and if Fate betrays you, the wise will at least praise you for having fallen honourably.

AEACUS. By Zeus, the Deliverer! what a brave man your master is.

XANTHIAS. A brave man! I should think so indeed, for he only knows how to drink and to make love!

AEACUS. He has convicted you of lying and did not thrash the impudent rascal who had dared to call himself the master.

XANTHIAS. Ah! he would have rued it if he had.

AEACUS. Well spoken! that's a reply that does a slave credit; 'tis thus that I like to act too.

XANTHIAS. How, pray?

AEACUS. I am beside myself with joy, when I can curse my master in secret.

XANTHIAS. And when you go off grumbling, after having been well thrashed?

AEACUS. I am delighted.

XANTHIAS. And when you make yourself important?

AEACUS. I know of nothing sweeter.

XANTHIAS. Ah! by Zeus! we are brothers. And when you are listening to what your masters are saying?

AEACUS. 'Tis a pleasure that drives me to distraction.

XANTHIAS. And when you repeat it to strangers?

AEACUS. Oh! I feel as happy as if I were emitting semen.

XANTHIAS. By Phoebus Apollo! reach me your hand; come hither, that I may embrace you; and, in the name of Zeus, the Thrashed one, tell me what all this noise means, these shouts, these quarrels, that I can hear going on inside yonder.

AEACUS. 'Tis Aeschylus and Euripides.

XANTHIAS. What do you mean?

AEACUS. The matter is serious, very serious indeed; all Hades is in commotion.

XANTHIAS. What's it all about?

AEACUS. We have a law here, according to which, whoever in each of the great sciences and liberal arts beats all his rivals, is fed at the Prytaneum and sits at Pluto's side ...

XANTHIAS. I know that.

AEACUS. ... until someone cleverer than he in the same style of thing comes along; then he has to give way to him.

XANTHIAS. And how has this law disturbed Aeschylus?

AEACUS. He held the chair for tragedy, as being the greatest in his art.

XANTHIAS. And who has it now?

AEACUS. When Euripides descended here, he started reciting his verses to the cheats, cut-purses, parricides, and brigands, who abound in Hades; his supple and tortuous reasonings filled them with enthusiasm, and they pronounced him the cleverest by far. So Euripides, elated with pride, took possession of the throne on which Aeschylus was installed.

XANTHIAS. And did he not get stoned?

AEACUS. No, but the folk demanded loudly that a regular trial should decide to which of the two the highest place belonged.

XANTHIAS. What folk? this mob of rascals? (*Points to the spectators.*)

AEACUS. Their clamour reached right up to heaven.

XANTHIAS. And had Aeschylus not his friends too?

AEACUS. Good people are very scarce here, just the same as on earth.

XANTHIAS. What does Pluto reckon to do?

AEACUS. To open a contest as soon as possible; the two rivals will show their skill, and finally a verdict will be given.

XANTHIAS. What! has not Sophocles also claimed the chair then?

AEACUS. No, no! he embraced Aeschylus and shook his hand, when he came down; he could have taken the seat, for Aeschylus vacated it for him; but according to Clidemides,[459] he prefers to act as his second; if Aeschylus triumphs, he will stay modestly where he is, but if not, he has declared that he will contest the prize with Euripides.

XANTHIAS. When is the contest to begin?

AEACUS. Directly! the battle royal is to take place on this very spot. Poetry is to be weighed in the scales.

XANTHIAS. What? How can tragedy be weighed?

AEACUS. They will bring rulers and compasses to measure the words, and those forms which are used for moulding bricks, also diameter measures and wedges, for Euripides says he wishes to torture every verse of his rival's tragedies.

XANTHIAS. If I mistake not, Aeschylus must be in a rage.

AEACUS. With lowered head he glares fiercely like a bull.

XANTHIAS. And who will be the judge?

AEACUS. The choice was difficult; it was seen that there was a dearth of able men. Aeschylus took exception to the Athenians ...

XANTHIAS. No doubt he thought there were too many thieves among them.

AEACUS. ... and moreover believed them too light-minded to judge of a poet's merits. Finally they fell back upon your master, because he understands tragic poetry.[460] But let us go in; when the masters are busy, we must look out for blows!

CHORUS. Ah! what fearful wrath will be surging in his heart! what a roar there'll be when he sees the babbler who challenges him sharpening his teeth! how savagely his eyes will roll! What a battle of words like plumed helmets and waving crests hurling themselves against fragile outbursts and wretched parings! We shall see the ingenious architect of style defending himself against immense periods. Then, the close hairs of his thick mane all a-bristle, the giant will knit his terrible brow; he will pull out verses as solidly bolted together as the framework of a ship and will hurl them forth with a roar, while the pretty speaker with the supple and sharpened tongue, who weighs each syllable and submits everything to the lash of his envy, will cut this grand style to mincemeat and reduce to ruins this edifice erected by one good sturdy puff of breath.[461]

EURIPIDES (*to Dionysus*). Your advice is in vain, I shall not vacate the chair, for I contend I am superior to him.

DIONYSUS. Aeschylus, why do you keep silent? You understand what he says.

EURIPIDES. He is going to stand on his dignity first; 'tis a trick he never failed to use in his tragedies.

DIONYSUS. My dear fellow, a little less arrogance, please.

EURIPIDES. Oh! I know him for many a day. I have long had a thorough hold of his ferocious heroes, for his high-flown language and of the monstrous blustering words which his great, gaping mouth hurls forth thick and close without curb or measure.

AESCHYLUS. It is indeed you, the son of a rustic goddess,[462] who dare to treat me thus, you, who only know how to collect together stupid sayings and to stitch the rags of your beggars?[463] I shall make you rue your insults.

DIONYSUS. Enough said, Aeschylus, calm the wild wrath that is turning your heart into a furnace.

AESCHYLUS. No, not until I have clearly shown the true value of this impudent fellow with his lame men.[464]

DIONYSUS. A lamb, a black lamb! Slaves, bring it quickly, the storm-cloud is about to burst.[465]

AESCHYLUS. Shame on your Cretan monologues![466] Shame on the infamous nuptials[467] that you introduce into the tragic art!

DIONYSUS. Curb yourself, noble Aeschylus, and as for you, my poor Euripides, be prudent, protect yourself from this hailstorm, or he may easily in his rage hit you full in the temple with some terrible word, that would let out your Telephus.[468] Come, Aeschylus, no flying into a temper! discuss the question coolly; poets must not revile each other like market wenches. Why, you shout at the very outset and burst out like a pine that catches fire in the forest.

EURIPIDES. I am ready for the contest and don't flinch; let him choose the attack or the defence; let him discuss everything, the dialogue, the choruses, the tragic genius, Peleus, Aeolus, Meleager[469] and especially Telephus.

DIONYSUS. And what do you propose to do, Aeschylus? Speak!

AESCHYLUS. I should have wished not to maintain a contest that is not equal or fair.

DIONYSUS. Why not fair?

AESCHYLUS. Because my poetry has outlived me, whilst his died with him and he can use it against me. However, I submit to your ruling.

DIONYSUS. Let incense and a brazier be brought, for I want to offer a prayer to the gods. Thanks to their favour, may I be able to decide between these ingenious rivals as a clever expert should! And do you sing a hymn in honour of the Muses.

CHORUS. Oh! ye chaste Muses, the daughters of Zeus, you who read the fine and subtle minds of thought-makers when they enter upon a contest of quibbles and tricks, look down on these two powerful athletes; inspire them, one with mighty words and the other with odds and ends of verses. Now the great mind contest is beginning.

DIONYSUS. And do you likewise make supplication to the gods before entering the lists.

AESCHYLUS. Oh, Demeter! who hast formed my mind, may I be able to prove myself worthy of thy Mysteries![470]

DIONYSUS. And you, Euripides, prove yourself meet to sprinkle incense on the brazier.

EURIPIDES. Thanks, but I sacrifice to other gods.[471]

DIONYSUS. To private gods of your own, which you have made after your own image?

EURIPIDES. Why, certainly!

DIONYSUS. Well then, invoke your gods.

EURIPIDES. Oh! thou Aether, on which I feed, oh! thou Volubility of Speech, oh! Craftiness, oh! Subtle Scent! enable me to crush the arguments of my opponent.

CHORUS. We are curious to see upon what ground these clever tilters are going to measure each other. Their tongue is keen, their wit is ready, their heart is full of audacity. From the one we must expect both elegance and polish of language, whereas the other, armed with his ponderous words, will fall hip and thigh upon his foe and with a single blow tear down and scatter all his vain devices.

DIONYSUS. Come, be quick and speak and let your words be elegant, but without false imagery or platitude.

EURIPIDES. I shall speak later of my poetry, but I want first to prove that Aeschylus is merely a wretched impostor; I shall relate by what means he tricked a coarse audience, trained in the school of Phrynichus.[472] First one saw some seated figure, who was veiled, some Achilles or Niobé,[473] who then strutted about the stage, but neither uncovered their face nor uttered a syllable.

DIONYSUS. I' faith! that's true!

EURIPIDES. Meanwhile, the Chorus would pour forth as many as four tirades one after the other, without stopping, and the characters would still maintain their stony silence.

DIONYSUS. I liked their silence, and these mutes pleased me no less than those characters that have such a heap to say nowadays.

EURIPIDES. 'Tis because you were a fool, understand that well.

DIONYSUS. Possibly; but what was his object?

EURIPIDES. 'Twas pure quackery; in this way the spectator would sit motionless, waiting, waiting for Niobé to say something, and the piece would go running on.

DIONYSUS. Oh! the rogue! how he deceived me! Well, Aeschylus, why are you so restless? Why this impatience, eh?

EURIPIDES. 'Tis because he sees himself beaten. Then when he had rambled on well, and got half-way through the piece, he would spout some dozen big, blustering, winged words, tall as mountains, terrible scarers, which the spectator admired without understanding what they meant.

DIONYSUS. Oh! great gods!

AESCHYLUS. Silence!

EURIPIDES. There was no comprehending one word.

DIONYSUS (*to Aeschylus*). Don't grind your teeth.

EURIPIDES. There were Scamanders, abysses, griffins with eagles' beaks chiselled upon brazen bucklers, all words with frowning crests and hard, hard to understand.

DIONYSUS. 'Faith, I was kept awake almost an entire night, trying to think out his yellow bird, half cock and half horse.[474]

AESCHYLUS. Why, fool, 'tis a device that is painted on the prow of a vessel.

DIONYSUS. Ah! I actually thought 'twas Eryxis, the son of Philoxenus.[475]

EURIPIDES. But what did you want with a cock in tragedy?

AESCHYLUS. But you, you foe of the gods, what have you done that is so good?

EURIPIDES. Oh! I have not made horses with cocks' heads like you, nor goats with deer's horns, as you may see 'em on Persian tapestries; but, when I received tragedy from your hands, it was quite bloated with enormous, ponderous words, and I began by lightening it of its heavy baggage and treated it with little verses, with subtle arguments, with the sap of white beet and decoctions of philosophical folly, the whole being well filtered together;[476] then I fed it with monologues, mixing in some Cephisophon;[477] but I did not chatter at random nor mix in any ingredients that first came to hand; from the outset I made my subject clear, and told the origin of the piece.

AESCHYLUS. Well, that was better than telling your own.[478]

EURIPIDES. Then, starting with the very first verse, each character played his part; all spoke, both woman and slave and master, young girl and old hag.[479]

AESCHYLUS. And was not such daring deserving of death?

EURIPIDES. No, by Apollo! 'twas to please the people.

DIONYSUS. Oh! leave that alone, do; 'tis not the best side of your case.

EURIPIDES. Furthermore, I taught the spectators the art of speech …

AESCHYLUS. 'Tis true indeed! Would that you had burst before you did it!

EURIPIDES. … the use of the straight lines and of the corners of language, the science of thinking, of reading, of understanding, plotting, loving deceit, of suspecting evil, of thinking of everything….

AESCHYLUS. Oh! true, true again!

EURIPIDES. I introduced our private life upon the stage, our common habits; and 'twas bold of me, for everyone was at home with these and could be my critic; I did not burst out into big noisy words to prevent their comprehension; nor did I terrify the audience by showing them Cycni[480] and Memnons[481] on chariots harnessed with steeds and jingling bells. Look at his disciples and look at mine. His are Phormisius and Megaenetus of Magnesia[482], all a-bristle with long beards, spears and trumpets, and grinning with sardonic and ferocious laughter, while my disciples are Clitophon and the graceful Theramenes.[483]

DIONYSUS. Theramenes? An able man and ready for anything; a man, who in imminent dangers knew well how to get out of the scrape by saying he was from Chios and not from Ceos.[484]

EURIPIDES. 'Tis thus that I taught my audience how to judge, namely, by introducing the art of reasoning and considering into tragedy. Thanks to me, they understand everything, discern all things, conduct their households better and ask themselves, "What is to be thought of this? Where is that? Who has taken the other thing?"

DIONYSUS. Yes, certainly, and now every Athenian who returns home, bawls to his slaves, "Where is the stew-pot? Who has eaten off the sprat's head? Where is the clove of garlic that was left over from yesterday? Who has been nibbling at my olives?" Whereas formerly they kept their seats with mouths agape like fools and idiots.

CHORUS. You hear him, illustrious Achilles,[485] and what are you going to reply? Only take care that your rage does not lead you astray, for he has handled you brutally. My noble friend, don't get carried away; furl all your sails, except the top-gallants, so that your ship may only advance slowly, until you feel yourself driven forward by a soft and favourable wind. Come then, you who were the first of the Greeks to construct imposing monuments of words and to raise the old tragedy above childish trifling, open a free course to the torrent of your words.

AESCHYLUS. This contest rouses my gall; my heart is boiling over with wrath. Am I bound to dispute with this fellow? But I will not let him think me unarmed and helpless. So, answer me! what is it in a poet one admires?

EURIPIDES. Wise counsels, which make the citizens better.

AESCHYLUS. And if you have failed in this duty, if out of honest and pure-minded men you have made rogues, what punishment do you think is your meet?

DIONYSUS. Death. I will reply for him.

AESCHYLUS. Behold then what great and brave men I bequeathed to him! They did not shirk the public burdens; they were not idlers, rogues and cheats, as they are to-day; their very breath was spears, pikes, helmets with white crests, breastplates and greaves; they were gallant souls encased in seven folds of ox-leather.

EURIPIDES. I must beware! he will crush me beneath the sheer weight of his hail of armour.

DIONYSUS. And how did you teach them this bravery? Speak, Aeschylus, and don't display so much haughty swagger.

AESCHYLUS. By composing a drama full of the spirit of Ares.

DIONYSUS. Which one?

AESCHYLUS. The Seven Chiefs before Thebes. Every man who had once seen it longed to be marching to battle.

DIONYSUS. And you did very wrongly; through you the Thebans have become more warlike; for this misdeed you deserve to be well beaten.

AESCHYLUS. You too might have trained yourself, but you were not willing. Then, by producing 'The Persae,' I have taught you to conquer all your enemies; 'twas my greatest work.

DIONYSUS. Aye, I shook with joy at the announcement of the death of Darius; and the Chorus immediately clapped their hands and shouted, "Triumph!"[486]

AESCHYLUS. Those are the subjects that poets should use. Note how useful, even from remotest times, the poets of noble thought have been! Orpheus taught us the mystic rites and the horrid nature of murder; Musaeus, the healing of ailments and the oracles; Hesiod, the tilling of the soil and the times for delving and harvest. And does not divine Homer owe his immortal glory to his noble teachings? Is it not he who taught the warlike virtues, the art of fighting and of carrying arms?

DIONYSUS. At all events he has not taught it to Pantacles,[487] the most awkward of all men; t'other day, when he was directing a procession, 'twas only after he had put on his helmet that he thought of fixing in the crest.

AESCHYLUS. But he has taught a crowd of brave warriors, such as Lamachus,[488] the hero of Athens. 'Tis from Homer that I borrowed the Patrocli and the lion-hearted Teucers,[489] whom I revived to the citizens, to incite them to show themselves worthy of these illustrious examples when the trumpets sounded. But I showed them neither Sthenoboea[490] nor shameless Phaedra; and I don't remember ever having placed an amorous woman on the stage.

EURIPIDES. No, no, you have never known Aphrodité.

AESCHYLUS. And I am proud of it. Whereas with you and those like you, she appears everywhere and in every shape; so that even you yourself were ruined and undone by her.[491]

DIONYSUS. That's true; the crimes you imputed to the wives of others, you suffered from in turn.

EURIPIDES. But, cursed man, what harm have my Sthenoboeas done to Athens?

AESCHYLUS. You are the cause of honest wives of honest citizens drinking hemlock, so greatly have your Bellerophons made them blush.[492]

EURIPIDES. Why, did I invent the story of Phaedra?

AESCHYLUS. No, the story is true enough; but the poet should hide what is vile and not produce nor represent it on the stage. The schoolmaster teaches little children and the poet men of riper age. We must only display what is good.

EURIPIDES. And when you talk to us of towering mountains—Lycabettus and of the frowning Parnes[493]—is that teaching us what is good? Why not use human language?

AESCHYLUS. Why, miserable man, the expression must always rise to the height of great maxims and of noble thoughts. Thus as the garment of the demi-gods is more magnificent, so also is their language more sublime. I ennobled the stage, while you have degraded it.

EURIPIDES. And how so, pray?

AESCHYLUS. Firstly you have dressed the kings in rags,[494] so that they might inspire pity.

EURIPIDES. Where's the harm?

AESCHYLUS. You are the cause why no rich man will now equip the galleys, they dress themselves in tatters, groan and say they are poor.

DIONYSUS. Aye, by Demeter! and he wears a tunic of fine wool underneath; and when he has deceived us with his lies, he may be seen turning up on the fish-market.[495]

AESCHYLUS. Moreover, you have taught boasting and quibbling; the wrestling schools are deserted and the young fellows have submitted their arses to outrage,[496] in order that they might learn to reel off idle chatter, and the sailors have dared to bandy words with their officers.[497] In my day they only knew how to ask for their ship's-biscuit and to shout "Yo ho! heave ho!"

DIONYSUS. ... and to let wind under the nose of the rower below them, to befoul their mate with filth and to steal when they went ashore. Nowadays they argue instead of rowing and the ship can travel as slow as she likes.

AESCHYLUS. Of what crimes is he not the author? Has he not shown us procurers, women who get delivered in the temples, have traffic with their brothers,[498] and say that life is not life.[499] 'Tis thanks to him that our city is full of scribes and buffoons, veritable apes, whose grimaces are incessantly deceiving the people; but there is no one left who knows how to carry a torch,[500] so little is it practised.

DIONYSUS. I' faith, that's true! I almost died of laughter at the last Panathenaea at seeing a slow, fat, pale-faced fellow, who ran well behind all the rest, bent completely double and evidently in horrible pain. At the gate of the Ceramicus the spectators started beating his belly, sides, flanks and thighs; these slaps knocked so much wind out of him that it extinguished his torch and he hurried away.

CHORUS. 'Tis a serious issue and an important debate; the fight is proceeding hotly and its decision will be difficult; for, as violently as the one attacks, as cleverly and as subtly does the other reply. But don't keep always to the same ground; you are not at the end of your specious artifices. Make use of every trick you have, no matter whether it be old or new! Out with everything boldly, blunt though it be; risk anything—that is smart and to the point. Perchance you fear that the audience is too stupid to grasp your subtleties, but be reassured, for that is no longer the case. They are all well-trained folk; each has his book, from which he learns the art of quibbling; such wits as they are happily endowed with have been rendered still keener through study. So have no fear! Attack everything, for you face an enlightened audience.

EURIPIDES. Let's take your prologues; 'tis the beginnings of this able poet's tragedies that I wish to examine at the outset. He was obscure in the description of his subjects.

DIONYSUS. And which prologue are you going to examine?

EURIPIDES. A lot of them. Give me first of all that of the 'Orestes.'[501]

DIONYSUS. All keep silent, Aeschylus, recite.

AESCHYLUS. "Oh! Hermes of the nether world, whose watchful power executes the paternal bidding, be my deliverer, assist me, I pray thee. I come, I return to this land."[502]

DIONYSUS. Is there a single word to condemn in that?

EURIPIDES. More than a dozen.

DIONYSUS. But there are but three verses in all.

EURIPIDES. And there are twenty faults in each.

DIONYSUS. Aeschylus, I beg you to keep silent; otherwise, besides these three iambics, there will be many more attacked.

AESCHYLUS. What? Keep silent before this fellow?

DIONYSUS. If you will take my advice.

EURIPIDES. He begins with a fearful blunder. Do you see the stupid thing?

DIONYSUS. Faith! I don't care if I don't.

AESCHYLUS. A blunder? In what way?

EURIPIDES. Repeat the first verse.

AESCHYLUS. "Oh! Hermes of the nether world, whose watchful power executes the paternal bidding."

EURIPIDES. Is not Orestes speaking in this fashion before his father's tomb?

AESCHYLUS. Agreed.

EURIPIDES. Does he mean to say that Hermes had watched, only that Agamemnon should perish at the hands of a woman and be the victim of a criminal intrigue?

AESCHYLUS. 'Tis not to the god of trickery, but to Hermes the benevolent, that he gives the name of god of the nether world, and this he proves by adding that Hermes is accomplishing the mission given him by his father.

EURIPIDES. The blunder is even worse than I had thought to make it out; for if he holds his office in the nether world from his father....

DIONYSUS. It means his father has made him a grave-digger.

AESCHYLUS. Dionysus, your wine is not redolent of perfume.[503]

DIONYSUS. Continue, Aeschylus, and you, Euripides, spy out the faults as he proceeds.

AESCHYLUS. "Be my deliverer, assist me, I pray thee. I come, I return to this land."

EURIPIDES. Our clever Aeschylus says the very same thing twice over.

AESCHYLUS. How twice over?

EURIPIDES. Examine your expressions, for I am going to show you the repetition. "I come, I return to this land." But I *come* is the same thing as I *return*.

DIONYSUS. Undoubtedly. 'Tis as though I said to my neighbour, "Lend me either your kneading-trough or your trough to knead in."

AESCHYLUS. No, you babbler, no, 'tis not the same thing, and the verse is excellent.

DIONYSUS. Indeed! then prove it.

AESCHYLUS. To come is the act of a citizen who has suffered no misfortune; but the exile both comes and returns.

DIONYSUS. Excellent! by Apollo! What do you say to that, Euripides?

EURIPIDES. I say that Orestes did not return to his country, for he came there secretly, without the consent of those in power.

DIONYSUS. Very good indeed! by Hermes! only I have not a notion what it is you mean.

EURIPIDES. Go on.

DIONYSUS. Come, be quick, Aeschylus, continue; and you look out for the faults.

AESCHYLUS. "At the foot of this tomb I invoke my father and beseech him to hearken to me and to hear."

EURIPIDES. Again a repetition, to hearken and to hear are obviously the same thing.

DIONYSUS. Why, wretched man, he's addressing the dead, whom to call thrice even is not sufficient.

AESCHYLUS. And you, how do you form your prologues?

EURIPIDES. I am going to tell you, and if you find a repetition, an idle word or inappropriate, let me be scouted!

DIONYSUS. Come, speak; 'tis my turn to listen. Let us hear the beauty of your prologues,

EURIPIDES. "Oedipus was a fortunate man at first ..."

AESCHYLUS. Not at all; he was destined to misfortune before he even existed, since Apollo predicted he would kill his father before ever he was born. How can one say he was fortunate at first?

EURIPIDES. "... and he became the most unfortunate of mortals afterwards."

AESCHYLUS. No, he did not become so, for he never ceased being so. Look at the facts! First of all, when scarcely born, he is exposed in the middle of winter in an earthenware vessel, for fear he might become the murderer of his father, if brought up; then he came to Polybus with his feet swollen; furthermore, while young, he marries an old woman, who is also his mother, and finally he blinds himself.

DIONYSUS. 'Faith! I think he could not have done worse to have been a colleague of Erasinidas.[504]

EURIPIDES. You can chatter as you will, my prologues are very fine.

AESCHYLUS. I will take care not to carp at them verse by verse and word for word;[505] but, an it please the gods, a simple little bottle will suffice me for withering every one of your prologues.

EURIPIDES. You will wither my prologues with a little bottle?[506]

AESCHYLUS. With only one. You make verses of such a kind, that one can adapt what one will to your iambics: a little bit of fluff, a little bottle, a little bag. I am going to prove it.

EURIPIDES. You will prove it?

AESCHYLUS. Yes.

DIONYSUS. Come, recite.

EURIPIDES. "Aegyptus, according to the most widely spread reports, having landed at Argos with his fifty daughters[507] ..."

AESCHYLUS. ... lost his little bottle.

EURIPIDES. What little bottle? May the plague seize you!

DIONYSUS. Recite another prologue to him. We shall see.

EURIPIDES. "Dionysus, who leads the choral dance on Parnassus with the thyrsus in his hand and clothed in skins of fawns[508] ..."

AESCHYLUS. ... lost his little bottle.

DIONYSUS. There again his little bottle upsets us.

EURIPIDES. He won't bother us much longer. I have a certain prologue to which he cannot adapt his tag: "There is no perfect happiness; this one is of noble origin, but poor; another of humble birth[509] ..."

AESCHYLUS. ... lost his little bottle.

DIONYSUS. Euripides!

EURIPIDES. What's the matter?

DIONYSUS. Clue up your sails, for this damned little bottle is going to blow a gale.

EURIPIDES. Little I care, by Demeter! I am going to make it burst in his hands.

DIONYSUS. Then out with it; recite another prologue, but beware, beware of the little bottle.

EURIPIDES. "Cadmus, the son of Agenor, while leaving the city of Sidon[510] ..."

AESCHYLUS. ... lost his little bottle.

DIONYSUS. Oh! my poor friend; buy that bottle, do, for it is going to tear all your prologues to ribbons.

EURIPIDES. What? Am I to buy it of him?

DIONYSUS. If you take my advice.

EURIPIDES. No, not I, for I have many prologues to which he cannot possibly fit his catchword: "Pelops, the son of Tantalus, having started for Pisa on his swift chariot[511] ..."

AESCHYLUS. ... lost his little bottle.

DIONYSUS. D'ye see? Again he has popped in his little bottle. Come, Aeschylus, he is going to buy it of you at any price, and you can have a splendid one for an obolus.

EURIPIDES. By Zeus, no, not yet! I have plenty of other prologues. "Oeneus in the fields one day[512] ..."

AESCHYLUS. ... lost his little bottle.

EURIPIDES. Let me first finish the opening verse: "Oeneus in the fields one day, having made an abundant harvest and sacrificed the first-fruits to the gods ..."

AESCHYLUS. ... lost his little bottle.

DIONYSUS. During the sacrifice? And who was the thief?

EURIPIDES. Allow him to try with this one: "Zeus, as even Truth has said[513] ..."

DIONYSUS (*to Euripides*). You have lost again; he is going to say, "lost his little bottle," for that bottle sticks to your prologues like a ringworm. But, in the name of the gods, turn now to his choruses.

EURIPIDES. I will prove that he knows nothing of lyric poetry, and that he repeats himself incessantly.

CHORUS. What's he going to say now? I am itching to know what criticisms he is going to make on the poet, whose sublime songs so far outclass those of his contemporaries. I cannot imagine with what he is going to reproach the king of the Dionysia, and I tremble for the aggressor.

EURIPIDES. Oh! those wonderful songs! But watch carefully, for I am going to condense them all into a single one.

DIONYSUS. And I am going to take pebbles to count the fragments.

EURIPIDES. "Oh, Achilles, King of Phthiotis, hearken to the shout of the conquering foe and haste to sustain the assault. We dwellers in the marshes do honour to Hermes, the author of our race. Haste to sustain the assault."

DIONYSUS. There, Aeschylus, you have already two assaults against you.

EURIPIDES. "Oh, son of Atreus, the most illustrious of the Greeks, thou, who rulest so many nations, hearken to me. Haste to the assault."

DIONYSUS. A third assault. Beware, Aeschylus.

EURIPIDES. "Keep silent, for the inspired priestesses are opening the temple of Artemis. Haste to sustain the assault. I have the right to proclaim that our warriors are leaving under propitious auspices. Haste to sustain the assault."[514]

DIONYSUS. Great gods, what a number of assaults! my kidneys are quite swollen with fatigue; I shall have to go to the bath after all these assaults.

EURIPIDES. Not before you have heard this other song arranged for the music of the cithara.

DIONYSUS. Come then, continue; but, prithee, no more "assaults."

EURIPIDES. "What! the two powerful monarchs, who reign over the Grecian youth, phlattothrattophlattothrat, are sending the Sphinx, that terrible harbinger of death, phlattothrattophlattothrat. With his avenging arm bearing a spear, phlattothrattophlattothrat, the impetuous bird delivers those who lean to the side of Ajax, phlattothrattophlattothrat, to the dogs who roam in the clouds, phlattothrattophlattothrat."[515]

DIONYSUS (*to Aeschylus*). What is this 'phlattothrat'? Does it come from Marathon or have you picked it out of some labourer's chanty?

AESCHYLUS. I took what was good and improved it still more, so that I might not be accused of gathering the same flowers as Phrynichus in the meadow of the Muse. But this man borrows from everybody, from the suggestions of prostitutes, from the sons of Melitus,[516] from the Carian flute-music, from wailing women, from dancing-girls. I am going to prove it, so let a lyre be brought. But what need of a lyre in his case? Where is the girl with the castanets? Come, thou Muse of Euripides; 'tis quite thy business to accompany songs of this sort.

DIONYSUS. This Muse has surely done fellation in her day, like a Lesbian wanton.[517]

AESCHYLUS. "Ye halcyons, who twitter over the ever-flowing billows of the sea, the damp dew of the waves glistens on your wings; and you spiders, who we-we-we-we-we-weave the long woofs of your webs in the corners of our houses with your nimble feet like the noisy shuttle, there where the dolphin by bounding in the billows, under the influence of the flute, predicts a favourable voyage; thou glorious ornaments of the vine, the slender tendrils that support the grape. Child, throw thine arms about my neck."[518] Do you note the harmonious rhythm?

DIONYSUS. Yes.

AESCHYLUS. Do you note it?

DIONYSUS. Yes, undoubtedly.

AESCHYLUS. And does the author of such rubbish dare to criticize my songs? he, who imitates the twelve postures of Cyrené in his poetry?[519] There you have his lyric melodies, but I still want to give you a sample of his monologues. "Oh! dark shadows of the night! what horrible dream are you sending me from the depths of your sombre abysses! Oh! dream, thou bondsman of Pluto, thou inanimate soul, child of the dark night, thou dread phantom in long black garments, how bloodthirsty, bloodthirsty is thy glance! how sharp are thy claws! Handmaidens, kindle the lamp, draw up the dew of the rivers in your vases and make the water hot; I wish to purify myself of this dream sent me by the gods. Oh! king of the ocean, that's right, that's right! Oh! my comrades, behold this wonder. Glycé has robbed me of my cock and has fled. Oh, Nymphs of the mountains! oh! Mania! seize her! How unhappy I am! I was full busy with my work, I was sp-sp-sp-sp-spinning the flax that was on my spindle, I was rounding off the clew that I was to go and sell in the market at dawn; and he flew off, flew off, cleaving the air with his swift wings; he left to me nothing but pain, pain! What tears, tears, poured, poured from my unfortunate eyes! Oh! Cretans, children of Ida, take your bows; help me, haste hither, surround the house. And thou, divine huntress, beautiful Artemis, come with thy hounds and search through the house. And thou also, daughter of Zeus, seize the torches in thy ready hands and go before me to Glycé's home, for I propose to go there and rummage everywhere."[520]

DIONYSUS. That's enough of choruses.

AESCHYLUS. Yes, faith, enough indeed! I wish now to see my verses weighed in the scales; 'tis the only way to end this poetic struggle.

DIONYSUS. Well then, come, I am going to sell the poet's genius the same way cheese is sold in the market.

CHORUS. Truly clever men are possessed of an inventive mind. Here again is a new idea that is marvellous and strange, and which another would not have thought of; as for myself I would not have believed anyone who had told me of it, I would have treated him as a driveller.

DIONYSUS. Come, hither to the scales.

AESCHYLUS AND EURIPIDES. Here we are.

DIONYSUS. Let each one hold one of the scales, recite a verse, and not let go until I have cried, "Cuckoo!"

AESCHYLUS AND EURIPIDES. We understand.

DIONYSUS. Well then, recite and keep your hands on the scales.

EURIPIDES. "Would it had pleased the gods that the vessel Argo had never unfurled the wings of her sails!"[521]

AESCHYLUS. "Oh! river Sperchius! oh! meadows, where the oxen graze!"[522]

DIONYSUS. Cuckoo! let go! Oh! the verse of Aeschylus sinks far the lower of the two.

EURIPIDES. And why?

DIONYSUS. Because, like the wool-merchants, who moisten their wares, he has thrown a river into his verse and has made it quite wet, whereas yours was winged and flew away.

EURIPIDES. Come, another verse! You recite, Aeschylus, and you, weigh.

DIONYSUS. Hold the scales again.

AESCHYLUS AND EURIPIDES. Ready.

DIONYSUS (*to Euripides*). You begin.

EURIPIDES. "Eloquence is Persuasion's only sanctuary."[523]

AESCHYLUS. "Death is the only god whom gifts cannot bribe."[524]

DIONYSUS. Let go! let go! Here again our friend Aeschylus' verse drags down the scale; 'tis because he has thrown in Death, the weightiest of all ills.

EURIPIDES. And I Persuasion; my verse is excellent.

DIONYSUS. Persuasion has both little weight and little sense. But hunt again for a big weighty verse and solid withal, that it may assure you the victory.

EURIPIDES. But where am I to find one—where?

DIONYSUS. I'll tell you one: "Achilles has thrown two and four."[525] Come, recite! 'tis the last trial.

EURIPIDES. "With his arm he seized a mace, studded with iron."[526]

AESCHYLUS. "Chariot upon chariot and corpse upon corpse."[527]

DIONYSUS (*to Euripides*) There you're foiled again.

EURIPIDES. Why?

DIONYSUS. There are two chariots and two corpses in the verse; why, 'tis a weight a hundred Egyptians could not lift.[528]

AESCHYLUS. 'Tis no longer verse against verse that I wish to weigh, but let him clamber into the scale himself, he, his children, his wife, Cephisophon[529] and all his works; against all these I will place but two of my verses on the other side.

DIONYSUS. I will *not* be their umpire, for they are dear to me and I will not have a foe in either of them; meseems the one is mighty clever, while the other simply delights me.

PLUTO. Then you are foiled in the object of your voyage.

DIONYSUS. And if I do decide?

PLUTO. You shall take with you whichever of the twain you declare the victor; thus you will not have come in vain.

DIONYSUS. That's all right! Well then, listen; I have come down to find a poet.

EURIPIDES. And with what intent?

DIONYSUS. So that the city, when once it has escaped the imminent dangers of the war, may have tragedies produced. I have resolved to take back whichever of the two is prepared to give good advice to the citizens. So first of all, what think you of Alcibiades? For the city is in most difficult labour over this question.

EURIPIDES. And what does it think about it?

DIONYSUS. What does it think? It regrets him, hates him, and yet wishes to have him, all at the same time. But tell me your opinion, both of you.

EURIPIDES. I hate the citizen who is slow to serve his country, quick to involve it in the greatest troubles, ever alert to his own interests, and a bungler where those of the State are at stake.

DIONYSUS. That's good, by Posidon! And you, what is your opinion?

AESCHYLUS. A lion's whelp should not be reared within the city. No doubt that's best; but if the lion has been reared, one must submit to his ways.

DIONYSUS. Zeus, the Deliverer! this puzzles me greatly. The one is clever, the other clear and precise. Now each of you tell me your idea of the best way to save the State.

EURIPIDES. If Cinesias were fitted to Cleocritus as a pair of wings, and the wind were to carry the two of them across the waves of the sea ...

DIONYSUS. 'Twould be funny. But what is he driving at?

EURIPIDES. ... they could throw vinegar into the eyes of the foe in the event of a sea-fight. But I know something else I want to tell you.

DIONYSUS. Go on.

EURIPIDES. When we put trust in what we mistrust and mistrust what we trust....

DIONYSUS. What? I don't understand. Tell us something less profound, but clearer.

EURIPIDES. If we were to mistrust the citizens, whom we trust, and to employ those whom we to-day neglect, we should be saved. Nothing succeeds with us; very well then, let's do the opposite thing, and our deliverance will be assured.

DIONYSUS. Very well spoken. You are the most ingenious of men, a true Palamedes![530] Is this fine idea your own or is it Cephisophon's?

EURIPIDES. My very own,—bar the vinegar, which is Cephisophon's.

DIONYSUS (*to Aeschylus*). And you, what have you to say?

AESCHYLUS. Tell me first who the commonwealth employs. Are they the just?

DIONYSUS. Oh! she holds *them* in abhorrence.

AESCHYLUS. What, are then the wicked those she loves?

DIONYSUS. Not at all, but she employs them against her will.

AESCHYLUS. Then what deliverance can there be for a city that will neither have cape nor cloak?[531]

DIONYSUS. Discover, I adjure you, discover a way to save her from shipwreck.

AESCHYLUS. I will tell you the way on earth, but I won't here.

DIONYSUS. No, send her this blessing from here.

AESCHYLUS. They will be saved when they have learnt that the land of the foe is theirs and their own land belongs to the foe; that their vessels are their true wealth, the only one upon which they can rely.[532]

DIONYSUS. That's true, but the dicasts devour everything.[533]

PLUTO (to Dionysus). Now decide.

DIONYSUS. 'Tis for you to decide, but I choose him whom my heart prefers.

EURIPIDES. You called the gods to witness that you would bear me through; remember your oath and choose your friends.

DIONYSUS. Yes, "my tongue has sworn."[534] ... But I choose Aeschylus.

EURIPIDES. What have you done, you wretch?

DIONYSUS. I? I have decided that Aeschylus is the victor. What then?

EURIPIDES. And you dare to look me in the face after such a shameful deed?

DIONYSUS. "Why shameful, if the spectators do not think so?"[535]

EURIPIDES. Cruel wretch, will you leave me pitilessly among the dead?

DIONYSUS. "Who knows if living be not dying,[536] if breathing be not feasting, if sleep be not a fleece?"[537]

PLUTO. Enter my halls. Come, Dionysus.

DIONYSUS. What shall we do there?

PLUTO. I want to entertain my guests before they leave.

DIONYSUS. Well said, by Zeus; 'tis the very thing to please me best.

CHORUS. Blessed the man who has perfected wisdom! Everything is happiness for him. Behold Aeschylus; thanks to the talent, to the cleverness he has shown, he returns to his country; and his fellow-citizens, his relations, his friends will all hail his return with joy. Let us beware of jabbering with Socrates and of disdaining the sublime notes of the tragic Muse. To pass an idle life reeling off grandiloquent speeches and foolish quibbles, is the part of a madman.

PLUTO. Farewell, Aeschylus! Go back to earth and may your noble precepts both save our city[538] and cure the mad; there are such, a many of them! Carry this rope from me to Cleophon, this one to Myrmex and Nichomachus, the public receivers, and this other one to Archenomous.[539] Bid them come here at once and without delay; if not, by Apollo, I will brand them with the hot iron.[540] I will make one bundle of them and Adimantus,[541] the son of Leucolophus,[542] and despatch the lot into hell with all possible speed.

AESCHYLUS. I will do your bidding, and do you make Sophocles occupy my seat. Let him take and keep it for me, against I should ever return here. In fact I award him the second place among the tragic poets. As for this impostor, watch that he never usurps my throne, even should he be placed there in spite of himself.

PLUTO (*to the Chorus of the Initiate*). Escort him with your sacred torches, singing to him as you go his own hymns and choruses.

CHORUS. Ye deities of the nether world, grant a pleasant journey to the poet who is leaving us to return to the light of day; grant likewise wise and healthy thoughts to our city. Put an end to the fearful calamities that overwhelm us, to the awful clatter of arms. As for Cleophon and the likes of him, let them go, an it please them, and fight in their own land.[543]

* * * * *

FINIS OF "THE FROGS"

* * * * *

Footnotes:

[382] These were comic poets contemporary with Aristophanes. Phrynichus, the best known, gained the second prize with his 'Muses' when the present comedy was put upon the stage. Amipsias had gained the first prize over our author's first edition of 'The Clouds' and again over his 'Birds.' Aristophanes is ridiculing vulgar and coarse jests, which, however, he does not always avoid himself.

[383] Instead of the expected "son of Zeus," he calls himself the "son of a wine-jar."

[384] At the sea-fight at Arginusae the slaves who had distinguished themselves by their bravery were presented with their freedom. This battle had taken place only a few months before the production of 'The Frogs.' Had Xanthias been one of these slaves he could then have treated his master as he says, for he would have been his equal.

[385] The door of the Temple of Heracles, situated in the deme of Melité, close to Athens. This temple contained a very remarkable statue of the god, the work of Eleas, the master of Phidias.

[386] A fabulous monster, half man and half horse.

[387] So also, in 'The Thesmophoriazusae,' Agathon is described as wearing a saffron robe, which was a mark of effeminacy.

[388] A woman's foot-gear.

[389] He speaks of him as though he were a vessel. Clisthenes, who was scoffed at for his ugliness, was completely beardless, which fact gave him the look of a eunuch. He was accused of prostituting himself.

[390] Heracles cannot believe it. Dionysus had no repute for bravery. His cowardice is one of the subjects for jesting which we shall most often come upon in 'The Frogs.'

[391] A tragedy by Euripides, produced some years earlier, some fragments of which are quoted by Aristophanes in his 'Thesmophoriazusae.'

[392] An actor of immense stature.

[393] The gluttony of Heracles was a byword. See 'The Birds.'

[394] Euripides, weary, it is said, of the ridicule and envy with which he was assailed in Athens, had retired in his old age to the court of Archelaus, King of Macedonia, where he had met with the utmost hospitality. We are assured that he perished through being torn to pieces by dogs, which set upon him in a lonely spot. His death occurred in 407 B.C., the year before the production of 'The Frogs.'

[395] This is a hemistich, the Scholiast says, from Euripides.

[396] The son of Sophocles. Once, during his father's lifetime, he gained the prize for tragedy, but it was suspected that the piece itself was largely the work of Sophocles himself. It is for this reason that Dionysus wishes to try him when he is dependent on his own resources, now that his father is dead. The death of the latter was quite recent at the time of the production of 'The Frogs,' and the fact lent all the greater interest to this piece.

[397] Agathon was a contemporary of Euripides, and is mentioned in terms of praise by Aristotle for his delineation of the character of Achilles, presumably in his tragedy of 'Telephus.' From the fragments which remain of this author it appears that his style was replete with ornament, particularly antithesis.

[398] Son of Caminus, an inferior poet, often made the butt of Aristophanes' jeers.

[399] A poet apparently, unknown.

[400] Expressions used by Euripides in different tragedies.

[401] Parody of a verse in Euripides' 'Andromeda,' a lost play.

[402] Heracles, being such a glutton, must be a past master in matters of cookery, but this does not justify him in posing as a dramatic critic.

[403] Xanthias, bent double beneath his load, gets more and more out of patience with his master's endless talk with Heracles.

[404] The mortar in which hemlock was pounded.

[405] An allusion to the effect of hemlock.

[406] A quarter of Athens where the Lampadephoria was held in honour of Athené, Hephaestus, and Prometheus, because the first had given the mortals oil, the second had invented the lamp, and the third had stolen fire from heaven. The principal part of this festival consisted in the *lampadedromia*, or torch-race. This name was given to a race in which the competitors for the prize ran with a torch in their hand; it was essential that the goal should be reached with the torch still alight. The signal for starting was given by throwing a torch from the top of the tower mentioned a few verses later on.

[407] Theseus had descended into Hades with Pirithous to fetch away Persephoné. Aristophanes doubtless wishes to say that in consequence of this descent Pluto established a toll across Acheron, in order to render access to his kingdom less easy, and so that the poor and the greedy, who could not or would not pay, might be kept out.

[408] Morsimus was a minor poet, who is also mentioned with disdain in 'The Knights,' and is there called the son of Philocles. Aristophanes jestingly likens anyone who helps to disseminate his verses to the worst of criminals.

[409] The Pyrrhic dance was a lively and quick-step dance. Cinesias was not a dancer, but a dithyrambic poet, who declaimed with much

gesticulation and movement that one might almost think he was performing this dance.

[410] Those initiated into the Mysteries of Demeter, who, according to the belief of the ancients, enjoyed a kind of beatitude after death.

[411] Xanthias, his strength exhausted and his patience gone, prepares to lay down his load. Asses were used for the conveyance from Athens to Eleusis of everything that was necessary for the celebration of the Mysteries. They were often overladen, and from this fact arose the proverb here used by Xanthias, as indicating any heavy burden.

[412] The Ancients believed that meeting this or that person or thing at the outset of a journey was of good or bad omen. The superstition is not entirely dead even to-day.

[413] Dionysus had seated himself *on* instead of *at* the oar.

[414] One of the titles given to Dionysus, because of the worship accorded him at Nysa, a town in Ethiopia, where he was brought up by the nymphs.

[415] This was the third day of the Anthesteria or feasts of Dionysus. All kinds of vegetables were cooked in pots and offered to Dionysus and Athené. It was also the day of the dramatic contests.

[416] Dionysus' temple, the Lenaeum, was situated in the district of Athens known as the *Linnae*, or Marshes, on the south side of the Acropolis.

[417] He points to the audience.

[418] A spectre, which Hecaté sent to frighten men. It took all kinds of hideous shapes. It was exorcised by abuse.

[419] This was one of the monstrosities which credulity attributed to the Empusa.

[420] He is addressing a priest of Bacchus, who occupied a seat reserved for him in the first row of the audience.

[421] A verse from the Orestes of Euripides.—Hegelochus was an actor who, in a recent representation, had spoken the line in such a manner as to lend it an absurd meaning; instead of saying, [Greek: gal_en_en], which means *calm*, he had pronounced it [Greek: gal_en], which means *a cat*.

[422] The priest of Bacchus, mentioned several verses back.

[423] High-flown expressions from Euripides' Tragedies.

[424] A second Chorus, comprised of Initiates into the Mysteries of Demeter and Dionysus.

[425] A philosopher, a native of Melos, and originally a dithyrambic poet. He was prosecuted on a charge of atheism.

[426] A comic and dithyrambic poet.

[427] This Thorycion, a toll collector at Aegina, which then belonged to Athens, had taken advantage of his position to send goods to Epidaurus, an Argolian town, thereby defrauding the treasury of the duty of 5 per cent, which was levied on every import and export.

[428] An allusion to Alcibiades, who is said to have obtained a subsidy for the Spartan fleet from Cyrus, satrap of Asia Minor.

[429] An allusion to the dithyrambic poet, Cinesias, who was accused of having sullied, by stooling against it, the pedestal of a statue of Hecaté at one of the street corners of Athens.

[430] Athené.

[431] The route of the procession of the Initiate was from the Ceramicus (a district of Athens) to Eleusis, a distance of twenty-five stadia.

[432] A shaft shot at the *choragi* by the poet, because they had failed to have new dresses made for the actors on this occasion.

[433] It was at the age of seven that children were entered on the registers of their father's tribe. Aristophanes is accusing Archidemus, who at that time was the head of the popular party, of being no citizen, because his name is not entered upon the registers of any tribe.

[434] At funerals women tore their hair, rent their garments, and beat their bosoms. Aristophanes parodies these demonstrations of grief and attributes them to the effeminate Clisthenes. Sebinus the Anaphlystian is a coined name containing an obscene allusion, implying he was in the habit of allowing connexion with himself a posteriori, and being masturbated by the other in turn.

[435] Callias, the son of Hipponicus, which the poet turns into Hippobinus, i.e. one who treads a mare, was an Athenian general, who had distinguished himself at the battle of Arginusae; he was notorious for his debauched habits, which he doubtless practised even on board his galleys. He is called a new Heracles, because of the legend that Heracles triumphed over fifty virgins in a single night; no doubt the poet alludes to some exploit of the kind here.

[436] A proverb applied to silly boasters. The Corinthians had sent an envoy to Megara, who, in order to enhance the importance of his city, incessantly repeated the phrase, "*The Corinth of Zeus.*"

[437] Demeter.

[438] Tartessus was an Iberian town, near the Avernian marshes, which were said to be tenanted by reptiles, the progeny of vipers and muraenae, a kind of fish.

[439] Tithrasios was a part of Libya, fabled to be peopled by Gorgons.

[440] "Invoke the god" was the usual formula which immediately followed the offering of the libation in the festival of Dionysus. Here he uses the words after a libation of a new kind and induced by fear.

[441] That is, Heracles, whose temple was at Melité, a suburban deme of Athens.

[442] Whose statues were placed to make the boundaries of land.

[443] One of the Thirty Tyrants, noted for his versatility.

[444] Celon and Hyperbolus were both dead, and are therefore supposed to have become the leaders and patrons of the populace in Hades, the same as they had been on earth.

[445] Already mentioned; one of the chiefs of the popular party in 406 B.C.

[446] Heracles had carried of Cerberus.

[447] Names of Thracian slaves.

[448] As was done to unruly children; he allows every kind of torture with the exception of the mildest.

[449] A deme of Attica, where there was a temple to Heracles. No doubt those present uttered the cry "Oh! oh!" in honour of the god.

[450] He pretends it was not a cry of pain at all, but of astonishment and admiration.

[451] Pretending that it was the thorn causing him pain, and not the lash of the whip.

[452] According to the Scholiast this is a quotation from the 'Laocoon,' a lost play of Sophocles.

[453] A general known for his cowardice; he was accused of not being a citizen, but of Thracian origin; in 406 B.C. he was in disfavour, and he perished shortly after in a popular tumult.

[454] According to Athenian law, the accused was acquitted when the voting was equal.

[455] He had helped to establish the oligarchical government of the Four Hundred, who had just been overthrown.

[456] The fight of Arginusae; the slaves who had fought there had been accorded their freedom.—The Plataeans had had the title of citizens since the battle of Marathon.

[457] Things were not going well for Athens at the time; it was only two years later, 404 B.C., that Lysander took the city.

[458] A demagogue; because he deceived the people. Aristophanes compares him with the washermen who cheated their clients by using some mixture that was cheaper than potash.

[459] Callistrates says that Clidemides was one of Sophocles' sons; Apollonius states him to have been an actor.

[460] Dionysus was, of course, the patron god of the drama and dramatic contests.

[461] The majestic grandeur of Aeschylus' periods, coupled with a touch of parody, is to be recognized in this piece.

[462] It is said that Euripides was the son of a fruit-seller.

[463] Euripides is constantly twitted by Aristophanes with his predilection for ragged beggars and vagabonds as characters in his plays.

[464] Bellerophon, Philoctetes, and Telephus, were all characters in different Tragedies of Euripides.

[465] Sailors, when in danger, sacrificed a black lamb to Typhon, the god of storms.

[466] An allusion to a long monologue of Icarus in the tragedy called 'The Cretans.'

[467] In 'Aeolus,' Macareus violates his own sister; in 'The Clouds,' this incest, which Euripides introduced upon the stage, is also mentioned.

[468] The title of one of Euripides' pieces.

[469] The titles of three lost Tragedies of Euripides.

[470] A verse from one of the lost Tragedies of Euripides; the poet was born at Eleusis.

[471] Aristophanes often makes this accusation of religious heterodoxy against Euripides.

[472] A dramatic poet, who lived about the end of the sixth century B.C., and a disciple of Thespis; the scenic art was then comparatively in its infancy.

[473] The Scholiast tells us that Achilles remained mute in the tragedy entitled 'The Phrygians' or 'The Ransom of Hector,' and that his face was veiled; he only spoke a few words at the beginning of the drama during a dialogue with Hermes.—We have no information about the Niobé mentioned here.

[474] The Scholiast tells us that this expression ([Greek: hippalektru_on]) was used in 'The Myrmidons' of Aeschylus; Aristophanes ridicules it again both in the 'Peace' and in 'The Birds.'

[475] An individual apparently noted for his uncouth ugliness.

[476] The beet and the decoctions are intended to indicate the insipidity of Euripides' style.

[477] An intimate friend of Euripides, who is said to have worked with him on his Tragedies, to have been 'ghost' to him in fact.

[478] An allusion to Euripides' obscure birth; his mother had been, so it was said, a vegetable-seller in the public market.

[479] Euripides had introduced every variety of character into his pieces, whereas Aeschylus only staged divinities or heroes.

[480] There are two Cycni, one, the son of Ares, was killed by Heracles according to the testimony of Hesiod in his description of the "Shield of Heracles"; the other, the son of Posidon, who, according to Pindar, perished under the blows of Achilles. It is not known in which Tragedy of Aeschylus this character was introduced.

[481] Memnon, the son of Aurora, was killed by Achilles; in the list of the Tragedies of Aeschylus there is one entitled 'Memnon.'

[482] These two were not poets, but Euripides supposes them disciples of Aeschylus, because of their rude and antiquated manners.

[483] Clitophon and Theramenes were elegants of effeminate habits and adept talkers.

[484] A proverb which was applied to versatile people; the two Greek names [Greek: Chios] and [Greek: Keios] might easily be mistaken for one another. Both, of course, are islands of the Cyclades.

[485] A verse from the 'Myrmidons' of Aeschylus; here Achilles is Aeschylus himself.

[486] The 'Persae' of Aeschylus (produced 472 B.C.) was received with transports of enthusiasm, reviving as it did memories of the glorious defeat of Xerxes at Salamis, where the poet had fought, only a few years before, 480 B.C.

[487] Nothing is known of this Pantacles, whom Eupolis, in his 'Golden Age,' also describes as awkward ([Greek: skaios]).

[488] Aristophanes had by this time modified his opinion of this general, whom he had so flouted in 'The Acharnians.'

[489] Son of Telamon, the King of Salamis and brother of Ajax.

[490] The wife of Proetus, King of Argos. Bellerophon, who had sought refuge at the court of this king after the accidental murder of his brother Bellerus, had disdained her amorous overtures. Therefore she denounced him to her husband as having wanted to attempt her virtue and urged him to cause his death. She killed herself immediately after the departure of the young hero.

[491] Cephisophon, Euripides' friend, is said to have seduced his wife.

[492] Meaning, they have imitated Sthenoboea in everything; like her, they have conceived adulterous passions and, again like her, they have poisoned themselves.

[493] Lycabettus, a mountain of Attica, just outside the walls of Athens, the "Arthur's Seat" of the city. Parnassus, the famous mountain of Phocis, the seat of the temple and oracle of Delphi and the home of the Muses. The whole passage is, of course, in parody of the grandiloquent style of Aeschylus.

[494] An allusion to Oeneus, King of Aetolia, and to Telephus, King of Mysia; characters put upon the stage by Euripides.

[495] It was only the rich Athenians who could afford fresh fish, because of their high price; we know how highly the gourmands prized the eels from the Copaic lake.

[496] If Aristophanes is to be believed, the orators were of depraved habits, and exacted infamous complaisances as payment for their lessons in rhetoric.

[497] Aristophanes attributes the general dissoluteness to the influence of Euripides; he suggests that the subtlety of his poetry, by sharpening the wits of the vulgar and even of the coarsest, has instigated them to insubordination.

[498] Augé, who was seduced by Heracles, was delivered in the temple of Athené (Scholiast); it is unknown in what piece this fact is mentioned.— Macareus violates his sister Canacé in the 'Aeolus.'

[499] i.e. they busy themselves with philosophic subtleties. This line is taken from 'The Phryxus,' of which some fragments have come down to us.

[500] In the torch-race the victor was the runner who attained the goal first without having allowed his torch to go out. This race was a very ancient institution. Aristophanes means to say that the old habits had fallen into disuse.

[501] A tetralogy composed of three tragedies, the 'Agamemnon,' the 'Choëphorae,' the 'Eumenides,' together with a satirical drama, the 'Proteus.'

[502] This is the opening of the 'Choëphorae.' Aeschylus puts the words in the mouth of Orestes, who is returning to his native land and visiting his father's tomb.

[503] i.e. your jokes are very coarse.

[504] He was one of the Athenian generals in command at Arginusae; he and his colleagues were condemned to death for not having given burial to the men who fell in that naval fight.

[505] As Euripides had done to those of Aeschylus; that sort of criticism was too low for him.

[506] [Greek: D_ekuthion ap_olesa], *oleum perdidi,* I have lost my labour, was a proverbial expression, which was also possibly the refrain of some song. Aeschylus means to say that all Euripides' phrases are cast in the same mould, and that his style is so poor and insipid that one can adapt to it any

foolery one wishes; as for the phrase he adds to every one of the phrases his rival recites, he chooses it to insinuate that the work of Euripides is *labour lost*, and that he would have done just as well not to meddle with tragedy. The joke is mediocre at its best and is kept up far too long.

[507] Prologue of the 'Archelaus' of Euripides, a tragedy now lost.

[508] From prologue of the 'Hypsipilé' of Euripides, a play now lost.

[509] From prologue of the 'Sthenoboea' of Euripides, a play now lost.

[510] From prologue of the 'Phryxus' of Euripides, a play now lost.

[511] From prologue of the 'Iphigeneia in Tauris' of Euripides.

[512] Prologue of 'The Meleager' by Euripides, lost.

[513] Prologue of 'The Menalippé Sapiens,' by Euripides, lost.

[514] The whole of these fragments are quoted at random and have no meaning. Euripides, no doubt, wants to show that the choruses of Aeschylus are void of interest or coherence. As to the refrain, "haste to sustain the assault," Euripides possibly wants to insinuate that Aeschylus incessantly repeats himself and that a wearying monotony pervades his choruses. However, all these criticisms are in the main devoid of foundation.

[515] This ridiculous couplet pretends to imitate the redundancy and nonsensicality of Aeschylus' language; it can be seen how superficial and unfair the criticism of Euripides is; probably this is just what Aristophanes wanted to convey by this long and wearisome scene.

[516] The Scholiast conjectures this Melitus to be the same individual who later accused Socrates.

[517] The most infamous practices were attributed to the Lesbian women, amongst others, that of *fellation*, that is the vile trick of taking a man's penis in the mouth, to give him gratification by sucking and licking it with the

tongue. Dionysus means to say that Euripides takes pleasure in describing shameful passions.

[518] Here the criticism only concerns the rhythm and not either the meaning or the style. This passage was sung to one of the airs that Euripides had adopted for his choruses and which have not come down to us; we are therefore absolutely without any data that would enable us to understand and judge a criticism of this kind.

[519] A celebrated courtesan, who was skilled in twelve different postures of Venus. Aeschylus returns to his idea, which he has so often indicated, that Euripides' poetry is low and impure; he at the same time scoffs at the artifices to which Euripides had recourse when inspiration and animation failed him.

[520] No monologue of Euripides that has been preserved bears the faintest resemblance to this specimen which. Aeschylus pretends to be giving here.

[521] Beginning of Euripides' 'Medea.'

[522] Fragment from Aeschylus 'Philoctetes.' The Sperchius is a river in Thessaly, which has its source in the Pindus range and its mouth in the Maliac gulf.

[523] A verse from Euripides' 'Antigoné.' Its meaning is, that it is better to speak well than to speak the truth, if you want to persuade.

[524] From the 'Niobe,' a lost play, of Aeschylus.

[525] From the 'Telephus' of Euripides, in which he introduces Achilles playing at dice. This line was also ridiculed by Eupolis.

[526] From Euripides' 'Meleager.' All these plays, with the one exception of the 'Medea,' are lost.

[527] From the 'Glaucus Potniensis,' a lost play of Aeschylus.

[528] i.e. one hundred porters, either because many of the Athenian porters were Egyptians, or as an allusion to the Pyramids and other great works, which had habituated them to carrying heavy burdens.

[529] Euripides' friend and collaborator.

[530] The invention of weights and measures, of dice, and of the game of chess are attributed to him, also that of four additional letters of the alphabet.

[531] i.e. that cannot decide for either party.

[532] i.e. that a country can always be invaded and that the fleet alone is a safe refuge. This is the same advice as that given by Pericles, and which Thucydides expresses thus, "Let your country be devastated, or even devastate it yourself, and set sail for Laconia with your fleet."

[533] An allusion to the fees of the dicasts, or jurymen; we have already seen that at this period it was two obols, and later three.

[534] A half-line from Euripides' 'Hippolytus.' The full line is: [Greek: h_e gl_ott' om_omok', h_e de phr_en an_omotos,] "my tongue has taken an oath, but my mind is unsworn," a bit of casuistry which the critics were never tired of bringing up against the author.

[535] A verse from the 'Aeolus' of Euripides, but slightly altered. Euripides said, "Why is is shameful, if the spectators, who enjoy it, do not think so?"

[536] A verse from the 'Phrixus' of Euripides; what follows is a parody.

[537] We have already seen Aeschylus pretending that it was possible to adapt any foolish expression one liked to the verses of Euripides: "a little bottle, a little bag, a little fleece."

[538] Pluto speaks as though he were an Athenian himself.

[539] That they should hang themselves. Cleophon is said to have been an influential alien resident who was opposed to concluding peace; Myrmex

and Nicomachus were two officials guilty of peculation cf public funds; Archenomus is unknown.

[540] He would brand them as fugitive slaves, if, despite his orders, they refused to come down.

[541] An Athenian admiral.

[542] The real name of the father of Adimantus was Leucolophides, which Aristophanes jestingly turns into Leucolophus, i.e. *White Crest*.

[543] i.e. in a foreign country; Cleophon, as we have just seen, was not an Athenian.

THE THESMOPHORIAZUSAE

or

The Women's Festival

INTRODUCTION

Like the 'Lysistrata,' the 'Thesmophoriazusae, or Women's Festival,' and the next following play, the 'Ecclesiazusae, or Women in Council' are comedies in which the fair sex play a great part, and also resemble that extremely *scabreux* production in the plentiful crop of doubtful 'double entendres' and highly suggestive situations they contain.

The play has more of a proper intrigue and formal dénouement than is general with our Author's pieces, which, like modern extravaganzas and musical comedies, are often strung on a very slender thread of plot. The idea of the 'Thesmophoriazusae' is as follows.

Euripides is summoned as a notorious woman-hater and detractor of the female sex to appear for trial and judgment before the women of Athens assembled to celebrate the Thesmophoria, a festival held in honour of the goddesses Demeter and Persephone, from which men were rigidly excluded. The poet is terror-stricken, and endeavours to persuade his confrère, the tragedian Agathon, to attend the meeting in the guise of a woman to plead his cause, Agathon's notorious effeminacy of costume and way of life lending itself to the deception; but the latter refuses point-blank. He then prevails on his father-in-law, Mnesilochus, to do him this favour, and shaves, depilates, and dresses him up accordingly. But so far from throwing oil on the troubled waters, Mnesilochus indulges in a long harangue full of violent abuse of the whole sex, and relates some scandalous stories of the naughty ways of peccant wives. The assembly suspects at once there is a man amongst them, and on examination of the old fellow's person, this is proved to be the case. He flies for sanctuary to the altar, snatching a child from the arms of one of the women as a hostage, vowing to kill it if they molest him further. On investigation, however, the infant turns out to be a wine-skin dressed in baby's clothes.

In despair Mnesilochus sends urgent messages to Euripides to come and rescue him from his perilous predicament. The latter then appears, and in successive characters selected from his different Tragedies—now Menelaus meeting Helen again in Egypt, now Echo sympathising with the chained Andromeda, presently Perseus about to release the heroine from her rock—pleads for his unhappy father-in-law. At length he succeeds in getting him away in the temporary absence of the guard, a Scythian archer, whom he entices from his post by the charms of a dancing-girl.

As may be supposed, the appearance of Mnesilochus among the women dressed in women's clothes, the examination of his person to discover his true sex and his final detection, afford fine opportunities for a display of the broadest Aristophanic humour. The latter part of the play also, where various pieces of Euripides are burlesqued, is extremely funny; and must have been still more so when represented before an audience familiar with every piece and almost every line parodied, and played by actors trained and got up to imitate every trick and mannerism of appearance and delivery of the tragic actors who originally took the parts.

The 'Thesmophoriazusae' was produced in the year 412 B.C., six years before the death of Euripides, who is held up to ridicule in it, as he is in 'The Wasps' and several other of our Author's comedies.

* * * * *

THE THESMOPHORIAZUSAE

or

The Women's Festival

DRAMATIS PERSONAE

EURIPIDES.
MNESILOCHUS, Father-in-law of Euripides.
AGATHON.
SERVANT OF AGATHON.
CHORUS attending AGATHON.
HERALD.
WOMEN.
CLISTHENES.
A PRYTANIS or Member of the Council.
A SCYTHIAN or Police Officer.
CHORUS OF THESMOPHORIAZUSAE—women keeping the Feast of
Demeter.

**SCENE: In front of Agathon's house; afterwards in the precincts of the
Temple of Demeter.**

* * * * *

THE THESMOPHORIAZUSAE

or

The Women's Festival

MNESILOCHUS. Great Zeus! will the swallow never appear to end the winter of my discontent? Why the fellow has kept me on the run ever since early this morning; he wants to kill me, that's certain. Before I lose my spleen entirely, Euripides, can you at least tell me whither you are leading me?

EURIPIDES. What need for you to hear what you are going to see?

MNESILOCHUS. How is that? Repeat it. No need for me to hear....

EURIPIDES. What you are going to see.

MNESILOCHUS. Nor consequently to see....

EURIPIDES. What you have to hear.[544]

MNESILOCHUS. What is this wiseacre stuff you are telling me? I must neither see nor hear.

EURIPIDES. Ah! but you have two things there that are essentially distinct.

MNESILOCHUS. Seeing and hearing.

EURIPIDES. Undoubtedly.

MNESILOCHUS. In what way distinct?

EURIPIDES. In this way. Formerly, when Ether separated the elements and bore the animals that were moving in her bosom, she wished to endow them with sight, and so made the eye round like the sun's disc and bored ears in the form of a funnel.

MNESILOCHUS. And because of this funnel I neither see nor hear. Ah! great gods! I am delighted to know it. What a fine thing it is to talk with wise men!

EURIPIDES. I will teach you many another thing of the sort.

MNESILOCHUS. That's well to know; but first of all I should like to find out how to grow lame, so that I need not have to follow you all about.

EURIPIDES. Come, hear and give heed!

MNESILOCHUS. I'm here and waiting.

EURIPIDES. Do you see that little door?

MNESILOCHUS. Yes, certainly.

EURIPIDES. Silence!

MNESILOCHUS. Silence about what? About the door?

EURIPIDES. Pay attention!

MNESILOCHUS. Pay attention and be silent about the door? Very well.

EURIPIDES. 'Tis there that Agathon, the celebrated tragic poet, dwells.[545]

MNESILOCHUS. Who is this Agathon?

EURIPIDES. 'Tis a certain Agathon....

MNESILOCHUS. Swarthy, robust of build?

EURIPIDES. No, another. You have never seen him?

MNESILOCHUS. He has a big beard?

EURIPIDES. No, no, evidently you have never seen him.

MNESILOCHUS. Never, so far as I know.

EURIPIDES. And yet you have pedicated him. Well, it must have been without knowing who he was. Ah! let us step aside; here is one of his slaves bringing a brazier and some myrtle branches; no doubt he is going to offer a sacrifice and pray for a happy poetical inspiration for Agathon.

SERVANT OF AGATHON. Silence! oh, people! keep your mouths sedately shut! The chorus of the Muses is moulding songs at my master's hearth. Let the winds hold their breath in the silent Ether! Let the azure waves cease murmuring on the shore!...

MNESILOCHUS. Brououou! brououou! (*Imitates the buzzing of a fly.*)

EURIPIDES. Keep quiet! what are you saying there?

SERVANT. ... Take your rest, ye winged races, and you, ye savage inhabitants of the woods, cease from your erratic wandering ...

MNESILOCHUS. Broum, broum, brououou.

SERVANT. ... for Agathon, our master, the sweet-voiced poet, is going ...

MNESILOCHUS. ... to be pedicated?

SERVANT. Whose voice is that?

MNESILOCHUS. 'Tis the silent Ether.

SERVANT. ... is going to construct the framework of a drama. He is rounding fresh poetical forms, he is polishing them in the lathe and is welding them; he is hammering out sentences and metaphors; he is working up his subject like soft wax. First he models it and then he casts it in bronze ...

MNESILOCHUS. ... and sways his buttocks amorously.

SERVANT. Who is the rustic who approaches this sacred enclosure?

237

MNESILOCHUS. Take care of yourself and of your sweet-voiced poet! I have a strong instrument here both well rounded and well polished, which will pierce your enclosure and penetrate your bottom.

SERVANT. Old man, you must have been a very insolent fellow in your youth!

EURIPIDES (*to the servant*). Let him be, friend, and, quick, go and call Agathon to me.

SERVANT. 'Tis not worth the trouble, for he will soon be here himself. He has started to compose, and in winter[546] it is never possible to round off strophes without coming to the sun to excite the imagination. (*He departs.*)

MNESILOCHUS. And what am I to do?

EURIPIDES. Wait till he comes.... Oh, Zeus! what hast thou in store for me to-day?

MNESILOCHUS. But, great gods, what is the matter then? What are you grumbling and groaning for? Tell me; you must not conceal anything from your father-in-law.

EURIPIDES. Some great misfortune is brewing against me.

MNESILOCHUS. What is it?

EURIPIDES. This day will decide whether it is all over with Euripides or not.

MNESILOCHUS. But how? Neither the tribunals nor the Senate are sitting, for it is the third of the five days consecrated to Demeter.[547]

EURIPIDES. That is precisely what makes me tremble; the women have plotted my ruin, and to-day they are to gather in the Temple of Demeter to execute their decision.

MNESILOCHUS. Why are they against you?

EURIPIDES. Because I mishandle them in my tragedies.

MNESILOCHUS. By Posidon, you would seem to have thoroughly deserved your fate. But how are you going to get out of the mess?

EURIPIDES. I am going to beg Agathon, the tragic poet, to go to the Thesmophoria.

MNESILOCHUS. And what is he to do there?

EURIPIDES. He would mingle with the women, and stand up for me, if needful.

MNESILOCHUS. Would he be openly present or secretly?

EURIPIDES. Secretly, dressed in woman's clothes.

MNESILOCHUS. That's a clever notion, thoroughly worthy of you. The prize for trickery is ours.

EURIPIDES. Silence!

MNESILOCHUS. What's the matter?

EURIPIDES. Here comes Agathon.

MNESILOCHUS. Where, where?

EURIPIDES. That's the man they are bringing out yonder on the machine.[548]

MNESILOCHUS. I am blind then! I see no man here, I only see Cyrené.[549]

EURIPIDES. Be still! He is getting ready to sing.

MNESILOCHUS. What subtle trill, I wonder, is he going to warble to us?

AGATHON. Damsels, with the sacred torch[550] in hand, unite your dance to shouts of joy in honour of the nether goddesses; celebrate the freedom of your country.

CHORUS. To what divinity is your homage addressed? I wish to mingle mine with it.

AGATHON. Oh! Muse! glorify Phoebus with his golden bow, who erected the walls of the city of the Simois.[551]

CHORUS. To thee, oh Phoebus, I dedicate my most beauteous songs; to thee, the sacred victor in the poetical contests.

AGATHON. And praise Artemis too, the maiden huntress, who wanders on the mountains and through the woods....

CHORUS. I, in my turn, celebrate the everlasting happiness of the chaste Artemis, the mighty daughter of Latona!

AGATHON. ... and Latona and the tones of the Asiatic lyre, which wed so well with the dances of the Phrygian Graces.[552]

CHORUS. I do honour to the divine Latona and to the lyre, the mother of songs of male and noble strains. The eyes of the goddess sparkle while listening to our enthusiastic chants. Honour to the powerful Phoebus! Hail! thou blessed son of Latona!

MNESILOCHUS. Oh! ye venerable Genetyllides,[553] what tender and voluptuous songs! They surpass the most lascivious kisses in sweetness; I feel a thrill of delight pass up my rectum as I listen to them. Young man, whoever you are, answer my questions, which I am borrowing from Aeschylus' 'Lycurgeia.'[554] Whence comes this effeminate? What is his country? his dress? What contradictions his life shows! A lyre and a hair-net! A wrestling school oil flask and a girdle![555] What could be more contradictory? What relation has a mirror to a sword? And you yourself, who are you? Do you pretend to be a man? Where is the sign of your manhood, your penis, pray? Where is the cloak, the footgear that belong to that sex? Are you a woman? Then where are your breasts? Answer me. But you keep silent. Oh! just as you choose; your songs display your character quite sufficiently.

AGATHON. Old man, old man, I hear the shafts of jealousy whistling by my ears, but they do not hit me. My dress is in harmony with my thoughts. A poet must adopt the nature of his characters. Thus, if he is placing women on the stage, he must contract all their habits in his own person.

MNESILOCHUS. Then you ride the high horse[556] when you are composing a Phaedra.

AGATHON. If the heroes are men, everything in him will be manly. What we don't possess by nature, we must acquire by imitation.

MNESILOCHUS. When you are staging Satyrs, call me; I will do my best to help you from behind with standing tool.

AGATHON. Besides, it is bad taste for a poet to be coarse and hairy. Look at the famous Ibycus, at Anacreon of Teos, and at Alcaeus,[557] who handled music so well; they wore headbands and found pleasure in the lascivious dances of Ionia. And have you not heard what a dandy Phrynichus was[558] and how careful in his dress? For this reason his pieces were also beautiful, for the works of a poet are copied from himself.

MNESILOCHUS. Ah! so it is for this reason that Philocles, who is so hideous, writes hideous pieces; Xenocles, who is malicious, malicious ones, and Theognis,[559] who is cold, such cold ones?

AGATHON. Yes, necessarily and unavoidably; and 'tis because I knew this that I have so well cared for my person.

MNESILOCHUS. How, in the gods' name?

EURIPIDES. Come, leave off badgering him; I was just the same at his age, when I began to write.

MNESILOCHUS. At! then, by Zeus! I don't envy you your fine manners.

EURIPIDES (*to Agathon*). But listen to the cause that brings me here.

AGATHON. Say on.

EURIPIDES. Agathon, wise is he who can compress many thoughts into few words.[560] Struck by a most cruel misfortune, I come to you as a suppliant.

AGATHON. What are you asking?

EURIPIDES. The women purpose killing me to-day during the Thesmophoria, because I have dared to speak ill of them.

AGATHON. And what can I do for you in the matter?

EURIPIDES. Everything. Mingle secretly with the women by making yourself pass as one of themselves; then do you plead my cause with your own lips, and I am saved. You, and you alone, are capable of speaking of me worthily.

AGATHON. But why not go and defend yourself?

EURIPIDES. 'Tis impossible. First of all, I am known; further, I have white hair and a long beard; whereas you, you are good-looking, charming, and are close-shaven; you are fair, delicate, and have a woman's voice.

AGATHON. Euripides!

EURIPIDES. Well?

AGATHON. Have you not said in one of your pieces, "You love to see the light, and don't you believe your father loves it too?"[561]

EURIPIDES. Yes.

AGATHON. Then never you think I am going to expose myself in your stead; 'twould be madness. 'Tis for you to submit to the fate that overtakes you; one must not try to trick misfortune, but resign oneself to it with good grace.

MNESILOCHUS. This is why you, you wretch, offer your posterior with a good grace to lovers, not in words, but in actual fact.

EURIPIDES. But what prevents your going there?

AGATHON. I should run more risk than you would.

EURIPIDES. Why?

AGATHON. Why? I should look as if I were wanting to trespass on secret nightly pleasures of the women and to ravish their Aphrodité [562]

MNESILOCHUS. Of wanting to ravish indeed! you mean wanting to be ravished—in the rearward mode. Ah! great gods! a fine excuse truly!

EURIPIDES. Well then, do you agree?

AGATHON. Don't count upon it.

EURIPIDES. Oh! I am unfortunate indeed! I am undone!

MNESILOCHUS. Euripides, my friend, my son-in-law, never despair.

EURIPIDES. What can be done?

MNESILOCHUS. Send him to the devil and do with me as you like.

EURIPIDES. Very well then, since you devote yourself to my safety, take off your cloak first.

MNESILOCHUS. There, it lies on the ground. But what do you want to do with me?

EURIPIDES. To shave off this beard of yours, and to remove your hair below as well.

MNESILOCHUS. Do what you think fit; I yield myself entirely to you.

EURIPIDES. Agathon, you have always razors about you; lend me one.

AGATHON. Take if yourself, there, out of that case.

EURIPIDES. Thanks. Sit down and puff out the right cheek.

MNESILOCHUS. Oh! oh! oh!

EURIPIDES. What are you shouting for? I'll cram a spit down your gullet, if you're not quiet.

MNESILOCHUS. Oh! oh! oh! oh! oh! oh! (*He springs up and starts running away.*)

EURIPIDES. Where are you running to now?

MNESILOCHUS. To the temple of the Eumenides.[563] No, by Demeter I won't let myself be gashed like that.

EURIPIDES. But you will get laughed at, with your face half-shaven like that.

MNESILOCHUS. Little care I.

EURIPIDES. In the gods' names, don't leave me in the lurch. Come here.

MNESILOCHUS. Oh! by the gods! (*Resumes his seat.*)

EURIPIDES. Keep still and hold up your head. Why do you want to fidget about like this?

MNESILOCHUS. Mu, mu.

EURIPIDES. Well! why, mu, mu? There! 'tis done and well done too!

244

MNESILOCHUS Ah! great god! It makes me feel quite light.

EURIPIDES. Don't worry yourself; you look charming. Do you want to see yourself?

MNESILOCHUS. Aye, that I do; hand the mirror here.

EURIPIDES. Do you see yourself?

MNESILOCHUS. But this is not I, it is Clisthenes![564]

EURIPIDES. Stand up; I am now going to remove your hair. Bend down.

MNESILOCHUS. Alas! alas! they are going to grill me like a pig.

EURIPIDES. Come now, a torch or a lamp! Bend down and take care of the tender end of your tail!

MNESILOCHUS. Aye, aye! but I'm afire! oh! oh! Water, water, neighbour, or my rump will be alight!

EURIPIDES. Keep up your courage!

MNESILOCHUS. Keep my courage, when I'm being burnt up?

EURIPIDES. Come, cease your whining, the worst is over.

MNESILOCHUS. Oh! it's quite black, all burnt below there all about the hole!

EURIPIDES. Don't worry! that will be washed off with a sponge.

MNESILOCHUS. Woe to him who dares to wash my rump!

EURIPIDES. Agathon, you refuse to devote yourself to helping me; but at any rate lend me a tunic and a belt. You cannot say you have not got them.

AGATHON. Take them and use them as you like; I consent.

MNESILOCHUS. What must be taken?

EURIPIDES. What must be taken? First put on this long saffron-coloured robe.

MNESILOCHUS. By Aphrodité! what a sweet odour! how it smells of a man's genitals![565] Hand it me quickly. And the belt?

EURIPIDES. Here it is.

MNESILOCHUS. Now some rings for my legs.

EURIPIDES. You still want a hair-net and a head-dress.

AGATHON. Here is my night-cap.

EURIPIDES. Ah! that's capital.

MNESILOCHUS. Does it suit me?

AGATHON. It could not be better.

EURIPIDES. And a short mantle?

AGATHON. There's one on the couch; take it.

EURIPIDES. He wants slippers.

AGATHON. Here are mine.

MNESILOCHUS. Will they fit me? You like a loose fit.[566]

AGATHON. Try them on. Now that you have all you need, let me be taken inside.[567]

EURIPIDES. You look for all the world like a woman. But when you talk, take good care to give your voice a woman's tone.

MNESILOCHUS. I'll try my best.

EURIPIDES. Come, get yourself to the temple.

MNESILOCHUS. No, by Apollo, not unless you swear to me ...

EURIPIDES. What?

MNESILOCHUS. ... that, if anything untoward happen to me, you will leave nothing undone to save me.

EURIPIDES Very well! I swear it by the Ether, the dwelling-place of the king of the gods.[568]

MNESILOCHUS. Why not rather swear it by the disciples of Hippocrates?[569]

EURIPIDES. Come, I swear it by all the gods, both great and small.

MNESILOCHUS. Remember, 'tis the heart, and not the tongue, that has sworn;[570] for the oaths of the tongue concern me but little.

EURIPIDES. Hurry yourself! The signal for the meeting has just been displayed on the Temple of Demeter. Farewell. [*Exit.*

MNESILOCHUS. Here, Thratta, follow me.[571] Look, Thratta, at the cloud of smoke that arises from all these lighted torches. Ah! beautiful Thesmophorae![572] grant me your favours, protect me, both within the temple and on my way back! Come, Thratta, put down the basket and take out the cake, which I wish to offer to the two goddesses. Mighty divinity, oh, Demeter, and thou, Persephoné, grant that I may be able to offer you many sacrifices; above all things, grant that I may not be recognized. Would that my young daughter might marry a man as rich as he is foolish and silly, so that she may have nothing to do but amuse herself. But where can a place be found for hearing well? Be off, Thratta, be off; slaves have no right to be present at this gathering.[573]

HERALD. Silence! Silence! Pray to the Thesmophorae, Demeter and Cora; pray to Plutus,[574] Calligenia,[575] Curotrophos,[576] the Earth, Hermes

247

and the Graces, that all may happen for the best at this gathering, both for the greatest advantage of Athens and for our own personal happiness! May the award be given her, who, by both deeds and words, has most deserved it from the Athenian people and from the women! Address these prayers to heaven and demand happiness for yourselves. Io Paean! Io Paean! Let us rejoice!

CHORUS. May the gods deign to accept our vows and our prayers! Oh! almighty Zeus, and thou, god with the golden lyre,[577] who reignest on sacred Delos, and thou, oh, invincible virgin, Pallas, with the eyes of azure and the spear of gold, who protectest our illustrious city, and thou, the daughter of the beautiful Latona, the queen of the forests,[578] who art adored under many names, hasten hither at my call. Come, thou mighty Posidon, king of the Ocean, leave thy stormy whirlpools of Nereus; come goddesses of the seas, come, ye nymphs, who wander on the mountains. Let us unite our voices to the sounds of the golden lyre, and may wisdom preside at the gathering of the noble matrons of Athens.

HERALD. Address your prayers to the gods and goddesses of Olympus, of Delphi, Delos and all other places; if there be a man who is plotting against the womenfolk or who, to injure them, is proposing peace to Euripides and the Medes, or who aspires to usurping the tyranny, plots the return of a tyrant, or unmasks a supposititious child; or if there be a slave who, a confidential party to a wife's intrigues, reveals them secretly to her husband, or who, entrusted with a message, does not deliver the same faithfully; if there be a lover who fulfils naught of what he has promised a woman, whom he has abused on the strength of his lies, if there be an old woman who seduces the lover of a maiden by dint of her presents and treacherously receives him in her house; if there be a host or hostess who sells false measure, pray the gods that they will overwhelm them with their wrath, both them and their families, and that they may reserve all their favours for you.

CHORUS. Let us ask the fulfilment of these wishes both for the city and for the people, and may the wisest of us cause her opinion to be accepted. But woe to those women who break their oaths, who speculate on the public misfortune, who seek to alter the laws and the decrees, who reveal our secrets to the foe and admit the Medes into our territory so that they may devastate it! I declare them both impious and criminal. Oh! almighty Zeus! see to it that the gods protect us, albeit we are but women!

HERALD. Hearken, all of you! this is the decree passed by the Senate of the Women under the presidency of Timoclea and at the suggestion of Sostrata; it is signed by Lysilla, the secretary: "There will be a gathering of the people on the morning of the third day of the Thesmophoria, which is a day of rest for us; the principal business there shall be the punishment that it is meet to inflict upon Euripides for the insults with which he has loaded us." Now who asks to speak?

FIRST WOMAN. I do.

HERALD. First put on this garland, and then speak. Silence! let all be quiet! Pay attention! for here she is spitting as orators generally do before they begin; no doubt she has much to say.

FIRST WOMAN. If I have asked to speak, may the goddesses bear me witness, it was not for sake of ostentation. But I have long been pained to see us women insulted by this Euripides, this son of the green-stuff woman,[579] who loads us with every kind of indignity. Has he not hit us enough, calumniated us sufficiently, wherever there are spectators, tragedians, and a chorus? Does he not style us gay, lecherous, drunken, traitorous, boastful? Does he not repeat that we are all vice, that we are the curse of our husbands? So that, directly they come back from the theatre, they look at us doubtfully and go searching every nook, fearing there may be some hidden lover. We can do nothing as we used to, so many are the false ideas which he has instilled into our husbands. Is a woman weaving a garland for herself? 'Tis because she is in love.[580] Does she let some vase drop while going or returning to the house? her husband asks her in whose honour she has broken it, "It can only be for that Corinthian stranger."[581] Is a maiden unwell? Straightway her brother says, "That is a colour that does not please me."[582] And if a childless woman wishes to substitute one, the deceit can no longer be a secret, for the neighbours will insist on being present at her delivery. Formerly the old men married young girls, but they have been so calumniated that none think of them now, thanks to the verse: "A woman is the tyrant of the old man who marries her."[583] Again, it is because of Euripides that we are incessantly watched, that we are shut up behind bolts and bars, and that dogs are kept to frighten off the gallants. Let that pass; but formerly it was we who had the care of the food, who fetched the flour from the storeroom, the oil and the wine; we can do it no more. Our husbands now carry little Spartan keys on their persons, made with three notches and full of malice and spite.[584] Formerly it sufficed to purchase a ring marked with the same sign for three obols, to open the most securely sealed-up door;[585] but now this pestilent Euripides has taught men to hang seals of worm-eaten wood about their necks.[586] My opinion, therefore, is that we should rid ourselves of our enemy by poison or by any other means, provided he dies. That is what I announce publicly; as to certain points, which I wish to keep secret, I propose to record them on the secretary's minutes.

CHORUS. Never have I listened to a cleverer or more eloquent woman. Everything she says is true; she has examined the matter from all sides and has weighed up every detail. Her arguments are close, varied, and happily chosen. I believe that Xenocles himself, the son of Carcinus, would seem to talk mere nonsense, if placed beside her.

SECOND WOMAN. I have only a very few words to add, for the last speaker has covered the various points of the indictment; allow me only to tell you what happened to me. My husband died at Cyprus, leaving me five children, whom I had great trouble to bring up by weaving chaplets on the myrtle market. Anyhow, I lived as well as I could until this wretch had persuaded the spectators by his tragedies that there were no gods; since then I have not sold as many chaplets by half. I charge you therefore and exhort you all to punish him, for does he not deserve it in a thousand respects, he who loads you with troubles, who is as coarse toward you as the green-stuff upon which his mother reared him? But I must back to the market to weave my chaplets; I have twenty to deliver yet.

CHORUS. This is even more animated and more trenchant than the first speech; all she has just said is full of good sense and to the point; it is clever, clear and well calculated to convince. Yes! we must have striking vengeance on the insults of Euripides.

MNESILOCHUS. Oh, women! I am not astonished at these outbursts of fiery rage; how could your bile not get inflamed against Euripides, who has spoken so ill of you? As for myself, I hate the man, I swear it by my children; 'twould be madness not to hate him! Yet, let us reflect a little; we are alone and our words will not be repeated outside. Why be so bent on his ruin? Because he has known and shown up two or three of our faults, when we have a thousand? As for myself, not to speak of other women, I have more than one great sin upon my conscience, but this is the blackest of them. I had been married three days and my husband was asleep by my side; I had a lover, who had seduced me when I was seven years old; impelled by his passion, he came scratching at the door; I understood at once he was there and was going down noiselessly. "Where are you going?" asked my husband. "I am suffering terribly with colic," I told him, "and am going to the closet." "Go," he replied, and started pounding together juniper berries, aniseed, and sage.[587] As for myself, I moistened the door-hinge[588] and went to find my lover, who embraced me, half-reclining upon Apollo's altar[589] and holding on to the sacred laurel with one hand. Well now! Consider! that is a thing of which Euripides has never spoken. And when we bestow our favours on slaves and muleteers for want of better, does he mention this? And when we eat garlic early in the morning after a night of wantonness, so that our husband, who has been keeping guard upon the city wall, may be reassured by the smell and suspect nothing,[590] has Euripides ever breathed a word of this? Tell me. Neither has he spoken of the woman who spreads open a large cloak before her husband's eyes to make him admire it in full daylight to conceal her lover by so doing and afford him the means of making his escape. I know another, who for ten whole days pretended to be suffering the pains of labour until she had secured a child; the husband hurried in all directions to buy drugs to hasten her deliverance, and meanwhile an old woman brought the infant in a stew-pot; to prevent its crying she had stopped up its mouth with honey.

With a sign she told the wife that she was bringing a child for her, who at once began exclaiming, "Go away, friend, go away, I think I am going to be delivered; I can feel him kicking his heels in the belly ... of the stew-pot."[591] The husband goes off full of joy, and the old wretch quickly picks the honey out of the child's mouth, which sets a-crying; then she seizes the babe, runs to the father and tells him with a smile on her face, "'Tis a lion, a lion, that is born to you; 'tis your very image. Everything about it is like you, even to its little tool, which is all twisty like a fir-cone." Are these not our everyday tricks? Why certainly, by Artemis, and we are angry with Euripides, who assuredly treats us no worse than we deserve!

CHORUS. Great gods! where has she unearthed all that? What country gave birth to such an audacious woman? Oh! you wretch! I should not have thought ever a one of us could have spoken in public with such impudence. 'Tis clear, however, that we must expect everything and, as the old proverb says, must look beneath every stone, lest it conceal some orator[592] ready to sting us. There is but one thing in the world worse than a shameless woman, and that's another woman.

THIRD WOMAN. By Aglaurus![593] you have lost your wits, friends! You must be bewitched to suffer this plague to belch forth insults against us all. Is there no one has any spirit at all? If not, we and our maid-servants will punish her. Run and fetch coals and let's depilate her cunt in proper style, to teach her not to speak ill of her sex.

MNESILOCHUS. Oh! no! have mercy, friends. Have we not the right to speak frankly at this gathering? And because I have uttered what I thought right in favour of Euripides, do you want to depilate me for my trouble?

THIRD WOMAN. What! we ought not to punish you, who alone have dared to defend the man who has done us so much harm, whom it pleases to put all the vile women that ever were upon the stage, who only shows us Melanippés Phaedras? But of Penelopé he has never said a word, because she was reputed chaste and good.

MNESILOCHUS. I know the reason. 'Tis because not a single Penelopé exists among the women of to-day, but all without exception are Phaedras.

THIRD WOMAN. Women, you hear how this creature still dares to speak of us all.

MNESILOCHUS. And, 'faith, I have not said all that I know. Do you want any more?

THIRD WOMAN. You cannot tell us any more; you have emptied your bag.

MNESILOCHUS. Why, I have not told the thousandth part of what we women do. Have I said how we use the hollow handles of our brooms to draw up wine unbeknown to our husbands.

THIRD WOMAN. The cursed jade!

MNESILOCHUS. And how we give meats to our lovers at the feast of the Apaturia and then accuse the cat....

THIRD WOMAN. She's mad!

MNESILOCHUS. ... Have I mentioned the woman who killed her husband with a hatchet? Of another, who caused hers to lose his reason with her potions? And of the Acharnian woman ...

THIRD WOMAN. Die, you bitch!

MNESILOCHUS. ... who buried her father beneath the bath?[594]

THIRD WOMAN. And yet we listen to such things?

MNESILOCHUS. Have I told how you attributed to yourself the male child your slave had just borne and gave her your little daughter?

THIRD WOMAN. This insult calls for vengeance. Look out for your hair!

MNESILOCHUS. By Zeus! don't touch me.

THIRD WOMAN. There!

MNESILOCHUS. There! tit for tat! (*They exchange blows.*)

THIRD WOMAN. Hold my cloak, Philista!

MNESILOCHUS. Come on then, and by Demeter ...

THIRD WOMAN. Well! what?

MNESILOCHUS. ... I'll make you disgorge the sesame-cake you have eaten.[595]

CHORUS. Cease wrangling! I see a woman[596] running here in hot haste. Keep silent, so that we may hear the better what she has to say.

CLISTHENES. Friends, whom I copy in all things, my hairless chin sufficiently evidences how dear you are to me; I am women-mad and make myself their champion wherever I am. Just now on the market-place I heard mention of a thing that is of the greatest importance to you; I come to tell it you, to let you know it, so that you may watch carefully and be on your guard against the danger which threatens you.

CHORUS. What is it, my child? I can well call you child, for you have so smooth a skin.

CLISTHENES. 'Tis said that Euripides has sent an old man here to-day, one of his relations ...

CHORUS. With what object? What is his purpose?

CLISTHENES. ... so that he may hear your speeches and inform him of your deliberations and intentions.

CHORUS. But how would a man fail to be recognized amongst women?

CLISTHENES. Euripides singed and depilated him and disguised him as a woman.

MNESILOCHUS. This is pure invention! What man is fool enough to let himself be depilated? As for myself, I don't believe a word of it.

CLISTHENES. Are you mad? I should not have come here to tell you, if I did not know it on indisputable authority.

CHORUS. Great gods! what is it you tell us! Come, women, let us not lose a moment; let us search and rummage everywhere! Where can this man have hidden himself escape our notice? Help us to look, Clisthenes; we shall thus owe you double thanks, dear friend.

CLISTHENES (*to a fourth woman*). Well there! let us see. To begin with you; who are you?

MNESILOCHUS (*aside*). Wherever am I to stow myself?

CLISTHENES. Each and every one must pass the scrutiny.

MNESILOCHUS (*aside*). Oh! great gods!

FOURTH WOMAN. You ask me who I am? I am the wife of Cleonymus.[597]

CLISTHENES. Do you know this woman?

CHORUS. Yes, yes, pass on to the rest.

CLISTHENES. And she who carries the child?

MNESILOCHUS (*aside*). I'm a dead man. (*He runs off.*)

CLISTHENES (*to Mnesilochus*). Hi! you there! where are you off to? Stop there. What are you running away for?

MNESILOCHUS. I want to relieve myself.

CLISTHENES. The shameless thing! Come, hurry yourself; I will wait here for you.

CHORUS. Wait for her and examine her closely; 'tis the only one we do not know.

CLISTHENES. You are a long time about your business.

MNESILOCHUS. Aye, my god, yes; 'tis because I am unwell, for I ate cress yesterday.[598]

CLISTHENES. What are you chattering about cress? Come here and be quick.

MNESILOCHUS. Oh! don't pull a poor sick woman about like that.

CLISTHENES. Tell me, who is your husband?

MNESILOCHUS. My husband? Do you know a certain individual at Cothocidae[599]…?

CLISTHENES. Whom do you mean? Give his name.

MNESILOCHUS. 'Tis an individual to whom the son of a certain individual one day….

CLISTHENES. You are drivelling! Let's see, have you ever been here before?

MNESILOCHUS. Why certainly, every year.

CLISTHENES. Who is your tent companion?[600]

MNESILOCHUS. 'Tis a certain…. Oh! my god!

CLISTHENES. You don't answer.

FIFTH WOMAN. Withdraw, all of you; I am going to examine her thoroughly about last year's mysteries. But move away, Clisthenes, for no man may hear what is going to be said. Now answer my questions! What was done first?

MNESILOCHUS. Let's see then. What was done first? Oh! we drank.

FIFTH WOMAN. And then?

MNESILOCHUS. We drank to our healths.

FIFTH WOMAN. You will have heard that from someone. And then?

MNESILOCHUS. Xenylla relieved herself in a cup, for there was no other vessel.

FIFTH WOMAN. You trifle. Here, Clisthenes, here! This is the man of whom you spoke.

CLISTHENES. What is to be done then?

FIFTH WOMAN. Take off his clothes, I can get nothing out of him.

MNESILOCHUS. What! are you going to strip a mother of nine children naked?

CLISTHENES. Come, undo your girdle, you shameless thing.

FIFTH WOMAN. Ah! what a sturdy frame! but she has no breasts like we have.

MNESILOCHUS. That's because I'm barren. I never had any children.

FIFTH WOMAN. Oh! indeed! just now you were the mother of nine.

CLISTHENES. Stand up straight. Hullo! what do I see there? Why, a penis sticking out behind.

FIFTH WOMAN. There's no mistaking it; you can see it projecting, and a fine red it is.

CLISTHENES. Where has it gone to now?

FIFTH WOMAN. To the front.

CLISTHENES. No.

FIFTH WOMAN. Ah! 'tis behind now.

CLISTHENES. Why, friend, 'tis for all the world like the Isthmus; you keep pulling your tool backwards and forwards just as the Corinthians do their ships.[601]

FIFTH WOMAN. Ah! the wretch! this is why he insulted us and defended Euripides.

MNESILOCHUS. Aye, wretch indeed, what troubles have I not got into now!

FIFTH WOMAN. What shall we do?

CLISTHENES. Watch him closely, so that he does not escape. As for me, I go to report the matter to the magistrates, the Prytanes.

CHORUS. Let us kindle our lamps; let us go firmly to work and with courage, let us take off our cloaks and search whether some other man has not come here too; let us pass round the whole Pnyx,[602] examine the tents and the passages.[603] Come, be quick, let us start off on a light toe[604] and rummage all round in silence. Let us hasten, let us finish our round as soon as possible. Look quickly for the traces that might show you a man hidden here, let your glance fall on every side; look well to the right and to the left. If we seize some impious fellow, woe to him! He will know how we punish the outrage, the crime, the sacrilege. The criminal will then acknowledge at last that gods exist; his fate will teach all men that the deities must be revered, that justice must be observed and that they must submit to the sacred laws. If not, then woe to them! Heaven itself will punish sacrilege; being aflame with fury and mad with frenzy, all their deeds will prove to mortals, both men and women, that the deity punishes injustice and impiety, and that she is not slow to strike. But I think I have now searched everywhere and that no other man is hidden among us.

SIXTH WOMAN. Where is he flying to? Stop him! stop him! Ah! miserable woman that I am, he has torn my child from my breast and has disappeared with it.

MNESILOCHUS. Scream as loud as you will, but he shall never suck your bosom more. If you do not let me go this very instant, I am going to cut open the veins of his thighs with this cutlass and his blood shall flow over the altar.

SIXTH WOMAN. Oh! great gods! oh! friends, help me! terrify him with your shrieks, triumph over this monster, permit him not to rob me of my only child.

CHORUS. Oh! oh! venerable Parcae, what fresh attack is this? 'Tis the crowning act of audacity and shamelessness! What has he done now, friends, what has he done?

MNESILOCHUS. Ah! this insolence passes all bounds, but I shall know how to curb it.

CHORUS. What a shameful deed! the measure of his iniquities is full!

SIXTH WOMAN. Aye, 'tis shameful that he should have robbed me of my child.

CHORUS. 'Tis past belief to be so criminal and so impudent!

MNESILOCHUS. Ah! you're not near the end of it yet.

SIXTH WOMAN. Little I care whence you come; you shall not return to boast of having acted so odiously with impunity, for you shall be punished.

MNESILOCHUS. You won't do it, by the gods!

CHORUS. And what immortal would protect you for your crime?

MNESILOCHUS. 'Tis in vain you talk! I shall not let go the child.

CHORUS. By the goddesses, you will not laugh presently over your crime and your impious speech. For with impiety, as 'tis meet, shall we reply to your impiety. Soon fortune will turn round and overwhelm you. Come! bring wood along. Let us burn the wretch, let us roast him as quickly as possible.

SIXTH WOMAN. Bring faggots, Mania! (*To Mnesilochus.*) You will be mere charcoal soon.

CHORUS. Grill away, roast me, but you, my child, take off this Cretan robe and blame no one but your mother for your death. But what does this mean? The little girl is nothing but a skin filled with wine and shod with Persian slippers.[605] Oh! you wanton, you tippling woman, who think of nothing but wine; you are a fortune to the drinking-shops and are our ruin; for the sake of drink, you neglect both your household and your shuttle!

SIXTH WOMAN. Faggots, Mania, plenty of them.

MNESILOCHUS. Bring as many as you like. But answer me; are you the mother of this brat?

SIXTH WOMAN. I carried it ten months.[606]

MNESILOCHUS. You carried it?

SIXTH WOMAN. I swear it by Artemis.

MNESILOCHUS. How much does it hold? Three cotylae?[607] Tell me.

SIXTH WOMAN. Oh! what have you done? You have stripped the poor child quite naked, and it is so small, so small.

MNESILOCHUS. So small?

SIXTH WOMAN. Yes, quite small, to be sure.

MNESILOCHUS. How old is it? Has it seen the feast of cups thrice or four times?

SIXTH WOMAN. It was born about the time of the last Dionysia.[608] But give it back to me.

MNESILOCHUS. No, may Apollo bear me witness.

SIXTH WOMAN. Well, then we are going to burn him.

MNESILOCHUS. Burn me, but then I shall rip this open instantly.

SIXTH WOMAN. No, no, I adjure you, don't; do anything you like to me rather than that.

MNESILOCHUS. What a tender mother you are; but nevertheless I shall rip it open. (*Tears open the wine-skin.*)

SIXTH WOMAN. Oh, my beloved daughter! Mania, hand me the sacred cup,   that
I may at least catch the blood of my child.

MNESILOCHUS. Hold it below; 'tis the sole favour I grant you.

SIXTH WOMAN. Out upon you, you pitiless monster!

MNESILOCHUS. This robe belongs to the priestess.[609]

SIXTH WOMAN. What belongs to the priestess?

MNESILOCHUS. Here, take it. (*Throws her the Cretan robe.*)

SEVENTH WOMAN. Ah! unfortunate Mica! who has robbed you of your daughter, your beloved child?

SIXTH WOMAN. That wretch. But as you are here, watch him well, while I go with Clisthenes to the Prytanes and denounce him for his crimes.

MNESILOCHUS. Ah! how can I secure safety? what device can I hit on? what can I think of? He whose fault it is, he who hurried me into this trouble, will not come to my rescue. Let me see, whom could I best send to him? Ha! I know a means taken from Palamedes; like him, I will write my misfortune on some oars, which I will cast into the sea. But there are no oars here. Where might I find some?[610] Where indeed? Bah! what if I took these statues[611] instead of oars, wrote upon them and then threw them towards this side and that. 'Tis the best thing to do. Besides, like oars they are of wood. Oh! my hands, keep up your courage, for my safety is at stake. Come, my beautiful tablets, receive the traces of my stylus and be the messengers of my sorry fate. Oh! oh! this B looks miserable enough! Where is it running to then? Come, off with you in all directions, to the right and to the left; and hurry yourselves, for there's much need indeed!

CHORUS. Let us address ourselves to the spectators to sing our praises, despite the fact that each one says much ill of women. If the men are to be believed, we are a plague to them; through us come all their troubles, quarrels, disputes, sedition, griefs and wars. But if we are truly such a pest, why marry us? Why forbid us to go out or show ourselves at the window? You want to keep this pest, and take a thousand cares to do it. If your wife goes out and you meet her away from the house, you fly into a fury. Ought you not rather to rejoice and give thanks to the gods? for if the pest has disappeared, you will no longer find it at home. If we fall asleep at friends' houses from the fatigue of playing and sporting, each of you comes prowling round the bed to contemplate the features of this pest. If we seat ourselves at the window, each one wants to see the pest, and if we withdraw through modesty, each wants all the more to see the pest perch herself there again. It is thus clear that we are better than you, and the proof of this is easy. Let us find out which is worse of the two sexes. We say, "'Tis you," while you aver, 'tis we. Come, let us compare them in detail, each individual man with a woman. Charminus is not equal to Nausimaché,[612] that's certain. Cleophon[613] is in every respect inferior to Salabaccho.[614] 'Tis long now since any of you has dared to contest the prize with Aristomaché, the heroine of Marathon, or with Stratonicé.[615]

Among the last year's Senators, who have just yielded their office to other citizens, is there one who equals Eubulé?[616] Therefore we maintain that men are greatly our inferiors. You see no woman who has robbed the State of fifty talents rushing about the city in a magnificent chariot; our greatest peculations are a measure of corn, which we steal from our husbands, and even then we return it them the very same day. But we could name many amongst you who do quite as much, and who are, even more than ourselves, gluttons, parasites, cheats and kidnappers of slaves. We know how to keep our property better than you. We still have our cylinders, our beams,[617] our baskets and our sunshades; whereas many among you have lost the wood of your spears as well as the iron, and many others have cast away their bucklers on the battlefield.

There are many reproaches we have the right to bring against men. The most serious is this, that the woman, who has given birth to a useful citizen, whether taxiarch or strategus[618] should receive some distinction; a place of honour should be reserved for her at the Sthenia, the Scirophoria,[619] and the other festivals that we keep. On the other hand, she of whom a coward was born or a worthless man, a bad trierarch[620] or an unskilful pilot, should sit with shaven head, behind her sister who had borne a brave man. Oh! citizens! is it just, that the mother of Hyperbolus should sit dressed in white and with loosened tresses beside that of Lamachus[621] and lend out money on usury? He, who may have done a deal of this nature with her, so far from paying her interest, should not even repay the capital, saying, "What, pay you interest? after you have given us this delightful son?"

MNESILOCHUS. I have contracted quite a squint by looking round for him, and yet Euripides does not come. Who is keeping him? No doubt he is ashamed of his cold Palamedes.[622] What will attract him? Let us see! By which of his pieces does he set most store? Ah! I'll imitate his Helen,[623] his lastborn. I just happen to have a complete woman's outfit.

SEVENTH WOMAN. What are you ruminating over now again? Why are you rolling up your eyes? You'll have no reason to be proud of your Helen, if you don't keep quiet until one of the Prytanes arrives.

MNESILOCHUS (*as Helen*). "These shores are those of the Nile with the beautiful nymphs, these waters take the place of heaven's rain and fertilize the white earth, that produces the black syrmea."[624]

SEVENTH WOMAN. By bright Hecaté, you're a cunning varlet.

MNESILOCHUS. "Glorious Sparta is my country and Tyndareus is my father."[625]

SEVENTH WOMAN. He your father, you rascal! Why, 'tis Phrynondas.[626]

MNESILOCHUS. "I was given the name of Helen."

SEVENTH WOMAN. What! you are again becoming a woman, before we have punished you for having pretended it a first time!

MNESILOCHUS. "A thousand warriors have died on my account on the banks of the Scamander."

SEVENTH WOMAN. Why have you not done the same?

MNESILOCHUS. "And here I am upon these shores; Menelaus, my unhappy husband, does not yet come. Ah! how life weighs upon me! Oh! ye cruel crows, who have not devoured my body! But what sweet hope is this that sets my heart a-throb? Oh, Zeus! grant it may not prove a lying one!"

EURIPIDES (*as Menelaus*). "To what master does this splendid palace belong? Will he welcome strangers who have been tried on the billows of the sea by storm and shipwreck?"[627]

MNESILOCHUS. "This is the palace of Proteus."[628]

EURIPIDES. "Of what Proteus?"

SEVENTH WOMAN. Oh! the thrice cursed rascal! how he lies! By the goddesses, 'tis ten years since Proteas[629] died.

EURIPIDES. "What is this shore whither the wind has driven our boat?"

MNESILOCHUS. "It's Egypt."

EURIPIDES. "Alas! how far we are from our own country!"

SEVENTH WOMAN. But don't believe that cursed fool. This is Demeter's Temple.

EURIPIDES. "Is Proteus in these parts?"

SEVENTH WOMAN. Ah, now, stranger, it must be sea-sickness that makes you so distraught! You have been told that Proteas is dead, and yet you ask if he is in these parts.

EURIPIDES. "He is no more! Oh! woe! where lie his ashes?"

MNESILOCHUS. 'Tis on his tomb you see me sitting.

SEVENTH WOMAN. You call an altar a tomb! Beware of the rope!

EURIPIDES. "And why remain sitting on this tomb, wrapped in this long veil, oh, stranger lady?"[630]

MNESILOCHUS. "They want to force me to marry a son of Proteus."

SEVENTH WOMAN. Ah! wretch, why tell such shameful lies? Stranger, this is a rascal who has slipped in amongst us women to rob us of our trinkets.

MNESILOCHUS (*to Seventh Woman*) "Shout! load me with your insults, for little care I."

EURIPIDES. "Who is the old woman who reviles you, stranger lady?"

MNESILOCHUS. "'Tis Theonoé, the daughter of Proteus."

SEVENTH WOMAN. I! Why, my name's Critylla, the daughter of Antitheus,[631] of the deme of Gargettus;[632] as for you, you are a rogue.

MNESILOCHUS. "Your entreaties are vain. Never shall I wed your brother; never shall I betray the faith I owe my husband Menelaus, who is fighting before Troy."

EURIPIDES. "What are you saying? Turn your face towards me."

MNESILOCHUS. "I dare not; my cheeks show the marks of the insults I have been forced to suffer."

EURIPIDES "Oh! great gods! I cannot speak, for very emotion.... Ah! what do I see? Who are you?"

MNESILOCHUS. "And you, what is your name? for my surprise is as great as yours."

EURIPIDES. "Are you Grecian or born in this country?"

MNESILOCHUS. "I am Grecian. But now your name, what is it?"

EURIPIDES. "Oh! how you resemble Helen!"

MNESILOCHUS. And you Menelaus, if I can judge by those pot-herbs.[633]

EURIPIDES. "You are not mistaken, 'tis that unfortunate mortal who stands before you."

MNESILOCHUS. "Ah! how you have delayed coming to your wife's arms! Press me to your heart, throw your arms about me, for I wish to cover you with kisses. Carry me away, carry me away, quick, quick, far, very far from here."

SEVENTH WOMAN. By the goddesses, woe to him who would carry you away! I should thrash him with my torch.

EURIPIDES. "Do you propose to prevent me from taking my wife, the daughter of Tyndareus, to Sparta?"

SEVENTH WOMAN You seem to me to be a cunning rascal too; you are in collusion with this man, and 'twas not for nothing that you kept babbling about Egypt. But the hour for punishment has come; here is the magistrate come with his archer.

EURIPIDES. This grows awkward. Let me hide myself.

MNESILOCHUS. And what is to become of me, poor unfortunate man?

EURIPIDES. Be at ease. I shall never abandon you, as long as I draw breath and one of my numberless artifices remains untried.

MNESILOCHUS. The fish has not bitten this time.

THE PRYTANIS. Is this the rascal of whom Clisthenes told us? Why are you trying to make yourself so small? Archer, arrest him, fasten him to the post, then take up your position there and keep guard over him. Let none approach him. A sound lash with your whip for him who attempts to break the order.

SEVENTH WOMAN. Excellent, for just now a rogue almost took him from me.

MNESILOCHUS. Prytanis, in the name of that hand which you know so well how to bend, when money is placed in it, grant me a slight favour before I die.

PRYTANIS. What favour?

MNESILOCHUS. Order the archer to strip me before lashing me to the post; the crows, when they make their meal on the poor old man, would laugh too much at this robe and head-dress.

PRYTANIS. 'Tis in that gear that you must be exposed by order of the Senate, so that your crime may be patent to the passers-by.

MNESILOCHUS. Oh! cursed robe, the cause of all my misfortune! My last hope is thus destroyed!

CHORUS. Let us now devote ourselves to the sports which the women are accustomed to celebrate here, when time has again brought round the mighty Mysteries of the great goddesses, the sacred days which Pauson[634] himself honours by fasting and would wish feast to succeed feast, that he might keep them all holy. Spring forward with a light step, whirling in mazy circles; let your hands interlace, let the eager and rapid dancers sway to the music and glance on every side as they move. Let the chorus sing likewise and praise the Olympian gods in their pious transport.

'Tis wrong to suppose that, because I am a woman and in this Temple, I am going to speak ill of men; but since we want something fresh, we are going through the rhythmic steps of the round dance for the first time.

Start off while you sing to the god of the lyre and to the chaste goddess armed with the bow. Hail! thou god who flingest thy darts so far,[635] grant us the victory! The homage of our song is also due to Heré, the goddess of marriage, who interests herself in every chorus and guards the approach to the nuptial couch. I also pray Hermes, the god of the shepherds, and Pan and the beloved Graces to bestow a benevolent smile upon our songs.

Let us lead off anew, let us double our zeal during our solemn days, and especially let us observe a close fast; let us form fresh measures that keep good time, and may our songs resound to the very heavens. Do thou, oh divine Bacchus, who art crowned with ivy, direct our chorus; 'tis to thee that both my hymns and my dances are dedicated; oh, Evius, oh, Bromius,[636] oh, thou son of Semelé, oh, Bacchus, who delightest to mingle with the dear choruses of the nymphs upon the mountains, and who repeatest, while dancing with them, the sacred hymn, Evius, Evius, Evoe. Echo, the nymph of Cithaeron returns thy words, which resound beneath the dark vaults of the thick foliage and in the midst of the rocks of the forest; the ivy enlaces thy brow with its tendrils charged with flowers.

SCYTHIAN ARCHER.[637] You shall stay here in the open air to wail.

MNESILOCHUS. Archer, I adjure you.

SCYTHIAN. 'Tis labour lost.

MNESILOCHUS. Loosen the wedge a little.[638]

SCYTHIAN. Aye, certainly.

MNESILOCHUS. Oh! by the gods! why, you are driving it in tighter.

SCYTHIAN. Is that enough?

MNESILOCHUS. Oh! la, la! oh! la, la! May the plague take you!

SCYTHIAN. Silence! you cursed old wretch! I am going to get a mat to lie upon, so as to watch you close at hand at my ease.

MNESILOCHUS. Ah! what exquisite pleasures Euripides is securing for me! But, oh, ye gods! oh, Zeus the Deliverer, all is not yet lost! I don't believe him the man to break his word; I just caught sight of him appearing in the form of Perseus, and he told me with a mysterious sign to turn myself into Andromeda. And in truth am I not really bound? 'Tis certain, then, that he is coming to my rescue; for otherwise he would not have steered his flight this way.[639]

EURIPIDES (*as Perseus*). Oh Nymphs, ye virgins who are dear to me, how am I to approach him? how can I escape the sight of this Scythian? And Echo, thou who reignest in the inmost recesses of the caves, oh! favour my cause and permit me to approach my spouse.

MNESILOCHUS (*as Andromeda*).[640] A pitiless ruffian has chained up the most unfortunate of mortal maids. Alas! I had barely escaped the filthy claws of an old fury, when another mischance overtook me! This Scythian does not take his eye off me and he has exposed me as food for the crows. Alas! what is to become of me, alone here and without friends! I am not seen mingling in the dances nor in the games of my companions, but heavily loaded with fetters I am given over to the voracity of a Glaucetes.[641] Sing no bridal hymn for me, oh women, but rather the hymn of captivity, and in tears. Ah! how I suffer! great gods! how I suffer! Alas! alas! and through my own relatives too![642] My misery would make Tartarus dissolve into tears! Alas! in my terrible distress, I implore the mortal who first shaved me and depilated me, then dressed me in this long robe, and then sent me to this Temple into the midst of the women, to save me. Oh, thou pitiless Fate! I am then accursed, great gods! Ah! who would not be moved at the sight of the appalling tortures under which I succumb? Would that the blazing shaft of the lightning would wither… this barbarian for me! (*pointing to the Scythian archer*) for the immortal light has no further charm for my eyes since I have been descending the shortest path to the dead, tied up, strangled, and maddened with pain.

EURIPIDES (as *Echo*). Hail! beloved girl. As for your father, Cepheus, who has exposed you in this guise, may the gods annihilate him.

MNESILOCHUS (*as Andromeda*). And who are you whom my misfortunes have moved to pity?

EURIPIDES. I am Echo, the nymph who repeats all she hears. 'Tis I, who last year lent my help to Euripides in this very place.[643] But, my child, give yourself up to the sad laments that belong to your pitiful condition.

MNESILOCHUS. And you will repeat them?

EURIPIDES. I will not fail you. Begin.

MNESILOCHUS. "Oh! thou divine Night! how slowly thy chariot threads its way through the starry vault, across the sacred realms of the Air and mighty Olympus."

EURIPIDES. Mighty Olympus.

MNESILOCHUS. "Why is it necessary that Andromeda should have all the woes for her share?"

EURIPIDES. For her share.

MNESILOCHUS. "Sad death!"

EURIPIDES. Sad death!

MNESILOCHUS. You weary me, old babbler.

EURIPIDES. Old babbler.

MNESILOCHUS. Oh! you are too unbearable.

EURIPIDES. Unbearable.

MNESILOCHUS. Friend, let me talk by myself. Do please let me. Come, that's enough.

EURIPIDES. That's enough.

MNESILOCHUS. Go and hang yourself!

EURIPIDES. Go and hang yourself!

MNESILOCHUS. What a plague!

EURIPIDES. What a plague!

MNESILOCHUS. Cursed brute!

EURIPIDES. Cursed brute!

MNESILOCHUS. Beware of blows!

EURIPIDES. Beware of blows!

SCYTHIAN. Hullo! what are you jabbering about?

EURIPIDES. What are you jabbering about?

SCYTHIAN. I go to call the Prytanes.

EURIPIDES. I go to call the Prytanes.

SCYTHIAN. This is odd!

EURIPIDES. This is odd!

SCYTHIAN. Whence comes this voice?

EURIPIDES. Whence comes this voice.

SCYTHIAN. Ah! beware!

EURIPIDES. Ah! beware!

SCYTHIAN (*to Mnesilochus*). Are you mocking me?

EURIPIDES. Are you mocking me?

MNESILOCHUS. No, 'tis this woman, who stands near you.

EURIPIDES. Who stands near you.

SCYTHIAN. Where is the hussy? Ah! she is escaping! Whither, whither are you escaping?

EURIPIDES. Whither, whither are you escaping?

SCYTHIAN. You shall not get away.

EURIPIDES. You shall not get away.

SCYTHIAN. You are chattering still?

EURIPIDES. You are chattering still?

SCYTHIAN. Stop the hussy.

EURIPIDES. Stop the hussy.

SCYTHIAN. What a babbling, cursed woman!

EURIPIDES (*as Perseus*). "Oh! ye gods! to what barbarian land has my swift flight taken me? I am Perseus, who cleaves the plains of the air with my winged feet, and I am carrying the Gorgon's head to Argos."

SCYTHIAN. What, are you talking about the head of Gorgos,[644] the scribe?

EURIPIDES. No, I am speaking of the head of the Gorgon.

SCYTHIAN. Why, yes! of Gorgus!

EURIPIDES. "But what do I behold? A young maiden, beautiful as the immortals, chained to this rock like a vessel in port?"

MNESILOCHUS. Take pity on me, oh, stranger! I am so unhappy and distraught! Free me from these bonds.

SCYTHIAN. Don't you talk! a curse upon your impudence! you are going to die, and yet you will be chattering!

EURIPIDES. "Oh! virgin! I take pity on your chains."

SCYTHIAN. But this is no virgin; 'tis an old rogue, a cheat and a thief.

EURIPIDES. You have lost your wits, Scythian. This is Andromeda, the daughter of Cepheus.

SCYTHIAN. But just look at this tool; is that like a woman?

EURIPIDES. Give me your hand, that I may descend near this young maiden. Each man has his own particular weakness; as for me I am aflame with love for this virgin.

SCYTHIAN. Oh! I'm not jealous; and as he has his back turned this way, why, I make no objection to your pedicating him.

EURIPIDES. "Ah! let me release her, and hasten to join her on the bridal couch."

SCYTHIAN. If this old man instils you with such ardent concupiscence, why, you can bore through the plank, and so get at his behind.

EURIPIDES. No, I will break his bonds.

SCYTHIAN. Beware of my lash!

EURIPIDES. No matter.

SCYTHIAN. This blade shall cut off your head.

EURIPIDES. "Ah! what can be done? what arguments can I use? This savage will understand nothing! The newest and most cunning fancies are a dead letter to the ignorant. Let us invent some artifice to fit in with his coarse nature."

SCYTHIAN. I can see the rascal is trying to outwit me.

MNESILOCHUS. Ah! Perseus! remember in what condition you are leaving me.

SCYTHIAN. Are you wanting to feel my lash again!

CHORUS.

Oh! Pallas, who art fond of dances, hasten hither at my call. Oh! thou chaste virgin, the protectress of Athens, I call thee in accordance with the sacred rites, thee, whose evident protection we adore and who keepest the keys of our city in thy hands. Do thou appear, thou whose just hatred has overturned our tyrants. The womenfolk are calling thee; hasten hither at their bidding along with Peace, who shall restore the festivals. And ye, august goddesses,[645] display a smiling and propitious countenance to our gaze; come into your sacred grove, the entry to which is forbidden to men; 'tis there in the midst of sacred orgies that we contemplate your divine features. Come, appear, we pray it of you, oh, venerable Thesmophoriae! If you have ever answered our appeal, oh! come into our midst.

EURIPIDES. Women, if you will be reconciled with me, I am willing, and I undertake never to say anything ill of you in future. Those are my proposals for peace.

CHORUS. And what impels you to make these overtures?

EURIPIDES. This unfortunate man, who is chained to the post, is my father-in-law; if you will restore him to me, you will have no more cause to complain of me; but if not, I shall reveal your pranks to your husbands when they return from the war.

CHORUS. We accept peace, but there is this barbarian whom you must buy over.

EURIPIDES. That's my business. (*He returns as an old woman and is accompanied by a dancing-girl and a flute-girl.*) Come, my little wench, bear in mind what I told you on the road and do it well. Come, go past him and gird up your robe. And you, you little dear, play us the air of a Persian dance.

SCYTHIAN. What is this music that makes me so blithe?

EURIPIDES (*as an old woman*). Scythian, this young girl is going to practise some dances, which she has to perform at a feast presently.

SCYTHIAN. Very well! let her dance and practise; I won't hinder her. How nimbly she bounds! one might think her a flea on a fleece.

EURIPIDES. Come, my dear, off with your robe and seat yourself on the Scythian's knee; stretch forth your feet to me, that I may take off your slippers.

SCYTHIAN. Ah! yes, seat yourself, my little girl, ah! yes, to be sure. What a firm little bosom! 'tis just like a turnip.

EURIPIDES (*to the flute-girl*). An air on the flute, quick! (*To the dancing-girl.*) Well! are you still afraid of the Scythian?

SCYTHIAN. What beautiful thighs!

EURIPIDES. Come! keep still, can't you?

SCYTHIAN. 'Tis altogether a very fine morsel to make a man's cock stand.

EURIPIDES. That's so! (*To the dancing-girl.*) Resume your dress, it is time to be going.

SCYTHIAN. Give me a kiss.

EURIPIDES (*to the dancing-girl*). Come, give him a kiss.

SCYTHIAN. Oh! oh! oh! my goodness, what soft lips! 'tis like Attic honey. But might she not stop with me?

EURIPIDES. Impossible, archer; good evening.

SCYTHIAN. Oh! oh! old woman, do me this pleasure.

EURIPIDES. Will you give a drachma?

SCYTHIAN. Aye, that I will.

EURIPIDES. Hand over the money.

SCYTHIAN. I have not got it, but take my quiver in pledge.

EURIPIDES. You will bring her back?

SCYTHIAN. Follow me, my beautiful child. And you, old woman, just keep guard over this man. But what is your name?

EURIPIDES. Artemisia. Can you remember that name?

SCYTHIAN. Artemuxia.[646] Good!

EURIPIDES (*aside*). Hermes, god of cunning, receive my thanks! everything is turning out for the best. (*To the Scythian.*) As for you, friend, take away this girl, quick. (*Exit the Scythian with the dancing-girl.*) Now let me loose his bonds. (*To Mnesilochus.*) And you, directly I have released you, take to your legs and run off full tilt to your home to find your wife and children.

MNESILOCHUS. I shall not fail in that as soon as I am free.

EURIPIDES (*releases Mnesilochus*). There! 'Tis done. Come, fly, before the archer lays his hand on you again.

MNESILOCHUS. That's just what I am doing. [*Exit with Euripides.*

SCYTHIAN. Ah! old woman! what a charming little girl! Not at all the prude, and so obliging! Eh! where is the old woman? Ah! I am undone! And the old man, where is he? Hi! old woman! old woman! Ah! but this is a dirty trick! Artemuxia! she has tricked me, that's what the little old woman has done! Get clean out of my sight, you cursed quiver! (*Picks it up and throws it across the stage.*) Ha! you are well named quiver, for you have made me quiver indeed.[647] Oh! what's to be done? Where is the old woman then? Artemuxia!

CHORUS. Are you asking for the old woman who carried the lyre?

SCYTHIAN. Yes, yes; have you seen her?

CHORUS. She has gone that way along with an old man.

SCYTHIAN. Dressed in a long robe?

CHORUS. Yes; run quick, and you will overtake them.

SCYTHIAN. Ah! rascally old woman! Which way has she fled? Artemuxia!

CHORUS. Straight on; follow your nose. But, hi! where are you running to now? Come back, you are going exactly the wrong way.

SCYTHIAN. Ye gods! ye gods! and all this while Artemuxia is escaping. [*Exit running.*

CHORUS. Go your way! and a pleasant journey to you! But our sports have lasted long enough; it is time for each of us to be off home; and may the two goddesses reward us for our labours!

* * * * *

FINIS OF "THE THESMOPHORIAZUSAE"

* * * * *

Footnotes:

[544] Aristophanes parodies Euripides' language, which is occasionally sillily sententious.

[545] He flourished about 420 B.C. and composed many tragedies, such as 'Telephus,' 'Thyestes,' which are lost. Some fragments of his work are to be found in Aristotle and in Athenaeus; he also distinguished himself as a musician. The banquet, which gave his name to one of Plato's dialogues, is supposed to have taken place at his house.

[546] The Thesmophoria were celebrated in the month of Pyanepsion, or November.

[547] The Thesmophoria lasted five days; they were dedicated to Demeter Thesmophoros, or Legislatress, in recognition of the wise laws she had given mankind. For many days before the solemn event, the women of high birth (who alone were entitled to celebrate it) had to abstain from all pleasures that appealed to the senses, even the most legitimate, and to live with the greatest sobriety. The presiding priest at the Thesmophoria was always chosen from the sacerdotal family of the Eumolpidae, the descendants of Eumolpus, the son of Posidon. At these feasts, the worship of Persephoné was associated with that of Demeter.

[548] Refers presumably to the [Greek: ekkukl_ema], a piece of machinery by means of which interiors were represented on the Greek stage—room and occupant being in some way wheeled out into view of the spectators bodily.

[549] A celebrated 'lady of pleasure'; Agathon is like her by reason of his effeminate, wanton looks and dissolute habits.

[550] Demeter is represented wandering, torch in hand, about the universe looking for her lost child Proserpine (Persephoné).

[551] Troy.

[552] Agathon, in accordance with his character, voluptuousness, is represented as preferring the effeminate music and lascivious dances of Asia.

[553] Goddesses who presided over generation; see also the 'Lysistrata.'

[554] A tetralogy, a series of four dramas connected by subject, of which the principal character was Lycurgus, king of the Thracians. When Bacchus returned to Thrace as conqueror of the Indies he dared to deride the god, and was punished by him in consequence. All four plays are lost.

[555] That is, the attributes of a man and those of a woman combined.

[556] That is, you make love in the posture known as 'the horse,' *equus*, in other words the woman atop of the man. There is a further joke intended here, inasmuch as Euripides, in his 'Phaedra,' represents the heroine as being passionately addicted to hunting and horses.

[557] Ibycus, a lyric poet of the sixth century, originally from Rhegium in Magna Graecia.—Anacreon, a celebrated erotic poet of the beginning of the fifth century.—Alcaeus, a lyric poet, born about 600 B.C. at Mytilené, in the island of Lesbos, was driven out of his country by a tyrant and sang of his loves, his services as a warrior, his travels and the miseries of his exile. He was a contemporary of Sappho, and conceived a passion for her, which she only rewarded with disdain.

[558] Phrynichus, a disciple of Thespis, improved the dramatic art, when still no more than a child; it was he who first introduced female characters upon the stage and made use of the iambic of six feet in tragedies. He flourished about 500 B.C.

[559] Philocles, Xenocles, and Theognis were dramatic poets and contemporaries of Aristophanes. The two first were sons of Carcinus, the poet and dancer.

[560] Fragment of Euripides' 'Aeolus,' a lost drama.

[561] Fragment of Euripides' well-known play, the 'Alcestis.'

[562] An allusion to the secret practices of mutual love which the women assembled for the Thesmophoria were credited by popular repute with indulging in.

[563] That is, to sanctuary.

[564] An effeminate often mentioned by Aristophanes.

[565] An allusion to the pederastic habits which the poet attributes to Agathon.

[566] An obscene allusion.

[567] On the machine upon which he is perched.

[568] A fragment of the 'Menalippé' of Euripides.

[569] The ether played an important part in the physical theories of Hippocrates, the celebrated physician.

[570] An allusion to a verse in his 'Hippolytus,' where Euripides says, "*The tongue has sworn, but the heart is unsworn.*" See also 'The Frogs.'

[571] The name of a slave; being disguised as a woman, Mnesilochus has himself followed by a female servant, a Thracian slave-woman.

[572] Demeter and Cora (or Persephoné), who were adored together during the Thesmophoria.

[573] Women slaves were forbidden by law to be present at the Thesmophoria; they remained at the door of the temple and there waited for the orders of their mistresses.

[574] The god of riches.

[575] The nurse of Demeter. According to another version, Calligenia was a surname of Demeter herself, who was adored as presiding over the growth of a child at its mother's breast.

[576] A surname of Demeter, who, by means of the food she produces as goddess of abundance, presides over the development of the bodies of children and young people. Curotrophos is derived from [Greek: trephein], to nourish, and [Greek: kouros], young boy.

[577] Apollo.

[578] Artemis.

[579] An insult which Aristophanes constantly repeats in every way he can; as we have seen before, Euripides' mother was, or was commonly said to be, a market-woman.

[580] Lovers sent each other chaplets and flowers.

[581] In parody of a passage in the 'Sthenoboea' of Euripides, which is preserved in Athenaeus.

[582] He believes her pregnant.

[583] A fragment from the 'Phoenix,' by Euripides.

[584] It seems that the Spartan locksmiths were famous for their skill.

[585] The women broke the seals their husbands had affixed, and then, with the aid of their ring bearing the same device, they replaced them as before.

[586] The impression of which was too complicated and therefore could not be imitated.

[587] As a remedy against the colic.

[588] So that it might not creak when opened.

[589] An altar in the form of a column in the front vestibule of houses and dedicated to Apollo.

[590] Because the smell of garlic is not inviting to gallants.

[591] The last words are the thoughts of the woman, who pretends to be in child-bed; she is, however, careful not to utter them to her husband.

[592] The proverb runs, "*There is a scorpion beneath every stone.*" By substituting *orator* for *scorpion*, Aristophanes means it to be understood that one is no less venomous than the other.

[593] There were two women named Aglaurus. One, the daughter of Actaeus, King of Attica, married Cecrops and brought him the kingship as her dowry; the other was the daughter of Cecrops, and was turned into stone for having interfered from jealousy with Hermes' courtship of Hersé her sister. It was this second Aglaurus the Athenian women were in the habit of invoking; they often associated with her her sister Pandrosus.

[594] Underneath the baths were large hollow chambers filled with steam to maintain the temperature of the water.

[595] By kicking her in the stomach.

[596] Clisthenes is always represented by Aristophanes as effeminate in the extreme in dress and habits.

[597] The coward, often mentioned with contempt by Aristophanes, had thrown away his shield.

[598] The ancients believed that cress reduced the natural secretions.

[599] A deme of Attica.

[600] The women lodged in pairs during the Thesmophoria in tents erected near the Temple of Demeter.

[601] The Corinthians were constantly passing their vessels across the isthmus from one sea to the other; we know that the Grecian ships were of very small dimensions.

[602] This was the name of the place where the Ecclesia, the public meeting of the people, took place; the chorus gives this name here to Demeter's temple, because the women are gathered there.

[603] The spaces left free between the tents, and which served as passage-ways.

[604] A choric dance began here.

[605] A woman's footgear.—On undressing the supposed child, Mnesilochus perceives that it is nothing but a skin of wine.

[606] Dr. P. Menier repeatedly points out in his "La médecine et les poètes latins," that the ancient writers constantly spoke of ten months as being a woman's period of gestation.

[607] A cotyla contained nearly half a pint.

[608] Both the Feast of Cups and the Dionysia were dedicated to Bacchus, the god of wine; it is for this reason that Mnesilochus refers to the former when guessing the wine-skin's age.

[609] The Cretan robe that had covered the wine-skin.

[610] An allusion to the tragedy by Euripides called 'Palamedes,' which belonged to the tetralogy of the Troades, and was produced in 414 B.C. Aristophanes is railing at the strange device which the poet makes Oeax resort to. Oeax was Palamedes' brother, and he is represented as inscribing

the death of the latter on a number of oars with the hope that at least one would reach the shores of Euboea and thus inform his father, Nauplias, the king of the fact.

[611] The images of the various gods which were invoked at the Thesmophoria, and the enumeration of which we have already had.

[612] Charminus, an Athenian general, who had recently been defeated at sea by the Spartans.—Nausimaché was a courtesan, but her name is purposely chosen because of its derivation ([Greek: naus], ship, and [Greek: mach_e], fight), so as to point more strongly to Charminus' disgrace.

[613] A general and an Athenian orator.

[614] A courtesan.

[615] Aristomaché ([Greek: mach_e], fight, and [Greek: arist_e], excellent) and Stratonicé ([Greek: stratos], army, and [Greek: nik_e], victory) are imaginary names, invented to show the decadence of the Athenian armies.

[616] Eubulé ([Greek: eu], well, and [Greek: bouleuesthai], to deliberate) is also an imaginary name. The poet wishes to say that in that year wisdom had not ruled the decisions of the Senate; they had allowed themselves to be humbled by the tyranny of the Four Hundred.

[617] The cylinder and the beams were the chief tools of the weaver. It was the women who did this work.

[618] The taxiarch had the command of 128 men; the strategus had the direction of an army.

[619] The Sthenia were celebrated in honour of Athené Sthenias, or the goddess of force; the women were then wont to attack each other with bitter sarcasms.—During the Scirophoria ([Greek: skiron], canopy) the statues of Athené, Demeter, Persephone, the Sun and Posidon were carried in procession under canopies with great pomp.

[620] The trierarchs were rich citizens, whose duty it was to maintain the galleys or triremes of the fleet.

[621] Hyperbolus is incessantly railed at by Aristophanes as a traitor and an informer. Lamachus, although our poet does not always spare him, was a brave general; he had been one of the commanders of the Sicilian Expedition.

[622] It will be remembered that Mnesilochus had employed a similar device to one imputed to Oeax by Euripides in his 'Palamedes,' in order to inform his father-in-law of his predicament.

[623] A tragedy, in which Menelaus is seen in Egypt, whither he has gone to seek Helen, who is detained there.

[624] These are the opening verses of Euripides' 'Helen,' with the exception of the last words, which are a parody.—Syrmea is a purgative plant very common in Egypt. Aristophanes speaks jestingly of the white soil of Egypt, because the slime of the Nile is very black.

[625] This reply and those that follow are fragments from 'Helen.'

[626] An infamous Athenian, whose name had become a byword for everything that was vile.

[627] The whole of this dialogue between Mnesilochus and Euripides is composed of fragments taken from 'Helen,' slightly parodied at times.

[628] King of Egypt.

[629] Son of Epicles, and mentioned by Thucydides.

[630] Aristophanes invents this in order to give coherence to what follows.

[631] An Athenian general whom Thucydides mentions.

[632] A deme of Attica.

[633] No doubt Euripides appeared on the stage carrying some herbs in his hand or wearing them in his belt, so as to recall his mother's calling. If the gibes of Aristophanes can be believed, she dealt in vegetables, as we have noted repeatedly.

[634] A ruined man, living in penury, presumably well known to the audience.

[635] Apollo.

[636] Surnames of Bacchus.

[637] The archers, or the police officers, at Athens were mostly Scythians. If not from that country always, they were known generally by that name.

[638] Which the archer had driven in to tighten up the rope binding the prison to the pillory.

[639] Perseus was returning from the land of the Gorgons mounted upon Pegasus, when, while high up in the air, he saw Andromeda bound to a rock and exposed to the lusts and voracity of a sea monster. Touched by the misfortune and the beauty of the princess, he turned the monster to stone by showing him the head of Medusa, released Andromeda and married her.— Euripides had just produced a tragedy on this subject.

[640] Mnesilochus speaks alternately in his own person and as though he were Andromeda, the effect being comical in the extreme.

[641] A notorious glutton, mentioned also in the 'Peace.'

[642] Through Euripides, his father-in-law.

[643] On the occasion of the presentation of the tragedy of 'Andromeda,' in which the nymph Echo plays an important part.

[644] Unknown; Aristophanes plays upon the similarity of name.

[645] That is, the Thesmophoriae, viz. Demeter and Persephoné.

[646] Throughout the whole scene the Scythian speaks with a grotesque barbarian accent.

[647] The pun depends in the Greek on the similarity of the final syllables of [Greek: subin_e], and [Greek: katabin_esi]. It can be given literally in English.

THE ECCLESIAZUSAE

or

Women In Council

INTRODUCTION

The 'Ecclesiazusae, or Women in Council,' was not produced till twenty years after the preceding play, the 'Thesmophoriazusae' (at the Great Dionysia of 392 B.C.), but is conveniently classed with it as being also largely levelled against the fair sex. "It is a broad, but very amusing, satire upon those ideal republics, founded upon communistic principles, of which Plato's well-known treatise is the best example. His 'Republic' had been written, and probably delivered in the form of oral lectures at Athens, only two or three years before, and had no doubt excited a considerable sensation. But many of its most startling principles had long ago been ventilated in the Schools."

Like the 'Lysistrata,' the play is a picture of woman's ascendancy in the State, and the topsy-turvy consequences resulting from such a reversal of ordinary conditions. The women of Athens, under the leadership of the wise Praxagora, resolve to reform the constitution. To this end they don men's clothes, and taking seats in the Assembly on the Pnyx, command a majority of votes and carry a series of revolutionary proposals—that the government be vested in a committee of women, and further, that property and women be henceforth held in common. The main part of the comedy deals with the many amusing difficulties that arise inevitably from this new state of affairs, the community of women above all necessitating special safeguarding clauses to secure the rights of the less attractive members of the sex to the service of the younger and handsomer men. Community of goods again, private property being abolished, calls for a regulation whereby all citizens are to dine at the public expense in the various public halls of the city, the particular place of each being determined by lot; and the drama winds up with one of these feasts, the elaborate menu of which is given in burlesque, and with the jubilations of the women over their triumph.

289

"This comedy appears to labour under the very same faults as the 'Peace.' The introduction, the secret assembly of the women, their rehearsal of their parts as men, the description of the popular assembly, are all handled in the most masterly manner; but towards the middle the action stands still. Nothing remains but the representation of the perplexities and confusion which arise from the new arrangements, especially in connection with the community of women, and from the prescribed equality of rights in love both for the old and ugly and for the young and beautiful. These perplexities are pleasant enough, but they turn too much on a repetition of the same joke."

We learn from the text of the play itself that the 'Ecclesiazusae' was drawn by lot for first representation among the comedies offered for competition at the Festival, the Author making a special appeal to his audience not to let themselves be influenced unfavourably by the circumstance; but whether the play was successful in gaining a prize is not recorded.

* * * * *

THE ECCLESIAZUSAE

or

Women In Council

DRAMATIS PERSONAE

PRAXAGORA.
BLEPYRUS, husband of Praxagora.
WOMEN.
A MAN.
CHREMES.
TWO CITIZENS.
HERALD.
AN OLD MAN.
A GIRL.
A YOUNG MAN.
THREE OLD WOMEN.
A SERVANT MAID.
HER MASTER.
CHORUS OF WOMEN.

SCENE: Before a house in a Public Square at Athens; a lamp is burning over the door. Time: a little after midnight.

* * * * *

THE ECCLESIAZUSAE

or

Women In Council

PRAXAGORA (*enters carrying a lamp in her hand*). Oh! thou shining light of my earthenware lamp, from this high spot shalt thou look abroad. Oh! lamp, I will tell thee thine origin and thy future; 'tis the rapid whirl of the potter's wheel that has lent thee thy shape, and thy wick counterfeits the glory of the sun;[648] mayst thou send the agreed signal flashing afar! In thee alone do we confide, and thou art worthy, for thou art near us when we practise the various postures in which Aphrodité delights upon our couches, and none dream even in the midst of her sports of seeking to avoid thine eye that watches our swaying bodies. Thou alone shinest into the depths of our most secret charms, and with thy flame dost singe the hairy growth of our privates. If we open some cellar stored with fruits and wine, thou art our companion, and never dost thou betray or reveal to a neighbour the secrets thou hast learned about us. Therefore thou shalt know likewise the whole of the plot that I have planned with my friends, the women, at the festival of the Scirophoria.[649]

I see none of those I was expecting, though dawn approaches; the Assembly is about to gather and we must take our seats in spite of Phyromachus,[650] who forsooth would say, "It is meet the women sit apart and hidden from the eyes of the men." Why, have they not been able then to procure the false beards that they must wear, or to steal their husbands cloaks? Ah! I see a light approaching; let us draw somewhat aside, for fear it should be a man.

FIRST WOMAN. Let us start, it is high time; as we left our dwellings, the cock was crowing for the second time.

PRAXAGORA. And I have spent the whole night waiting for you. But come, let us call our neighbour by scratching at her door; and gently too, so that her husband may hear nothing.

SECOND WOMAN. I was putting on my shoes, when I heard you scratching, for I was not asleep, so there! Oh! my dear, my husband (he is a Salaminian) never left me an instant's peace, but was at me, for ever at me, all night long, so that it was only just now that I was able to filch his cloak.

FIRST WOMAN. I see Clinareté coming too, along with Scstraté and their next-door neighbour Philaeneté.

PRAXAGORA. Hurry yourselves then, for Glycé has sworn that the last comer shall forfeit three measures of wine and a *choenix* of pease.

FIRST WOMAN. Don't you see Melisticé, the wife of Smicythion, hurrying hither in her great shoes? Methinks she is the only one of us all who has had no trouble in getting rid of her husband.

SECOND WOMAN. And can't you see Gusistraté, the tavern-keeper's wife, with a lamp in her hand, and the wives of Philodoretus and Chaeretades?

PRAXAGORA. I can see many others too, indeed the whole of the flower of
Athens.

THIRD WOMAN. Oh! my dear, I have had such trouble in getting away! My husband ate such a surfeit of sprats last evening that he was coughing and choking the whole night long.

PRAXAGORA. Take your seats, and, since you are all gathered here at last, let us see if what we decided on at the feast of the Scirophoria has been duly done.

FOURTH WOMAN. Yes. Firstly, as agreed, I have let the hair under my armpits grow thicker than a bush; furthermore, whilst my husband was at the Assembly, I rubbed myself from head to foot with oil and then stood the whole day long in the sun.[651]

FIFTH WOMAN. So did I. I began by throwing away my razor, so that I might get quite hairy, and no longer resemble a woman.

PRAXAGORA. Have you the beards that we had all to get ourselves for the Assembly?

FOURTH WOMAN. Yea, by Hecaté! Is this not a fine one?

FIFTH WOMAN. Aye, much finer than Epicrates'.[652]

PRAXAGORA (*to the other women*). And you?

FOURTH WOMAN. Yes, yes; look, they all nod assent.

PRAXAGORA. I see that you have got all the rest too, Spartan shoes, staffs and men's cloaks, as 'twas arranged.

SIXTH WOMAN. I have brought Lamias'[653] club, which I stole from him while he slept.

PRAXAGORA. What, the club that makes him puff and pant with its weight?

SIXTH WOMAN. By Zeus the Deliverer, if he had the skin of Argus, he would know better than any other how to shepherd the popular herd.

PRAXAGORA. But come, let us finish what has yet to be done, while the stars are still shining; the Assembly, at which we mean to be present, will open at dawn.

FIRST WOMAN. Good; you must take up your place at the foot of the platform and facing the Prytanes.

SIXTH WOMAN. I have brought this with me to card during the Assembly. (*She shows some wool.*)

PRAXAGORA. During the Assembly, wretched woman?

SIXTH WOMAN. Aye, by Artemis! shall I hear any less well if I am doing a bit of carding? My little ones are all but naked.

PRAXAGORA. Think of her wanting to card! whereas we must not let anyone see the smallest part of our bodies.[654] 'Twould be a fine thing if one of us, in the midst of the discussion, rushed on to the speaker's platform and, flinging her cloak aside, showed her hairy privates. If, on the other hand, we are the first to take our seats closely muffled in our cloaks, none will know us. Let us fix these beards on our chins, so that they spread all over our bosoms. How can we fail then to be mistaken for men? Agyrrhius has deceived everyone, thanks to the beard of Pronomus;[655] yet he was no better than a woman, and you see how he now holds the first position in the city. Thus, I adjure you by this day that is about to dawn, let us dare to copy him and let us be clever enough to possess ourselves of the management of affairs. Let us save the vessel of State, which just at present none seems able either to sail or row.

SIXTH WOMAN. But where shall we find orators in an Assembly of women?

PRAXAGORA. Nothing simpler. Is it not said, that the cleverest speakers are those who submit themselves oftenest to men? Well, thanks to the gods, we are that by nature.

SIXTH WOMAN. There's no doubt of that; but the worst of it is our inexperience.

PRAXAGORA. That's the very reason we are gathered here, in order to prepare the speech we must make in the Assembly. Hasten, therefore, all you who know aught of speaking, to fix on your beards.

SEVENTH WOMAN. Oh! you great fool! is there ever a one among us cannot use her tongue?

PRAXAGORA. Come, look sharp, on with your beard and become a man. As for me, I will do the same in case I should have a fancy for getting on to the platform. Here are the chaplets.

SECOND WOMAN. Oh! great gods! my dear Praxagora, do look here! Is it not laughable?

PRAXAGORA. How laughable?

SECOND WOMAN. Our beards look like broiled cuttle-fishes.

PRAXAGORA. The priest is bringing in—the cat.[656] Make ready, make ready! Silence, Ariphrades![657] Go and take your seat. Now, who wishes to speak?

SEVENTH WOMAN. I do.

PRAXAGORA. Then put on this chaplet[658] and success be with you.

SEVENTH WOMAN. There, 'tis done!

PRAXAGORA. Well then! begin.

SEVENTH WOMAN. Before drinking?

PRAXAGORA. Hah! she wants to drink![659]

SEVENTH WOMAN. Why, what else is the meaning of this chaplet?

PRAXAGORA. Get you hence! you would probably have played us this trick also before the people.

SEVENTH WOMAN. Well! don't the men drink then in the Assembly?

PRAXAGORA. Now she's telling us the men drink!

SEVENTH WOMAN. Aye, by Artemis, and neat wine too. That's why their decrees breathe of drunkenness and madness. And why libations, why so many ceremonies, if wine plays no part in them? Besides, they abuse each other like drunken men, and you can see the archers dragging more than one uproarious drunkard out of the Agora.

PRAXAGORA. Go back to your seat, you are wandering.

SEVENTH WOMAN. Ah! I should have done better not to have muffled myself in this beard; my throat's afire and I feel I shall die of thirst.

PRAXAGORA. Who else wishes to speak?

EIGHTH WOMAN. I do.

PRAXAGORA. Quick then, take the chaplet, for time's running short. Try to speak worthily, let your language be truly manly, and lean on your staff with dignity.

EIGHTH WOMAN. I had rather have seen one of your regular orators giving you wise advice; but, as that is not to be, it behoves me to break silence; I cannot, for my part indeed, allow the tavern-keepers to fill up their wine-pits with water.[660] No, by the two goddesses....

PRAXAGORA. What? by the two goddesses![661] Wretched woman, where are your senses?

EIGHTH WOMAN. Eh! what?... I have not asked you for a drink!

PRAXAGORA. No, but you want to pass for a man, and you swear by the two goddesses. Otherwise 'twas very well.

EIGHTH WOMAN. Well then. By Apollo....

PRAXAGORA. Stop! All these details of language must be adjusted; else it is quite useless to go to the Assembly.

SEVENTH WOMAN. Pass me the chaplet; I wish to speak again, for I think I have got hold of something good. You women who are listening to me....

PRAXAGORA. Women again; why, wretched creature, 'tis men that you are addressing.

297

SEVENTH WOMAN. 'Tis the fault of Epigonus;[662] I caught sight of him over yonder, and I thought I was speaking to women.

PRAXAGORA. Come, withdraw and remain seated in future. I am going to take this chaplet myself and speak in your name. May the gods grant success to my plans!

My country is as dear to me as it is to you, and I groan, I am grieved at all that is happening in it. Scarcely one in ten of those who rule it is honest, and all the others are bad. If you appoint fresh chiefs, they will do still worse. It is hard to correct your peevish humour; you fear those who love you and throw yourselves at the feet of those who betray you. There was a time when we had no assemblies, and then we all thought Agyrrhius a dishonest man;[663] now they are established, he who gets money thinks everything is as it should be, and he who does not, declares all who sell their votes to be worthy of death.

FIRST WOMAN. By Aphrodité, that is well spoken.

PRAXAGORA. Why, wretched woman, you have actually called upon Aphrodité.
Oh! what a fine thing 'twould have been had you said that in the Assembly!

FIRST WOMAN. I should never have done that!

PRAXAGORA. Well, mind you don't fall into the habit.—When we were discussing the alliance,[664] it seemed as though it were all over with Athens if it fell through. No sooner was it made than we were vexed and angry, and the orator who had caused its adoption was compelled to seek safety in flight.[665] Is there talk of equipping a fleet? The poor man says, yes, but the rich citizen and the countryman say, no. You were angered against the Corinthians and they with you; now they are well disposed towards you, be so towards them. As a rule the Argives are dull, but the Argive Hieronymus[666] is a distinguished chief. Herein lies a spark of hope; but Thrasybulus is far from Athens[667] and you do not recall him.

FIRST WOMAN. Oh! what a brilliant man!

PRAXAGORA. That's better! that's fitting applause.—Citizens, 'tis you who are the cause of all this trouble. You vote yourselves salaries out of the public funds and care only for your own personal interests; hence the State limps along like Aesimus.[668] But if you hearken to me, you will be saved. I assert that the direction of affairs must be handed over to the women, for 'tis they who have charge and look after our households.

SECOND WOMAN. Very good, very good, 'tis perfect! Say on, say on.

PRAXAGORA. They are worth more than you are, as I shall prove. First of all they wash all their wool in warm water, according to the ancient practice; you will never see them changing their method. Ah! if Athens only acted thus, if it did not take delight in ceaseless innovations, would not its happiness be assured? Then the women sit down to cook, as they always did; they carry things on their head as was their wont; they keep the Thesmophoria, as they have ever done; they knead their cakes just as they used to; they make their husbands angry as they have always done; they receive their lovers in their houses as was their constant custom; they buy dainties as they always did; they love unmixed wine as well as ever; they delight in being loved just as much as they always have. Let us therefore hand Athens over to them without endless discussions, without bothering ourselves about what they will do; let us simply hand them over the power, remembering that they are mothers and will therefore spare the blood of our soldiers; besides, who will know better than a mother how to forward provisions to the front? Woman is adept at getting money for herself and will not easily let herself be deceived; she understands deceit too well herself. I omit a thousand other advantages. Take my advice and you will live in perfect happiness.

FIRST WOMAN. How beautiful this is, my dearest Praxagora, how clever! But where, pray, did you learn all these pretty things?

PRAXAGORA. When the countryfolk were seeking refuge in the city,[669] I lived on the Pnyx with my husband, and there I learnt to speak through listening to the orators.

FIRST WOMAN. Then, dear, 'tis not astonishing that you are so eloquent and clever; henceforward you shall be our leader, so put your great ideas into execution. But if Cephalus[670] belches forth insults against you, what answer will you give him in the Assembly?

PRAXAGORA. I shall say that he drivels.

FIRST WOMAN. But all the world knows that.

PRAXAGORA. I shall furthermore say that he is a raving madman.

FIRST WOMAN. There's nobody who does not know it.

PRAXAGORA. That he, as excellent a statesman as he is, is a clumsy tinker.[671]

FIRST WOMAN. And if the blear-eyed Neoclides[672] comes to insult you?

PRAXAGORA. To him I shall say, "Go and look at a dog's backside".[673]

FIRST WOMAN. And if they fly at you?

PRAXAGORA. Oh! I shall shake them off as best I can; never fear, I know how to use this tool.[674]

FIRST WOMAN. But there is one thing we don't think of. If the archers drag you away, what will you do?

PRAXAGORA. With my arms akimbo like this, I will never, never let myself be taken round the middle.

FIRST WOMAN. If they seize you, we will bid them let you go.

SECOND WOMAN. That's the best way. But how are we going to lift up our arm[675] in the Assembly, we, who only know how to lift our legs in the act of love?

PRAXAGORA. 'Tis difficult; yet it must be done, and the arm shown naked to the shoulder in order to vote. Quick now, put on these tunics and these Laconian shoes, as you see the men do each time they go to the Assembly or for a walk. Then this done, fix on your beards, and when they are arranged in the best way possible, dress yourselves in the cloaks you have abstracted from your husbands; finally start off leaning on your staffs and singing some old man's song as the villagers do.

SECOND WOMAN. Well spoken; and let us hurry to get to the Pnyx before the women from the country, for they will no doubt not fail to come there.

PRAXAGORA. Quick, quick, for 'tis all the custom that those who are not at the Pnyx early in the morning, return home empty-handed.

CHORUS. Move forward, citizens, move forward; let us not forget to give ourselves this name and may that of *woman* never slip out of our mouths; woe to us, if it were discovered that we had laid such a plot in the darkness of night. Let us go to the Assembly then, fellow-citizens; for the Thesmothetae have declared that only those who arrive at daybreak with haggard eye and covered with dust, without having snatched time to eat anything but a snack of garlic-pickle, shall alone receive the triobolus. Walk up smartly, Charitimides,[676] Smicythus and Draces, and do not fail in any point of your part; let us first demand our fee and then vote for all that may perchance be useful for our partisans.... Ah! what am I saying? I meant to say, for our fellow-citizens. Let us drive away these men of the city,[677] who used to stay at home and chatter round the table in the days when only an obolus was paid, whereas now one is stifled by the crowds at the Pnyx.[678] No! during the Archonship of generous Myronides,[679] none would have dared to let himself be paid for the trouble he spent over public business; each one brought his own meal of bread, a couple of onions, three olives and some wine in a little wine-skin. But nowadays we run here to earn the three obols, for the citizen has become as mercenary as the stonemason. (*The Chorus marches away.*)

BLEPYRUS (*husband of Praxagora*). What does this mean? My wife has vanished! it is nearly daybreak and she does not return! Wanting to relieve myself, lo! I awake and hunt in the darkness for my shoes and my cloak; but grope where I will, I cannot find them. Meanwhile my need grew each moment more urgent and I had only just time to seize my wife's little mantle and her Persian slippers. But where shall I find a spot suitable for my purpose. Bah! One place is as good as another at night-time, for no one will see me. Ah! what fatal folly 'twas to take a wife at my age, and how I could thrash myself for having acted so foolishly! 'Tis a certainty she's not gone out for any honest purpose. However, that's not our present business.

A MAN. Who's there? Is that not my neighbour Blepyrus? Why, yes, 'tis himself and no other. Tell me, what's all that yellow about you? Can it be Cinesias[680] who has befouled you so?

BLEPYRUS. No, no, I only slipped on my wife's tunic[681] to come out in.

MAN. And where is your cloak?

BLEPYRUS. I cannot tell you, for I hunted for it vainly on the bed.

MAN. And why did you not ask your wife for it?

BLEPYRUS. Ah! why indeed! because she is not in the house; she has run away, and I greatly fear that she may be doing me an ill turn.

MAN. But, by Posidon, 'tis the same with myself. My wife has disappeared with my cloak, and what is still worse, with my shoes as well, for I cannot find them anywhere.

BLEPYRUS. Nor can I my Laconian shoes; but as I had urgent need, I popped my feet into these slippers, so as not to soil my blanket, which is quite new.

MAN. What does it mean? Can some friend have invited her to a feast?

BLEPYRUS. I expect so, for she does not generally misconduct herself, as far as I know.

MAN. Come, I say, you seem to be making ropes. Are you never going to be done? As for myself, I would like to go to the Assembly, and it is time to start, but the thing is to find my cloak, for I have only one.

BLEPYRUS. I am going to have a look too, when I have done; but I really think there must be a wild pear obstructing my rectum.

MAN. Is it the one which Thrasybulus spoke about to the Lacedaemonians?[682]

BLEPYRUS. Oh! oh! oh! how the obstruction holds! Whatever am I to do? 'Tis not merely for the present that I am frightened; but when I have eaten, where is it to find an outlet now? This cursed Achradusian fellow[683] has bolted the door. Let a doctor be fetched; but which is the cleverest in this branch of the science? Amynon?[684] Perhaps he would not come. Ah! Antithenes![685] Let him be brought to me, cost what it will. To judge by his noisy sighs, that man knows what a rump wants, when in urgent need. Oh! venerated Ilithyia![686] I shall burst unless the door gives way. Have pity! pity! Let me not become the night-stool of the comic poets.[687]

CHREMES. Hi! friend, what are you after there? Easing yourself!

BLEPYRUS. Oh! there! it is over and I can get up again at last.

CHREMES. What's this? You have your wife's tunic on.

BLEPYRUS. Aye, 'twas the first thing that came to my hand in the darkness. But where do you hail from?

CHREMES. From the Assembly.

BLEPYRUS. Is it already over then?

CHREMES. Certainly.

BLEPYRUS. Why, it is scarcely daylight.

CHREMES. I did laugh, ye gods, at the vermilion rope-marks that were to be seen all about the Assembly.[688]

BLEPYRUS. Did you get the triobolus?

CHREMES. Would it had so pleased the gods! but I arrived just too late, and am quite ashamed of it; I bring back nothing but this empty wallet.

BLEPYRUS. But why is that?

CHREMES. There was a crowd, such as has never been seen at the Pnyx, and the folk looked pale and wan, like so many shoemakers, so white were they in hue; both I and many another had to go without the triobolus.

BLEPYRUS. Then if I went now, I should get nothing.

CHREMES. No, certainly not, nor even had you gone at the second cock-crow.

BLEPYRUS. Oh! what a misfortune! Oh, Antilochus![689] no triobolus! Even death would be better! I am undone! But what can have attracted such a crowd at that early hour?

CHREMES. The Prytanes started the discussion of measures nearly concerning the safety of the State; immediately, that blear-eyed fellow, the son of Neoclides,[690] was the first to mount the platform. Then the folk shouted with their loudest voice, "What! he dares to speak, and that, too, when the safety of the State is concerned, and he a man who has not known how to save even his own eyebrows!" He, however, shouted louder than they all, and looking at them asked, "Why, what ought I to have done?"

BLEPYRUS. Pound together garlic and laserpitium juice, add to this mixture some Laconian spurge, and rub it well into the eyelids at night. That's what I should have answered, had I been there.

CHREMES. After him that clever rascal Evaeon[691] began to speak; he was naked, so far as we all could see, but he declared he had a cloak; he propounded the most popular, the most democratic, doctrines. "You see," he said, "I have the greatest need of sixteen drachmae, the cost of a new cloak, my health demands it; nevertheless I wish first to care for that of my fellow-citizens and of my country. If the fullers were to supply tunics to the indigent at the approach of winter, none would be exposed to pleurisy. Let him who has neither beds nor coverlets go to sleep at the tanners' after taking a bath; and if they shut the door in winter, let them be condemned to give him three goat-skins."

BLEPYRUS. By Dionysus, a fine, a very fine notion! Not a soul will vote against his proposal, especially if he adds that the flour-sellers must supply the poor with three measures of corn, or else suffer the severest penalties of the law; 'tis only in this way that Nausicydes[692] can be of any use to us.

CHREMES. Then we saw a handsome young man rush into the tribune, he was all pink and white like young Nicias,[693] and he began to say that the direction of matters should be entrusted to the women; this the crowd of shoemakers[694] began applauding with all their might, while the country-folk assailed him with groans.

BLEPYRUS. And, 'faith, they did well.

CHREMES. But they were outnumbered, and the orator shouted louder than they, saying much good of the women and much ill of you.

BLEPYRUS. And what did he say?

CHREMES. First he said you were a rogue...

BLEPYRUS. And you?

CHREMES. Let me speak ... and a thief....

BLEPYRUS. I alone?

CHREMES. And an informer.

BLEPYRUS. I alone?

CHREMES. Why, no, by the gods! all of us.

BLEPYRUS. And who avers the contrary?

CHREMES. He maintained that women were both clever and thrifty, that they never divulged the Mysteries of Demeter, while you and I go about babbling incessantly about whatever happens at the Senate.

BLEPYRUS. By Hermes, he was not lying!

CHREMES. Then he added, that the women lend each other clothes, trinkets of gold and silver, drinking-cups, and not before witnesses too, but all by themselves, and that they return everything with exactitude without ever cheating each other; whereas, according to him, we are ever ready to deny the loans we have effected.

BLEPYRUS. Aye, by Posidon, and in spite of witnesses.

CHREMES. Again, he said that women were not informers, nor did they bring lawsuits, nor hatch conspiracies; in short, he praised the women in every possible manner.

BLEPYRUS. And what was decided?

CHREMES. To confide the direction of affairs to them; 'tis the one and only innovation that has not yet been tried at Athens.

BLEPYRUS. And it was voted?

CHREMES. Yes.

BLEPYRUS. And everything that used to be the men's concern has been given over to the women?

CHREMES. You express it exactly.

BLEPYRUS. Thus 'twill be my wife who will go to the Courts now in my stead.

CHREMES. And it will be she who will keep your children in your place.

BLEPYRUS. I shall no longer have to tire myself out with work from daybreak onwards?

CHREMES. No, 'twill be the women's business, and you can stop at home and take your ease.

BLEPYRUS. Well, what I fear for us fellows now is, that, holding the reins of government, they will forcibly compel us ...

CHREMES. To do what?

BLEPYRUS. ... to work them.

CHREMES. And if we are not able?

BLEPYRUS. They will give us no dinner.

CHREMES. Well then, do your duty; dinner and love form a double enjoyment.

BLEPYRUS. Ah! but I hate compulsion.

CHREMES. But if it be for the public weal, let us resign ourselves. 'Tis an old saying, that our absurdest and maddest decrees always somehow turn out for our good. May it be so in this case, oh gods, oh venerable Pallas! But I must be off; so, good-bye to you!

BLEPYRUS. Good-bye, Chremes.

CHORUS. March along, go forward. Is there some man following us? Turn round, examine everywhere and keep a good look-out; be on your guard against every trick, for they might spy on us from behind. Let us make as much noise as possible as we tramp. It would be a disgrace for all of us if we allowed ourselves to be caught in this deed by the men. Come, wrap yourselves up well, and search both right and left, so that no mischance may happen to us. Let us hasten our steps; here we are close to the meeting-place, whence we started for the Assembly, and here is the house of our leader, the author of this bold scheme, which is now decreed by all the citizens. Let us not lose a moment in taking off our false beards, for we might be recognized and denounced. Let us stand under the shadow of this wall; let us glance round sharply with our eye to beware of surprises, while we quickly resume our ordinary dress. Ah! here is our leader, returning from the Assembly. Hasten to relieve your chins of these flowing manes. Look at your comrades yonder; they have already made themselves women again some while ago.

PRAXAGORA. Friends, success has crowned our plans. But off with these cloaks and these boots quick, before any man sees you; unbuckle the Laconian straps and get rid of your staffs; and do you help them with their toilet. As for myself, I am going to slip quietly into the house and replace my husband's cloak and other gear where I took them from, before he can suspect anything.

CHORUS. There! 'tis done according to your bidding. Now tell us how we can be of service to you, so that we may show you our obedience, for we have never seen a cleverer woman than you.

PRAXAGORA. Wait! I only wish to use the power given me in accordance with your wishes; for, in the market-place, in the midst of the shouts and danger, I appreciated your indomitable courage.

BLEPYRUS. Eh, Praxagora! where do you come from?

PRAXAGORA. How does that concern you, friend?

BLEPYRUS. Why, greatly! what a silly question!

PRAXAGORA. You don't think I have come from a lover's?

BLEPYRUS. No, perhaps not from only one.

PRAXAGORA. You can make yourself sure of that.

BLEPYRUS. And how?

PRAXAGORA. You can see whether my hair smells of perfume.

BLEPYRUS. What? cannot a woman possibly be loved without perfume, eh!

PRAXAGORA. The gods forfend, as far as I am concerned.

BLEPYRUS. Why did you go off at early dawn with my cloak?

PRAXAGORA. A companion, a friend who was in labour, had sent to fetch me.

BLEPYRUS. Could you not have told me?

PRAXAGORA. Oh, my dear, would you have me caring nothing for a poor woman in that plight?

BLEPYRUS. A word would have been enough. There's something behind all this.

PRAXAGORA. No, I call the goddesses to witness! I went running off; the poor woman who summoned me begged me to come, whatever might betide.

BLEPYRUS. And why did you not take your mantle? Instead of that, you carry off mine, you throw your dress upon the bed and you leave me as the dead are left, bar the chaplets and perfumes.

PRAXAGORA. 'Twas cold, and I am frail and delicate; I took your cloak for greater warmth, leaving you thoroughly warm yourself beneath your coverlets.

BLEPYRUS. And my shoes and staff, those too went off with you?

PRAXAGORA. I was afraid they might rob me of the cloak, and so, to look like a man, I put on your shoes and walked with a heavy tread and struck the stones with your staff.

BLEPYRUS. D'you know you have made us lose a *sextary* of wheat, which I should have bought with the *triobolus* of the Assembly?

PRAXAGORA. Be comforted, for she had a boy.

BLEPYRUS. Who? the Assembly?

PRAXAGORA. No, no, the woman I helped. But has the Assembly taken place then?

BLEPYRUS. Did I not tell you of it yesterday?

PRAXAGORA. True; I remember now.

BLEPYRUS. And don't you know the decrees that have been voted?

PRAXAGORA. No indeed.

BLEPYRUS. Go to! you can eat cuttle-fish[695] now, for 'tis said the government is handed over to you.

PRAXAGORA. To do what—to spin?

BLEPYRUS. No, that you may rule ...

PRAXAGORA. What?

BLEPYRUS. ... over all public business.

PRAXAGORA. Oh! by Aphrodité! how happy Athens will be!

BLEPYRUS. Why so?

PRAXAGORA. For a thousand reasons. None will dare now to do shameless deeds, to give false testimony or lay informations.

BLEPYRUS. Stop! in the name of the gods! Do you want me to die of hunger?

CHORUS. Good sir, let your wife speak.

PRAXAGORA. There will be no more thieves, nor envious people, no more rags nor misery, no more abuse and no more prosecutions and lawsuits.

BLEPYRUS. By Posidon! 'tis grand, if true.

PRAXAGORA. The results will prove it; you will confess it, and even these good people (*pointing to the spectators*) will not be able to say a word.

CHORUS. You have served your friends, but now it behoves you to apply your ability and your care to the welfare of the people. Devote the fecundity of your mind to the public weal; adorn the citizens' lives with a thousand enjoyments and teach them to seize every favourable opportunity. Devise some ingenious method to secure the much-needed salvation of Athens; but let neither your acts nor your words recall anything of the past, for 'tis only innovations that please. Don't delay the realization of your plans, for speedy execution is greatly esteemed by the public.

PRAXAGORA. I believe my ideas are good, but what I fear is, that the public will cling to the old customs and refuse to accept my reforms.

BLEPYRUS. Have no fear about that. Love of novelty and disdain for the past, these are the dominating principles among us.

PRAXAGORA. Let none contradict nor interrupt me until I have explained my plan. I want all to have a share of everything and all property to be in common; there will no longer be either rich or poor; no longer shall we see one man harvesting vast tracts of land, while another has not ground enough to be buried in, nor one man surround himself with a whole army of slaves, while another has not a single attendant; I intend that there shall only be one and the same condition of life for all.

BLEPYRUS. But how do you mean for all?

PRAXAGORA. Go and eat your excrements![696]

BLEPYRUS. Come, share and share alike!

PRAXAGORA. No, no, but you shall not interrupt me. This is what I was going to say: I shall begin by making land, money, everything that is private property, common to all. Then we shall live on this common wealth, which we shall take care to administer with wise thrift.

BLEPYRUS. And how about the man who has no land, but only gold and silver coins, that cannot be seen?

PRAXAGORA. He must bring them to the common stock, and if he fails he will be a perjured man.

BLEPYRUS. That won't worry him much, for has he not gained them by perjury?

PRAXAGORA. But his riches will no longer be of any use to him.

BLEPYRUS. Why?

PRAXAGORA. The poor will no longer be obliged to work; each will have all that he needs, bread, salt fish, cakes, tunics, wine, chaplets and chick-pease; of what advantage will it be to him not to contribute his share to the common wealth? What do you think of it?

BLEPYRUS. But is it not the folk who rob most that have all these things?

PRAXAGORA. Yes, formerly, under the old order of things; but now that all goods are in common, what will he gain by not bringing his wealth into the general stock?

BLEPYRUS. If someone saw a pretty wench and wished to satisfy his fancy for her, he would take some of his reserve store to make her a present and stay the night with her; this would not prevent him claiming his share of the common property.

PRAXAGORA. But he can sleep with her for nothing; I intend that women shall belong to all men in common, and each shall beget children by any man that wishes to have her.

BLEPYRUS. But all will go to the prettiest woman and beseech her to go with him.

PRAXAGORA. The ugliest and the most flat-nosed will be side by side with the most charming, and to win the latter's favours, a man will first have to get into the former.

BLEPYRUS. But we old men, shall we have penis enough if we have to satisfy the ugly first?

PRAXAGORA. They will make no resistance.

BLEPYRUS. To what?

PRAXAGORA. Never fear; they will make no resistance.

BLEPYRUS. Resistance to what?

PRAXAGORA. To the pleasure of the thing. 'Tis thus that matters will be ordered for you.

BLEPYRUS. 'Tis right well conceived for you women, for every wench's hole will be occupied; but as regards us poor men, you will leave those who are ugly to run after the handsome fellows.

PRAXAGORA. The ugly will follow the handsomest into the public places after supper and see to it that the law, which forbids the women to sleep with the big, handsome men before having satisfied the ugly shrimps, is complied with.

BLEPYRUS. Thus ugly Lysicrates' nose will be as proud as the handsomest face?

PRAXAGORA. Yes, by Apollo! this is a truly popular decree, and what a set-back 'twill be for one of those elegants with their fingers loaded with rings, when a man with heavy shoes says to him, "Give way to me and wait till I have done; you will pass in after me."

BLEPYRUS. But if we live in this fashion, how will each one know his children?

PRAXAGORA. The youngest will look upon the oldest as their fathers.

BLEPYRUS. Ah! how heartily they will strangle all the old men, since even now, when each one knows his father, they make no bones about strangling him! then, my word! won't they just scorn and shit upon the old folks!

PRAXAGORA. But those around will prevent it. Hitherto, when anyone saw an old man beaten, he would not meddle, because it did not concern him; but now each will fear the sufferer may be his own father and such violence will be stopped.

BLEPYRUS. What you say is not so silly after all; but 'twould be highly unpleasant were Epicurus and Leucolophas to come up and call me father.

PRAXAGORA. But 'twould be far worse, were ...

BLEPYRUS. Were what?

PRAXAGORA. ... Aristyllus to embrace you and style you his father.

BLEPYRUS. Ah! let him look to himself if he dares!

PRAXAGORA. For you would smell vilely of mint if he kissed you. But he was born before the decree was carried, so that you have not to fear his kiss.

BLEPYRUS. 'Twould be awful. But who will do the work?

PRAXAGORA. The slaves. Your only cares will be to scent yourself, and to go and dine, when the shadow of the gnomon is ten feet long on the dial.

BLEPYRUS. But how shall we obtain clothing? Tell me that!

PRAXAGORA. You will first wear out those you have, and then we women will weave you others.

BLEPYRUS. Now another point: if the magistrates condemn a citizen to the payment of a fine, how is he going to do it? Out of the public funds? That would not be right surely.

PRAXAGORA. But there will be no more lawsuits.

BLEPYRUS. What a disaster for many people!

PRAXAGORA. I have decreed it. Besides, friend, why should there be lawsuits?

BLEPYRUS. Oh! for a thousand reasons, on my faith! Firstly, because a debtor denies his obligation.

PRAXAGORA. But where will the lender get the money to lend, if all is in common? unless he steals it out of the treasury?

BLEPYRUS. That's true, by Demeter! But then again, tell me this; here are some men who are returning from a feast and are drunk and they strike some passer-by; how are they going to pay the fine? Ah! you are puzzled now!

PRAXAGORA. They will have to take it out of their pittance; and being thus punished through their belly, they will not care to begin again.

BLEPYRUS. There will be no more thieves then, eh?

PRAXAGORA. Why steal, if you have a share of everything?

BLEPYRUS. People will not be robbed any more at night?

PRAXAGORA. No, whether you sleep at home or in the street, there will be no more danger, for all will have the means of living. Besides, if anyone wanted to steal your cloak, you would give it him yourself. Why not? You will only have to go to the common store and be given a better one.

BLEPYRUS. There will be no more playing at dice?

PRAXAGORA. What object will there be in playing?

BLEPYRUS. But what kind of life is it you propose to set up?

PRAXAGORA. The life in common. Athens will become nothing more than a single house, in which everything will belong to everyone; so that everybody will be able to go from one house to the other at pleasure.

BLEPYRUS. And where will the meals be served?

PRAXAGORA. The law-courts and the porticoes will be turned into dining-halls.

BLEPYRUS. And what will the speaker's platform be used for?

PRAXAGORA. I shall place the bowls and the ewers there; and young children will sing the glory of the brave from there, also the infamy of cowards, who out of very shame will no longer dare to come to the public meals.

BLEPYRUS. Well thought of, by Apollo! And what will you do with the urns?

PRAXAGORA. I shall have them taken to the market-place, and standing close to the statue of Harmodius,[697] I shall draw a lot for each citizen, which by its letter will show the place where he must go to dine.[698] Thus, those for whom I have drawn a Beta, will go to the royal portico;[699] if 'tis a Theta, they will go to the portico of Theseus;[700] if 'tis a Kappa, to that of the flour-market.[701]

BLEPYRUS. To cram[702] himself there like a capon?

PRAXAGORA. No, to dine there.

BLEPYRUS. And the citizen whom the lot has not given a letter showing where he is to dine will be driven off by everyone?

PRAXAGORA. But that will not occur. Each man will have plenty; he will not leave the feast until he is well drunk, and then with a chaplet on his head and a torch in his hand; and then the women running to meet you in the cross-roads will say, "This way, come to our house, you will find a beautiful young girl there."—"And I," another will call from her balcony, "have one so pretty and as white as milk; but before touching her, you must sleep with me." And the ugly men, watching closely after the handsome fellows, will say, "Hi! friend, where are you running to? Go in, but you must do nothing, for 'tis the ugly and the flat-nosed to whom the law gives the first right of admission; amuse yourself in the porch while you wait, in handling your fig-leaves and playing with your tool." Well, tell me, does that picture suit you?

BLEPYRUS. Marvellously well.

PRAXAGORA. I must now go to the market-place to receive the property that is going to be placed in common and to choose a woman with a loud voice as my herald. I have all the cares of State on my shoulders, since the power has been entrusted to me. I must likewise go to busy myself about establishing the common meals, and you will attend your first banquet to-day.

BLEPYRUS. Are we going to banquet?

PRAXAGORA. Why, undoubtedly! Furthermore, I propose abolishing the courtesans.

BLEPYRUS. And what for?

PRAXAGORA. 'Tis clear enough why; so that, instead of them, *we* may have the first-fruits of the young men. It is not meet that tricked-out slaves should rob free-born women of their pleasures. Let the courtesans be free to sleep with the slaves and to depilate their privates for them.

BLEPYRUS. I will march at your side, so that I may be seen and that everyone may say, "Admire our leader's husband!" [*Exeunt Blepyrus and Praxagora.*

[*The Chorus which followed this scene is lost.*]

FIRST CITIZEN. Come, let us collect and examine all my belongings before taking them to the market-place. Come hither, my beautiful sieve, I have nothing more precious than you, come, all clotted with the flour of which I have poured so many sacks through you; you shall act the part of Canephoros[703] in the procession of my chattels. Where is the sunshade carrier?[704] Ah! this stew-pot shall take his place. Great gods, how black it is! it could not be more so if Lysicrates[705] had boiled the drugs in it with which he dyes his hair. Hither, my beautiful mirror. And you, my tripod, bear this urn for me; you shall be the waterbearer;[706] and you, cock, whose morning song has so often roused me in the middle of the night to send me hurrying to the Assembly, you shall be my flute-girl. Scaphephoros,[707] do you take the large basin, place in it the honeycombs and twine the olive-branches over them, bring the tripods and the phial of perfume; as for the humble crowd of little pots, I will just leave them behind.

SECOND CITIZEN. What folly to carry one's goods to the common store; I have a little more sense than that. No, no, by Posidon, I want first to ponder and calculate over the thing at leisure. I shall not be fool enough to strip myself of the fruits of my toil and thrift, if it is not for a very good reason;

let us see first, which way things turn. Hi! friend, what means this display of goods? Are you moving or are you going to pawn your stuff?

FIRST CITIZEN. Neither.

SECOND CITIZEN. Why then are you setting all these things out in line? Is it a procession that you are starting off to the public crier, Hiero?

FIRST CITIZEN. No, but in accordance with the new law, that has been decreed, I am going to carry all these things to the marketplace to make a gift of them to the State.

SECOND CITIZEN. Oh! bah! you don't mean that.

FIRST CITIZEN. Certainly.

SECOND CITIZEN. Oh! Zeus the Deliverer! you unfortunate man!

FIRST CITIZEN. Why?

SECOND CITIZEN. Why? 'Tis as clear as noonday.

FIRST CITIZEN. Must the laws not be obeyed then?

SECOND CITIZEN. What laws, you poor fellow?

FIRST CITIZEN. Those that have been decreed.

SECOND CITIZEN. Decreed! Are you mad, I ask you?

FIRST CITIZEN. Am I mad?

SECOND CITIZEN. Oh! this is the height of folly!

FIRST CITIZEN. Because I obey the law? Is that not the first duty of an honest man?

SECOND CITIZEN. Say rather of a ninny.

FIRST CITIZEN. Don't you propose taking what belongs to you to the common stock?

SECOND CITIZEN. I'll take good care I don't until I see what the majority are doing.

FIRST CITIZEN. There's but one opinion, namely, to contribute every single thing one has.

SECOND CITIZEN. I am waiting to see it, before I believe that.

FIRST CITIZEN. At least, so they say in every street.

SECOND CITIZEN. And they will go on saying so.

FIRST CITIZEN. Everyone talks of contributing all he has.

SECOND CITIZEN. And will go on talking of it.

FIRST CITIZEN. You weary me with your doubts and dubitations.

SECOND CITIZEN. Everybody else will doubt it.

FIRST CITIZEN. The pest seize you!

SECOND CITIZEN. It *will* take you. What? give up your goods! Is there a man of sense who will do such a thing? Giving is not one of our customs. Receiving is another matter; 'tis the way of the gods themselves. Look at the position of their hands on their statues; when we ask a favour, they present their hands turned palm up so as not to give, but to receive.

FIRST CITIZEN. Wretch, let me do what is right. Come, I'll make a bundle of all these things. Where is my strap?

SECOND CITIZEN. Are you really going to carry them in?

FIRST CITIZEN. Undoubtedly, and there are my three tripods strung together already.

SECOND CITIZEN. What folly! Not to wait to see what the others do, and then …

FIRST CITIZEN. Well, and then what?

SECOND CITIZEN. … wait and put it off again.

FIRST CITIZEN. What for?

SECOND CITIZEN. That an earthquake may come or an ill-omened flash of lightning, that a weasel may run across the street and that none carry in anything more, you fool!

FIRST CITIZEN. 'Twould be a fine matter, were I to find no room left for placing all this.

SECOND CITIZEN. You are much more likely to lose your stuff. As for placing it, you can be at ease, for there will be room enough as long as a month hence.

FIRST CITIZEN. Why?

SECOND CITIZEN. I know these folk; a decree is soon passed, but it is not so easily attended to.

FIRST CITIZEN. All will contribute their property, my friend.

SECOND CITIZEN. But what if they don't?

FIRST CITIZEN. But there is no doubt that they will.

SECOND CITIZEN. But *anyhow*, what if they don't?

FIRST CITIZEN. We shall compel them to do so.

SECOND CITIZEN. And what if they prove the stronger?

FIRST CITIZEN. I shall leave my goods and go off.

SECOND CITIZEN. And what if they sell them for you?

FIRST CITIZEN. The plague take you!

SECOND CITIZEN. And if it does?

FIRST CITIZEN. 'Twill be a good riddance.

SECOND CITIZEN. You are bent on contributing then?

FIRST CITIZEN. 'Pon my soul, yes! Look, there are all my neighbours carrying in all they have.

SECOND CITIZEN. Ha, ha! 'Tis no doubt Antisthenes.[708] He's a fellow who would rather sit on his pot for thirty days than not!

FIRST CITIZEN. The pest seize you!

SECOND CITIZEN. And perhaps Callimachus[709] is going to take in more money than Callias owns? That man want to ruin himself!

FIRST CITIZEN. How you weary me!

SECOND CITIZEN. Ah! I weary you! But, wretch, see what comes of decrees of this kind. Don't you remember the one reducing the price of salt, eh?

FIRST CITIZEN. Why, certainly I do.

SECOND CITIZEN. And do you remember that about the copper coinage?

FIRST CITIZEN. Ah! that cursed money did me enough harm. I had sold my grapes and had my mouth stuffed with pieces of copper;[710] indeed I was going to the market to buy flour, and was in the act of holding out my bag wide open, when the herald started shouting, "Let none in future accept pieces of copper; those of silver are alone current."

SECOND CITIZEN. And quite lately, were we not all swearing that the impost of one-fortieth, which Euripides[711] had conceived, would bring five talents to the State, and everyone was vaunting Euripides to the skies? But when the thing was looked at closely, it was seen that this fine decree was mere moonshine and would produce nothing, and you would have willingly burnt this very same Euripides alive.

FIRST CITIZEN. The cases are quite different, my good fellow. We were the rulers then, but now 'tis the women.

SECOND CITIZEN. Whom, by Posidon, I will never allow to piss on my nose.

FIRST CITIZEN. I don't know what the devil you're chattering about. Slave, pick up that bundle.

HERALD. Let all citizens come, let them hasten at our leader's bidding! 'Tis the new law. The lot will teach each citizen where he is to dine; the tables are already laid and loaded with the most exquisite dishes; the couches are covered with the softest of cushions; the wine and water is already being mixed in the ewers; the slaves are standing in a row and waiting to pour scent over the guests; the fish is being grilled, the hares are on the spit and the cakes are being kneaded, chaplets are being plaited and the fritters are frying; the youngest women are watching the pea-soup in the saucepans, and in the midst of them all stands Smaeus,[712] dressed as a knight, washing the crockery. And Geres[713] has come, dressed in a grand tunic and finely shod; he is joking with another young fellow and has already divested himself of his heavy shoes and his cloak.[714] The pantryman is waiting, so come and use your jaws.

SECOND CITIZEN. Aye, I'll go. Why should I delay, since the Republic commands me?

FIRST CITIZEN. And where are you going to, since you have not deposited your belongings?

SECOND CITIZEN. To the feast.

FIRST CITIZEN. If the women have any wits, they will first insist on your depositing your goods.

SECOND CITIZEN. But I am going to deposit them.

FIRST CITIZEN. When?

SECOND CITIZEN. I am not the man to make delays.

FIRST CITIZEN. How do you mean?

SECOND CITIZEN. There will be many less eager than I.

FIRST CITIZEN. In the meantime you are going to dine.

SECOND CITIZEN. What else should I do? Every sensible man must give his help to the State.

FIRST CITIZEN. But if admission is forbidden you?

SECOND CITIZEN. I shall duck my head and slip in.

FIRST CITIZEN. And if the women have you beaten?

SECOND CITIZEN. I shall summon them.

FIRST CITIZEN. And if they laugh you in the face?

SECOND CITIZEN. I shall stand near the door ...

FIRST CITIZEN. And then?

SECOND CITIZEN. ... and seize upon the dishes as they pass.

FIRST CITIZEN. Then go there, but after me. Sicon and Parmeno,[715] pick up all the baggage.

SECOND CITIZEN. Come, I will help you carry it.

FIRST CITIZEN. No, no, I should be afraid of your pretending to the leader that what I am depositing belonged to you.

SECOND CITIZEN. Let me see! let me think of some good trick by which I can keep my goods and yet take my share of the common feast. Ha! that's a good notion! Quick! I'll go and dine, ha, ha! [*Exit laughing.*

FIRST OLD WOMAN. How is this? no men are coming? And yet it must be fully time! 'Tis then for naught that I have painted myself with white lead, dressed myself in my beautiful yellow robe, and that I am here, frolicking and humming between my teeth to attract some passer-by! Oh, Muses, alight upon my lips, inspire me with some soft Ioniar love-song!

A YOUNG GIRL. You rotten old thing, you have placed yourself at the window before me. You were expecting to strip my vines during my absence and to trap some man in your snares with your songs. If you sing, I shall follow suit; all this singing will weary the spectators, but is nevertheless very pleasant and very diverting.

FIRST OLD WOMAN. Ha! here is an old man; take him and lead him away. As for you, you young flute-player, let us hear some airs that are worthy of you and me. Let him who wishes to taste pleasure come to my side. These young things know nothing about it; 'tis only the women of ripe age who understand the art of love, and no one could know how to fondle the lover who possessed me so well as myself; the young girls are all flightiness.

YOUNG GIRL. Don't be jealous of the young girls; voluptuousness resides in the pure outline of their beautiful limbs and blossoms on their rounded bosoms; but you, old woman, you who are tricked out and perfumed as if for your own funeral, are an object of love only for grim Death himself.

FIRST OLD WOMAN. May your hole be stopped; may you be unable to find your couch when you want to be fucked. And on your couch, when your lips seek a lover, may you embrace only a viper!

YOUNG GIRL. Alas! alas! what is to become of me? There is no lover! I am left here alone; my mother has gone out and the rest care little for me. Oh! my dear nurse, I adjure you to call Orthagoras, and may heaven bless you.

FIRST OLD WOMAN. Ah! poor child, desire is consuming you like an Ionian woman; I think you are no stranger to the wanton arts of the Lesbian women, but you shall not rob me of my pleasures; you will not be able to reduce or filch the time that first belongs to me, for your own gain. Sing as much as you please, peep out like a cat lying in wait, but none shall pass through your door without first having been to see me.

YOUNG GIRL. If anyone enter your house, 'twill be to carry out your corpse.

FIRST OLD WOMAN. That's new to me.

YOUNG GIRL. What! you rotten wretch, can anything be new to an old hag like you?

FIRST OLD WOMAN. My old age will not harm you.

YOUNG GIRL. Ah! shame on your painted cheeks!

FIRST OLD WOMAN. Why do you speak to me at all?

YOUNG GIRL. And why do you place yourself at the window?

FIRST OLD WOMAN. I am singing to myself about my lover, Epigenes.

YOUNG GIRL. Can you have any other lover than that old fop Geres?

FIRST OLD WOMAN. Epigenes will show you that himself, for he is coming to me. See, here he is.

YOUNG GIRL. He's not thinking of you in the least, you old witch.

FIRST OLD WOMAN. Aye, but he is, you little pest.

YOUNG GIRL. Let's see what he will do. I will leave my window.

FIRST OLD WOMAN. And I likewise. You will see I am not far wrong.

A YOUNG MAN. Ah! could I but sleep with the young girl without first satisfying the old flat-nose! 'Tis intolerable for a free-born man.

FIRST OLD WOMAN. Willy nilly, you must first gratify my desire. There shall be no nonsense about that, for my authority is the law and the law must be obeyed in a democracy. But come, let me hide, to see what he's going to do.

YOUNG MAN. Ah! ye gods, if I were to find the sweet child alone! for the wine has fired my lust.

YOUNG GIRL. I have tricked that cursed old wretch; she has left her window, thinking I would stay at home.

FIRST OLD WOMAN. Ah! here is the lover we were talking of. This way, my love, this way, come here and haste to rest the whole night in my arms. I worship your lovely curly hair; I am consumed with ardent desire. Oh! Eros, in thy mercy, compel him to my bed.

YOUNG MAN (*standing beneath the young girl's window and singing*).[716] Come down and haste to open the door unless you want to see me fall dead with desire. Dearest treasure, I am burning to yield myself to most voluptuous sport, lying on your bosom, to let my hands play with your buttocks. Aphrodité, why dost thou fire me with such delight in her? Oh! Eros, I beseech thee, have mercy and make her share my couch. Words cannot express the tortures I am suffering. Oh! my adored one, I adjure you, open your door for me and press me to your heart; 'tis for you that I am suffering. Oh! my jewel, my idol, you child of Aphrodité, the confidante of the Muses, the sister of the Graces, you living picture of Voluptuousness, oh! open for me, press me to your heart, 'tis for you that I am suffering.

FIRST OLD WOMAN. Are you knocking? Is it I you seek?

YOUNG MAN. What an idea!

FIRST OLD WOMAN. But you were tapping at the door.

YOUNG MAN. Death would be sweeter.

FIRST OLD WOMAN. Why do you come with that torch in your hand?

YOUNG MAN. I am looking for a man from Anaphlystia.[717]

FIRST OLD WOMAN. What's his name?

YOUNG MAN. Oh! 'tis not Sebinus,[718] whom no doubt you are expecting.

FIRST OLD WOMAN. By Aphrodité, you *must*, whether you like it or not.

YOUNG MAN. We are not now concerned with cases dated sixty years back; they are remanded for a later day; we are dealing only with those of less than twenty.[719]

FIRST OLD WOMAN. That was under the old order of things, sweetheart, but now you must first busy yourself with us.

YOUNG MAN. Aye, *if I want to*, according to the rules of draughts, where we may either take or leave.

FIRST OLD WOMAN. But 'tis not according to the rules of draughts that you take your seat at the banquet.[720]

YOUNG MAN. I don't know what you mean; 'tis at this door I want to knock.

328

FIRST OLD WOMAN. Not before knocking at mine first.

YOUNG MAN. For the moment I really have no need for old leather.

FIRST OLD WOMAN. I know that you love me; perhaps you are surprised to find me at the door. But come, let me kiss you.

YOUNG MAN. No, no, my dear, I am afraid of your lover.

FIRST OLD WOMAN. Of whom?

YOUNG MAN. The most gifted of painters.

FIRST OLD WOMAN. Why, whom do you mean to speak of?

YOUNG MAN. The artist who paints the little bottles on coffins.[721] But get you indoors, lest he should find you at the door.

FIRST OLD WOMAN. I know what you want.

YOUNG MAN. I can say as much of you.

FIRST OLD WOMAN. By Aphrodité, who has granted me this good chance, I won't let you go.

YOUNG MAN. You are drivelling, you little old hag.

FIRST OLD WOMAN. Rubbish! I am going to lead you to my couch.

YOUNG MAN. What need for buying hooks? I will let her down to the bottom of the well and pull up the buckets with her old carcase, for she's crooked enough for that.

FIRST OLD WOMAN. A truce to your jeering, poor boy, and follow me.

YOUNG MAN. Nothing compels me to do so, unless you have paid the levy of five hundredths for me.[722]

FIRST OLD WOMAN. Look, by Aphrodité, there is nothing that delights me as much as sleeping with a lad of your years.

YOUNG MAN. And I abhor such as you, and I will never, never consent.

FIRST OLD WOMAN. But, by Zeus, here is something will force you to it.

YOUNG MAN. What's that?

FIRST OLD WOMAN. A decree, which orders you to enter my house.

YOUNG MAN. Read it out then, and let's hear.

FIRST OLD WOMAN. Listen. "The women have decreed, that if a young man desires a young girl, he can only possess her after having satisfied an old woman; and if he refuses and goes to seek the maiden, the old women are authorized to seize him by his privates and so drag him in."

YOUNG MAN. Alas! I shall become a Procrustes.[723]

FIRST OLD WOMAN. Obey the law.

YOUNG MAN. But if a fellow-citizen, a friend, came to pay my ransom?

FIRST OLD WOMAN. No man may dispose of anything above a medimnus.[724]

YOUNG MAN. But may I not enter an excuse?

FIRST OLD WOMAN. There's no evasion.

YOUNG MAN. I shall declare myself a merchant and so escape service.[725]

FIRST OLD WOMAN. Beware what you do!

YOUNG MAN. Well! what is to be done?

FIRST OLD WOMAN. Follow me.

YOUNG MAN. Is it absolutely necessary?

FIRST OLD WOMAN. Yes, as surely as if Diomedes had commanded it.[726]

YOUNG MAN. Well then, first spread out a layer of origanum[727] upon four pieces of wood; bind fillets round your head, bring phials of scent and place a bowl filled with lustral water before your door.[728]

FIRST OLD WOMAN. Will you buy a chaplet for me too?

YOUNG MAN. Aye, if you outlast the tapers; for I expect to see you fall down dead as you go in.

YOUNG GIRL. Where are you dragging this unfortunate man to?

FIRST OLD WOMAN. 'Tis my very own property that I am leading in.

YOUNG GIRL. You do ill. A young fellow like him is not of the age to suit you. You ought to be his mother rather than his wife. With these laws in force, the earth will be filled with Oedipuses.[729]

FIRST OLD WOMAN. Oh! you cursed pest! 'tis envy that makes you say this; but I will be revenged.

YOUNG MAN. By Zeus the Deliverer, what a service you have done me, by freeing me of this old wretch! with what ardour I will show you my gratitude in a form both long and thick!

SECOND OLD WOMAN. Hi! you there! where are you taking that young man to, in spite of the law? The decree ordains that he must first sleep with me.

YOUNG MAN. Oh! what a misfortune! Where does *this* hag come from? 'Tis a more frightful monster than the other even.

SECOND OLD WOMAN. Come here.

YOUNG MAN (*to the young girl*). Oh! I adjure you, don't let me be led off by her!

SECOND OLD WOMAN. 'Tis not I; 'tis the law that leads you off.

YOUNG MAN. No, 'tis not the law, but an Empusa[730] with a body covered with blemishes and blotches.

SECOND OLD WOMAN. Follow me, my handsome little friend, come along quick without any more ado.

YOUNG MAN. Oh! let me first do the needful, so that I may gather my wits somewhat. Else I should be so terrified that you would see me letting out something yellow.

SECOND OLD WOMAN. Never mind! you can stool, if you want, in my house.

YOUNG MAN. Oh! I fear doing more than I want to; but I offer you two good securities.

SECOND OLD WOMAN. I don't require them.

THIRD OLD WOMAN. Hi! friend, where are you off to with that woman?

YOUNG MAN. I am not going with her, but am being dragged by force. Oh! whoever you are, may heaven bless you for having had pity on me in my dire misfortune. (*Turns round and sees the Third Old Woman.*) Oh Heracles! oh Heracles! oh Pan! Oh ye Corybantes! oh ye Dioscuri! Why, she is still more awful! Oh! what a monster! great gods! Are you an ape plastered with white lead, or the ghost of some old hag returned from the dark borderlands of death?

THIRD OLD WOMAN. No jesting! Follow me.

SECOND OLD WOMAN. No, come this way.

THIRD OLD WOMAN. I will never let you go.

SECOND OLD WOMAN. Nor will I.

YOUNG MAN. But you will rend me asunder, you cursed wretches.

SECOND OLD WOMAN. 'Tis I he must go with according to the law.

THIRD OLD WOMAN. Not if an uglier old woman than yourself appears.

YOUNG MAN. But if you kill me at the outset, how shall I afterwards go to find this beautiful girl of mine?

THIRD OLD WOMAN. That's your business. But begin by obeying.

YOUNG MAN. Of which one must I rid myself first?

SECOND OLD WOMAN. Don't you know? Come here.

YOUNG MAN. Then let the other one release me.

THIRD OLD WOMAN. Come to my house.

YOUNG MAN. If this dame will let me go.

SECOND OLD WOMAN. No, by all the gods, I'll not let you go.

THIRD OLD WOMAN. Nor will I.

YOUNG MAN. You would make very bad boatwomen.

SECOND OLD WOMAN. Why?

YOUNG MAN. Because you would tear your passengers to pieces in dragging them on board.

SECOND OLD WOMAN. Then come along, do, and hold your tongue.

THIRD OLD WOMAN. No, by Zeus, come with me.

YOUNG MAN. 'Tis clearly a case of the decree of Cannonus;[731] I must cut myself in two in order to fuck you both. But how am I to work two oars at once?

SECOND OLD WOMAN. Easily enough; you have only to eat a full pot of onions.[732]

YOUNG MAN. Oh! great gods! here I am close to the door and being dragged in!

THIRD OLD WOMAN (*to Second Old Woman*). You will gain nothing by this, for I shall rush into your house with you.

YOUNG MAN. Oh, no! no! 'twould be better to suffer a single misfortune than two.

THIRD OLD WOMAN. Ah! by Hecaté, 'twill be all the same whether you wish it or not.

YOUNG MAN. What a fate is mine, that I must gratify such a stinking harridan the whole night through and all day; then, when I am rid of her, I have still to tackle a hag of brick-colour hue! Am I not truly unfortunate? Ah! by Zeus the Deliverer! under what fatal star must I have been born, that I must sail in company with such monsters! But if my bark sinks in the sewer of these strumpets, may I be buried at the very threshold of the door; let this hag be stood upright on my grave, let her be coated alive with pitch and her legs covered with molten lead up to the ankles, and let her be set alight as a funeral lamp.

A SERVANT-MAID TO PRAXAGORA (*she comes from the banquet*). What happiness is the people's! what joy is mine, and above all that of my mistress! Happy are ye, who form choruses before our house! Happy all ye, both neighbours and fellow-citizens! Happy am I myself! I am but a servant, and yet I have poured on my hair the most exquisite essences. Let thanks be rendered to thee, oh, Zeus! But a still more delicious aroma is that of the wine of Thasos; its sweet bouquet delights the drinker for a long enough, whereas the others lose their bloom and vanish quickly. Therefore, long life to the wine-jars of Thasos! Pour yourselves out unmixed wine, it will cheer you the whole night through, if you choose the liquor that possesses most fragrance. But tell me, friends, where is my mistress's husband?

CHORUS. Wait for him here; he will no doubt pass this way.

MAID-SERVANT. Ah! there he is just going to dinner. Oh! master! what joy! what blessedness is yours!

BLEPYRUS. Ah! d'you think so?

MAID-SERVANT. None can compare his happiness to yours; you have reached its utmost height, you who, alone out of thirty thousand citizens, have not yet dined.

CHORUS Aye, here is undoubtedly a truly happy man.

MAID-SERVANT. Where are you off to?

BLEPYRUS. I am going to dine.

MAID-SERVANT. By Aphrodité, you will be the last of all, far and away the last. Yet my mistress has bidden me take you and take with you these young girls. Some Chian wine is left and lots of other good things. Therefore hurry, and invite likewise all the spectators whom we have pleased, and such of the judges as are not against us, to follow us; we will offer them everything they can desire. Let our hospitality be large and generous; forget no one, neither old nor young men, nor children. Dinner is ready for them all; they have but to go ... home.[733]

CHORUS. I am betaking myself to the banquet with this torch in my hand according to custom. But why do you tarry, Blepyrus? Take these young girls with you and, while you are away a while, I will whet my appetite with some dining-song. I have but a few words to say: let the wise judge me because of whatever is wise in this piece, and those who like a laugh by whatever has made them laugh. In this way I address pretty well everyone.

335

If the lot has assigned my comedy to be played first of all, don't let that be a disadvantage to me; engrave in your memory all that shall have pleased you in it and judge the competitors equitably as you have bound yourselves by oath to do. Don't act like vile courtesans, who never remember any but their last lover. It is time, friends, high time to go to the banquet, if we want to have our share of it. Open your ranks and let the Cretan rhythms regulate your dances.[734]

SEMI-CHORUS. Ready; we are ready!

CHORUS. And you others, let your light steps too keep time. Very soon will be served a very fine menu[*]—oysters-saltfish-skate-sharks'-heads left-over-vinegar-dressing-laserpitium-leek-with-honey-sauce-thrush blackbird-pigeon-dove-roast-cock's-brains-wagtail-cushat-hare-stewed in-new-wine-gristle-of-veal-pullet's-wings.[735] Come, quick, seize hold of a plate, snatch up a cup, and let's run to secure a place at table. The rest will have their jaws at work by this time.

[* Transcriber's note: In the original, all following words until 'wings' are connected with hyphens, i.e. they form *one* word.]

SEMI-CHORUS. Let up leap and dance, Io! evoë! Let us to dinner, Io! evoë.
For victory is ours, victory is ours! Ho! Victory! Io! evoë!

* * * * *

FINIS OF "THE ECCLESIAZUSAE"

* * * * *

Footnotes:

[648] A parody of the pompous addresses to inanimate objects so frequent in the prologues and monodies of Euripides.

[649] A festival which was kept in Athens in the month of scirophorion (June), whence its name; the statues of Athené, Demeter, Persephoné, Apollo and Posidon were borne through the city with great pomp with banners or canopies ([Greek: skira]) over them.

[650] Unknown.

[651] So as to get sunburnt and thus have a more manly appearance.

[652] A demagogue, well known on account of his long flowing beard; he was nicknamed by his fellow-citizens [Greek: Sakesphoros] that is, shield-bearer, because his beard came down to his waist and covered his body like a shield.

[653] Unknown.

[654] Whereas the arms must be extended to do carding, and folk could not fail to recognize her as a woman by their shape.

[655] Agyrrhius was an Athenian general, who commanded at Lesbos; he was effeminate and of depraved habits. No doubt he had let his beard grow to impose on the masses and to lend himself that dignity which he was naturally wanting in.—Pronomus was a flute-player, who had a fine beard.

[656] Young pigs were sacrificed at the beginning of the sittings; here the comic writer substitutes a cat for the pig. perhaps because of its lasciviousness.

[657] A pathic; Aristophanes classes him with the women, because of his effeminacy.

[658] The orators wore green chaplets, generally of olive leaves; guests also wore them at feasts, but then flowers were mingled with the leaves.

[659] An allusion to the rapacity of the orators, who only meddled in political discussions with the object of getting some personal gain through their influence; also to the fondness for strong drink we find attributed in so many passages to the Athenian women.

[660] A sort of cistern dug in the ground, in which the ancients kept their wine.

[661] This was a form of oath that women made use of; hence it is barred by Praxagora.

[662] Another pathic, like Ariphrades, mentioned above.

[663] Before the time of Pericles, when manners had not yet become corrupt, the fame of each citizen was based on fact; worthy men were honoured, and those who resembled Agyrrhius, already mentioned, were detested. For this general, see note a little above.

[664] The alliance with Corinth, Boeotia and Argolis against Sparta in 393 B.C.

[665] Conon, who went to Asia Minor and was thrown into prison at Sardis by the Persian Satrap.

[666] An Argive to whom Conon entrusted the command of his fleet when he went to the court of the King of Persia.—In this passage the poet is warning his fellow-citizens not to alienate the goodwill of the allies by their disdain, but to know how to honour those among them who had distinguished themselves by their talents.

[667] The Lacedaemonians, after having recalled their king, Agesilas, who gained the victory of Coronea, were themselves beaten at sea off Cnidus by Conon and Pharnabazus. 'Twas no doubt this victory which gave a *spark of hope* to the Athenians, who had suffered so cruelly during so many years; but Aristophanes declares that, in order to profit by this return of fortune, they must recall Thrasybulus, the deliverer of Athens in 401 B.C. He was then ostensibly employed in getting the islands of the Aegean sea and the towns of the Asiatic coast to return under the Athenian power, but this was really only an honourable excuse for thrusting him aside for reasons of jealousy.

[668] Unknown.

[669] During the earlier years of the Peloponnesian war, when the annual invasion of Attica by the Lacedaemonians drove the country population into the city.

[670] A demagogue, otherwise unknown.

[671] Cephalus' father was said to have been a tinker.

[672] The comic poets accused him of being an alien by birth and also an informer and a rogue. See the 'Plutus.'

[673] There was a Greek saying, "*Look into the backside of a dog and of three foxes*" which, says the Scholiast, used to be addressed to those who had bad eyes. But the precise point of the joke here is difficult to see.

[674] An obscene allusion; [Greek: hupokrouein] means both *pulsare* and *subagitare*,—to strike, and also to move to the man in sexual intercourse.

[675] In order to vote.

[676] The Chorus addresses the leaders amongst the women by the names of men. Charitimides was commander of the Athenian navy.

[677] The countryfolk affected to despise the townspeople, whom they dubbed idle and lazy.

[678] The fee of the citizens who attended the Assembly had varied like that of the dicasts, or jurymen.

[679] An Athenian general, who gained brilliant victories over the Thebans during the period prior to the Peloponnesian war.

[680] A dithyrambic poet, and notorious for his dissoluteness; he was accused of having daubed the statues of Hecate at the Athenian cross-roads with ordure.

[681] The women wore yellow tunics, called [Greek: krok_otoi], because of their colour.

[682] This Thrasybulus, not to be confounded with the more famous Thrasybulus, restorer of the Athenian democracy, in 403 B.C., had undertaken to speak against the Spartans, who had come with proposals of peace, but afterwards excused himself, pretending to be labouring under a sore throat, brought on by eating wild pears (B.C. 393). The Athenians suspected him of having been bribed by the Spartans.

[683] A coined word, derived from [Greek: *achras*], a wild pear.

[684] Amynon was not a physician, according to the Scholiast, but one of those orators called [Greek: europr_oktoi] (*laticuli*) 'wide-arsed,' because addicted to habits of pathic vice, and was invoked by Blepyrus for that reason.

[685] A doctor notorious for his dissolute life.

[686] The Grecian goddess who presided over child-birth.

[687] He is afraid lest some comic poet should surprise him in his ridiculous position and might cause a laugh at his expense upon the stage.

---

[688] In accordance with a quaint Athenian custom a rope daubed with vermilion was drawn across from end to end of the Agora (market-place) by officials of the city at the last moment before the Ecclesia, or Public Assembly, was to meet. Any citizen trying to evade his duty to be present was liable to have his white robe streaked red, and so be exposed to general ridicule on finally putting in an appearance on the Pnyx.

[689] A parody on a verse in 'The Myrmidons' of Aeschylus.—Antilochus was the son of Nestor; he was killed by Memnon, when defending his father.

[690] See above.

[691] He was very poor, and his cloak was such a mass of holes that one might doubt his having one at all. This surname, Evaeon ([Greek: eu ai_on], delicious life) had doubtless been given him on the 'lucus a non' principle because of his wretchedness.

[692] Apparently a wealthy corn-factor.

[693] Presumably this refers to the grandson of Nicias, the leader of the expedition to Sicily; he must have been sixteen or seventeen years old about that time, since, according to Lysias, Niceratus, the son of the great Nicias, was killed in 405 B.C. and had left a son of tender age behind him, who bore the name of his grandfather.

[694] That is, the pale-faced folk in the Assembly already referred to— really the women there present surreptitiously.

[695] To eat cuttle-fish was synonymous with enjoying the highest felicity.

[696] A common vulgar saying, used among the Athenians, as much as to say, *To the devil with interruptions!*

[697] This stood in the centre of the market-place.

[698] It was the custom at Athens to draw lots to decide in which Court each dicast should serve; Praxagora proposes to apply the same system to decide the dining station for each citizen.

[699] In Greek [Greek: h_e basileius]([Greek: stoa], understood), the first letter a [Greek: b_eta.]

[700] Commencing with a [Greek: Th_eta].

[701] [Greek: Ha alphitop_olis stoa]; why [Greek: kappa], it is hard to say; from some popular nickname probably, which is unknown to us.

[702] The pun cannot be kept in English; it is between [Greek: kaptein], to gobble, to cram oneself, and [Greek: kappa], the designating letter.

[703] That is, one of the beautiful maidens selected to bear the baskets containing the sacred implements in procession at the Festival of Demeter, Bacchus and Athené.

[704] The slave-girl who attended each Canephoros, and sheltered her from the sun's rays.

[705] Mentioned a little above for his ugliness; the Scholiast says he was a general.

[706] Hydriaphoros; the wives of resident aliens ([Greek: metoikoi]) were allowed to take part in these processions, but in a subordinate position; they carried vessels full of water for the service of the sacrifice.

[707] Scaphephoros, bearer of the vases containing the honey required for the sacrifices. The office was assigned to the [Greek: metoikoi] as a recognition of their semi-citizenship.

[708] A miser, who, moreover, was obstinately constipated.

[709] Presumably a man in extreme poverty.

[710] The ancients carried small coins in their mouth; this custom still obtains to-day in the East.

[711] This Euripides was the son of the tragic poet.

[712] This Smaeus was a notorious debauchee; the phrase contains obscene allusions, implying that he was ready both to ride a woman or to lick her privates—[Greek: kel_etizein] or [Greek: lesbiazein].

[713] Geres, an old fop, who wanted to pass as a young man.

[714] According to Greek custom, these were left at the entrance of the banqueting-hall.

[715] The names of his slaves.

[716] A specimen of the *serenades* ([Greek: paraklausithura]) of the Greeks.

[717] An Attic deme. There is an obscene jest here; the word [Greek: anaphlan] means to masturbate.

[718] [Greek: Ton Sebinon], a coined name, representing [Greek: ton se binounta], 'the man who is to tread you.'

[719] The passage is written in the language of the Bar. It is an allusion to the slowness of justice at Athens.

[720] i.e. the new law must be conformed to all round.

[721] It was customary to paint phials or little bottles on the coffins of the poor; these emblems took the place of the perfumes that were sprinkled on the bodies of the rich.

[722] i.e. unless I am your slave; no doubt this tax of five hundredths was paid by the master on the assumed value of his slave.—We have, however, no historical data to confirm this.

[723] Nickname of the notorious brigand. The word means 'one who stretches and tortures,' from [Greek: prokrouein], and refers to his habit of fitting all his captives to the same bedstead—the 'bed of Procrustes'—stretching them if too short to the required length, lopping their limbs as required if they were too long. Here a further pun is involved, [Greek: prokrouein] meaning also 'to go with a woman first.'

[724] Athenian law declared it illegal for a woman to contract any debt exceeding the price of a *medimnus* of corn; this law is now supposed to affect the men.

[725] Merchants were exempt from military service; in this case, it is another kind of service that the old woman wants to exact from the young man.

[726] A Thracian brigand, who forced strangers to share his daughters' bed, or be devoured by his horses.

[727] Dead bodies were laid out on a layer of origanum, which is an aromatic plant.

[728] The young man is here describing the formalities connected with the laying out of the dead.

[729] Who had married his mother Jocasta without knowing it.

[730] A hideous spectre that Hecaté was supposed to send to frighten men.

[731] Which provided that where a number of criminals were charged with the same offence, each must be tried separately.

[732] As an aphrodisiac.

[733] We have already seen similar waggish endings to phrases in the 'Lysistrata'; the figure is called [Greek: para prosdokian]—'contrary to expectation.'

[734] Nothing is known as to these Cretan rhythms. According to the Scholiast, this is a jest, because the Cretans, who were great eaters, sat down to table early in the morning. This is what the Chorus supposes it is going to do, since 'The Ecclesiazusae' was played first, i.e. during the forenoon.

[735] This wonderful word consists, in the original Greek, of seventy-seven syllables. For similar burlesque compounds see the 'Lysistrata,' 457, 458; 'Wasps,' 505 and 520. Compare Shakespeare, 'Love's Labour's Lost,' Act V. sc. 1: "I marvel thy master hath not eaten thee for a word; for thou art not so long by the head as *honorificabilitudinitatibus*." This is outdone by Rabelais' *Antipericatametaanaparbeugedamphicribrationibus*.

PLUTUS[*]

[* Transcriber's note: This caption is missing in the original.]

INTRODUCTION

The 'Plutus' differs widely from all other works of its Author, and, it must be confessed, is the least interesting and diverting of them all. "In its absence of personal interests and personal satire," and its lack of strong comic incidents, "it approximates rather to a whimsical allegory than a comedy properly so called."

The plot is of the simplest. Chremylus, a poor but just man, accompanied by his body-servant Cario—the redeeming feature, by the by, of an otherwise dull play, the original type of the comic valet of the stage of all subsequent periods—consults the Delphic Oracle concerning his son, whether he ought not to be instructed in injustice and knavery and the other arts whereby worldly men acquire riches. By way of answer the god only tells him that he is to follow whomsoever he first meets upon leaving the temple, who proves to be a blind and ragged old man. But this turns out to be no other than Plutus himself, the god of riches, whom Zeus has robbed of his eyesight, so that he may be unable henceforth to distinguish between the just and the unjust. However, succoured by Chremylus and conducted by him to the Temple of Aesculapius, Plutus regains the use of his eyes. Whereupon all just men, including the god's benefactor, are made rich and prosperous, and the unjust reduced to indigence.

The play was, it seems, twice put upon the stage—first in 408 B.C., and again in a revised and reinforced edition, with allusions and innuendoes brought up to date, in 388 B.C., a few years before the Author's death. The text we possess—marred, however, by several considerable lacunae—is now generally allowed to be that of the piece as played at the later date, when it won the prize.

* * * * *

PLUTUS

DRAMATIS PERSONAE

CHREMYLUS.
CARIO, Servant of Chremylus.
PLUTUS, God of Riches.
BLEPSIDEMUS, friend of Chremylus.
WIFE OF CHREMYLUS.
POVERTY.
A JUST MAN.
AN INFORMER, or Sycophant.
AN OLD WOMAN.
A YOUTH.
HERMES.
A PRIEST OF ZEUS.
CHORUS OF RUSTICS.

SCENE: In front of a farmhouse—a road leading up to it.

* * * * *

PLUTUS

CARIO. What an unhappy fate, great gods, to be the slave of a fool! A servant may give the best of advice, but if his master does not follow it, the poor slave must inevitably have his share in the disaster; for fortune does not allow him to dispose of his own body, it belongs to his master who has bought it. Alas! 'tis the way of the world. But the god, Apollo, whose oracles the Pythian priestess on her golden tripod makes known to us, deserves my censure, for 'tis assured he is a physician and a cunning diviner; and yet my master is leaving his temple infected with mere madness and insists on following a blind man. Is this not opposed to all good sense? 'Tis for us, who see clearly, to guide those who don't; whereas he clings to the trail of a blind fellow and compels me to do the same without answering my questions with ever a word. (*To Chremylus.*) Aye, master, unless you tell me why we are following this unknown fellow, I will not be silent, but I will worry and torment you, for you cannot beat me because of my sacred chaplet of laurel.

CHREMYLUS. No, but if you worry me I will take off your chaplet, and then you will only get a sounder thrashing.

CARIO. That's an old song! I am going to leave you no peace till you have told me who this man is; and if I ask it, 'tis entirely because of my interest in you.

CHREMYLUS. Well, be it so. I will reveal it to you as being the most faithful and the most rascally of all my servants.[736] I honoured the gods and did what was right, and yet I was none the less poor and unfortunate.

CARIO. I know it but too well.

CHREMYLUS. Other amassed wealth—the sacrilegious, the demagogues, the informers,[737] indeed every sort of rascal.

CARIO. I believe you.

CHREMYLUS. Therefore I came to consult the oracle of the god, not on my own account, for my unfortunate life is nearing its end, but for my only son; I wanted to ask Apollo, if it was necessary for him to become a thorough knave and renounce his virtuous principles, since that seemed to me to be the only way to succeed in life.

CARIO. And with what responding tones did the sacred tripod resound?[738]

CHREMYLUS. You shall know. The god ordered me in plain terms to follow the first man I should meet upon leaving the temple and to persuade him to accompany me home.

CARIO. And who was the first one you met?

CHREMYLUS. This blind man.

CARIO. And you are stupid enough not to understand the meaning of such an answer? Why, the god was advising you thereby, and that in the clearest possible way, to bring up your son according to the fashion of your country.

CHREMYLUS. What makes you think that?

CARIO. Is it not evident to the blind, that nowadays to do nothing that is right is the best way to get on?

CHREMYLUS. No, that is not the meaning of the oracle; there must be another, that is nobler. If this blind man would tell us who he is and why and with what object he has led us here, we should no doubt understand what our oracle really does mean.

CARIO (*to Plutus*). Come, tell us at once who you are, or I give effect to my threat. (*He menaces him.*) And quick too, be quick, I say.

PLUTUS. I'll thrash you.

CARIO (*to Chremylus*). Ha! is it thus he tells us his name?

349

CHREMYLUS. 'Tis to you and not to me that he replies thus; your mode of questioning him was ill-advised. (*To Plutus.*) Come, friend, if you care to oblige an honest man, answer me.

PLUTUS. I'll knock you down.

CARIO. Ah! what a pleasant fellow and what a delightful prophecy the god has given you!

CHREMYLUS. By Demeter, you'll have no reason to laugh presently.

CARIO. If you don't speak, you wretch, I will surely do you an ill turn.

PLUTUS. Friends, take yourselves off and leave me.

CHREMYLUS. That we very certainly shan't.

CARIO. This, master, is the best thing to do. I'll undertake to secure him the most frightful death; I will lead him to the verge of a precipice and then leave him there, so that he'll break his neck when he pitches over.

CHREMYLUS. Well then, I leave him to you, and do the thing quickly.

PLUTUS. Oh, no! Have mercy!

CHREMYLUS. Will you speak then?

PLUTUS. But if you learn who I am, I know well that you will ill-use me and will not let me go again.

CHREMYLUS. I call the gods to witness that you have naught to fear if you will only speak.

PLUTUS. Well then, first unhand me.

CHREMYLUS. There! we set you free.

PLUTUS. Listen then, since I must reveal what I had intended to keep a secret. I am Plutus.[739]

CHREMYLUS. Oh! you wretched rascal! You Plutus all the while, and you never said so!

CARIO. You, Plutus, and in this piteous guise!

CHREMYLUS. Oh, Phoebus Apollo! oh, ye gods of heaven and hell! Oh, Zeus! is it really and truly as you say?

PLUTUS. Aye.

CHREMYLUS. Plutus' very own self?

PLUTUS. His own very self and none other.

CHREMYLUS. But tell me, whence come you to be so squalid?

PLUTUS. I have just left Patrocles' house, who has not had a bath since his birth.[740]

CHREMYLUS. But your infirmity; how did that happen? Tell me.

PLUTUS. Zeus inflicted it on me, because of his jealousy of mankind. When I was young, I threatened him that I would only go to the just, the wise, the men of ordered life; to prevent my distinguishing these, he struck me with blindness! so much does he envy the good!

CHREMYLUS. And yet, 'tis only the upright and just who honour him.

PLUTUS. Quite true.

CHREMYLUS. Therefore, if ever you recovered your sight, you would shun the wicked?

PLUTUS. Undoubtedly.

CHREMYLUS. You would visit the good?

PLUTUS. Assuredly. It is a very long time since I saw them.

CHREMYLUS. That's not astonishing. I, who see clearly, don't see a single one.

PLUTUS. Now let me leave you, for I have told you everything.

CHREMYLUS. No, certainly not! we shall fasten ourselves on to you faster than ever.

PLUTUS. Did I not tell you, you were going to plague me?

CHREMYLUS. Oh! I adjure you, believe what I say and don't leave me; for you will seek in vain for a more honest man than myself.

CARIO. There is only one man more worthy; and that is I.

PLUTUS. All talk like this, but as soon as they secure my favours and grow rich, their wickedness knows no bounds.

CHREMYLUS. And yet all men are not wicked.

PLUTUS. All. There's no exception.

CARIO. You shall pay for that opinion.

CHREMYLUS. Listen to what happiness there is in store for you, if you but stay with us. I have hope; aye, I have good hope with the god's help to deliver you from that blindness, in fact to restore your sight.

PLUTUS. Oh! do nothing of the kind, for I don't wish to recover it.

CHREMYLUS. What's that you say?

CARIO. This fellow hugs his own misery.

PLUTUS. If you were mad enough to cure me, and Zeus heard of it, he would overwhelm me with his anger.

CHREMYLUS. And is he not doing this now by leaving you to grope your wandering way?

PLUTUS. I don't know; but I'm horribly afraid of him.

CHREMYLUS. Indeed? Ah! you are the biggest poltroon of all the gods! Why, Zeus with his throne and his lightnings would not be worth an obolus if you recovered your sight, were it but for a few instants.

PLUTUS. Impious man, don't talk like that.

CHREMYLUS. Fear nothing! I will prove to you that you are far more powerful and mightier than he.

PLUTUS. I mightier than he?

CHREMYLUS. Aye, by heaven! For instance, what is the origin of the power that Zeus wields over the other gods?[741]

CARIO. 'Tis money; he has so much of it.

CHREMYLUS. And who gives it to him?

CARIO (*pointing to Plutus*). This fellow.

CHREMYLUS. If sacrifices are offered to him, is not Plutus their cause?

CARIO. Undoubtedly, for 'tis wealth that all demand and clamour most loudly for.

CHREMYLUS. Thus 'tis Plutus who is the fount of all the honours rendered to Zeus, whose worship he can wither up at the root, if it so please him.

PLUTUS. And how so?

CHREMYLUS. Not an ox, nor a cake, nor indeed anything at all could be offered, if you did not wish it.

PLUTUS. Why?

CHREMYLUS. Why? but what means are there to buy anything if you are not there to give the money? Hence if Zeus should cause you any trouble, you will destroy his power without other help.

PLUTUS. So 'tis because of me that sacrifices are offered to him?

CHREMYLUS. Most assuredly. Whatever is dazzling, beautiful or charming in the eyes of mankind, comes from you. Does not everything depend on wealth?

CARIO. I myself was bought for a few coins; if I'm a slave, 'tis only because I was not rich.

CHREMYLUS. And what of the Corinthian courtesans?[742] If a poor man offers them proposals, they do not listen; but if it be a rich one, instantly they offer their buttocks for his pleasure.

CARIO. 'Tis the same with the lads; they care not for love, to them money means everything.

CHREMYLUS. You speak of those who accept all comers; yet some of them are honest, and 'tis not money they ask of their patrons.

CARIO. What then?

CHREMYLUS. A fine horse, a pack of hounds.

CARIO. Aye, they would blush to ask for money and cleverly disguise their shame.

CHREMYLUS. 'Tis in you that every art, all human inventions, have had their origin; 'tis through you that one man sits cutting leather in his shop.

CARIO. That another fashions iron or wood.

CHREMYLUS. That yet another chases the gold he has received from you.

CARIO. That one is a fuller.

CHREMYLUS. That t'other washes wool.

CARIO. That this one is a tanner.

CHREMYLUS. And that other sells onions.

CARIO. And if the adulterer, caught red-handed, is depilated,[743] 'tis on account of you.[744]

PLUTUS. Oh! great gods! I knew naught of all this!

CARIO. Is it not he who lends the Great King all his pride?

CHREMYLUS. Is it not he who draws the citizens to the Assembly?[745]

CARIO. And tell me, is it not you who equip the triremes?[746]

CHREMYLUS. And who feed our mercenaries at Corinth?[747]

CARIO. Are not you the cause of Pamphilus' sufferings?[748]

CHREMYLUS. And of the needle-seller's[749] with Pamphilus?

CARIO. Is it not because of you that Agyrrhius[750] lets wind so loudly?

CHREMYLUS. And that Philepsius[751] rolls off his fables?

CARIO. That troops are sent to succour the Egyptians?[752]

CHREMYLUS. And that Laïs is kept by Philonides?[753]

CARIO. That the tower of Timotheus[754] …

CHREMYLUS. ... (*To Cario.*) May it fall upon your head! (*To Plutus.*) In short, Plutus, 'tis through you that everything is done; be it known to you that you are the sole cause both of good and evil.

CARIO. In war, 'tis the flag under which you serve that victory favours.

PLUTUS. What! I can do so many things by myself and unaided?

CHREMYLUS. And many others besides; wherefore men are never tired of your gifts. They get weary of all else,—of love ...

CARIO. Of bread.

CHREMYLUS. Of music.

CARIO. Of sweetmeats.

CHREMYLUS. Of honours.

CARIO. Of cakes.

CHREMYLUS. Of battles.

CARIO. Of figs.

CHREMYLUS. Of ambition.

CARIO. Of gruel.

CHREMYLUS. Of military advancement.

CARIO. Of lentils.[755]

CHREMYLUS. But of you they never tire. Has a man got thirteen talents, he has all the greater ardour to possess sixteen; is that wish achieved, he will want forty or will complain that he knows not how to make the two ends meet.

PLUTUS. All this, methinks, is very true; there is but one point that makes me feel a bit uneasy.

CHREMYLUS. And that is?

PLUTUS. How could I use this power, which you say I have?

CHREMYLUS. Ah! they were quite right who said, there's nothing more timorous than Plutus.

PLUTUS. No, no; it was a thief who calumniated me. Having broken into a house, he found everything locked up and could take nothing, so he dubbed my prudence fear.

CHREMYLUS. Don't be disturbed; if you support me zealously, I'll make you more sharp-sighted than Lynceus.[756]

PLUTUS. And how should you be able to do that, you, who are but a mortal?

CHREMYLUS. I have great hope, after the answer Apollo gave me, shaking his sacred laurels the while.

PLUTUS. Is *he* in the plot then?

CHREMYLUS. Aye, truly.

PLUTUS. Take care what you say.

CHREMYLUS. Never fear, friend; for, be well assured, that if it has to cost me my life, I will carry out what I have in my head.

CARIO. And I will help you, if you permit it.

CHREMYLUS. We shall have many other helpers as well—all the worthy folk who are wanting for bread.

PLUTUS. Ah! ha! they'll prove sorry helpers.

CHREMYLUS. No, not so, once they've grown rich. But you, Cario, run quick ...

CARIO. Where?

CHREMYLUS. ... to call my comrades, the other husbandmen, that each of them may come here to take his share of the gifts of Plutus.

CARIO. I'm off. But let someone come from the house to take this morsel of meat.[757]

CHREMYLUS. I'll see to that; you run your hardest. As for you, Plutus, the most excellent of all the gods, come in here with me; this is the house you must fill with riches today, by fair means or foul.[758]

PLUTUS. I don't like at all going into other folks' houses in this manner; I have never got any good from it. If I got inside a miser's house, straightway he would bury me deep underground; if some honest fellow among his friends came to ask him for the smallest coin, he would deny ever having seen me. Then if I went to a fool's house, he would sacrifice me as a prey to gaming and to girls, and very soon I should be completely stripped and pitched out of doors.

CHREMYLUS. That's because you have never met a man who knew how to avoid the two extremes; moderation is the strong point in my character. I love saving as much as anybody, and I know how to spend, when 'tis needed. But let us go in; I want to make you known to my wife and to my only son, whom I love most of all after yourself.

PLUTUS. Aye, after myself, I'm very sure of that.

CHREMYLUS. Why should I hide the truth from you?

CARIO. Come, you active workers, who, like my master, eat nothing but garlic and the poorest food, you who are his friends and his neighbours, hasten your steps, hurry yourselves; there's not a moment to lose; this is the critical hour, when your presence and your support is needed by him.

CHORUS. Why, don't you see we are speeding as fast as men can, who are already enfeebled by age? But do you deem it fitting to make us run like this before ever telling us why your master has called us?

CARIO. I've grown hoarse with the telling, but you won't listen. My master is going to drag you all out of the stupid, sapless life you are leading and ensure you one full of all delights.

CHORUS. And how is he going to manage that?

CARIO. My poor friends, he has brought with him a disgusting old fellow, all bent and wrinkled, with a most pitiful appearance, bald and toothless; upon my word, I even believe he is circumcised like some vile barbarian.

CHORUS. These are news worth their weight in gold! What are you saying?
Repeat it to me; no doubt it means he is bringing back a heap of wealth.

CARIO. No, but a heap of all the infirmities attendant on old age.

CHORUS. If you are tricking us, you shall pay us for it. Beware of our sticks!

CARIO. Do you deem me so brazen as all that, and my words mere lies?

CHORUS. What serious airs the rascal puts on! Look! his legs are already shrieking, "oh! oh!" they are asking for the shackles and wedges.

CARIO. 'Tis in the tomb that 'tis your lot to judge. Why don't you go there? Charon has given you your ticket.[759]

CHORUS. Plague take you! you cursed rascal, who rail at us and have not even the heart to tell us why your master has made us come. We were pressed for time and tired out, yet we came with all haste, and in our hurry we have passed by lots of wild onions without even gathering them.

CARIO. I will no longer conceal the truth from you. Friends, 'tis Plutus whom my master brings, Plutus, who will give you riches.

CHORUS. What! we shall really all become rich!

CARIO. Aye, certainly; you will then be Midases, provided you grow ass's ears.

CHORUS. What joy, what happiness! If what you tell me is true, I long to dance with delight.

CARIO. And I too, threttanello![760] I want to imitate Cyclops and lead your troop by stamping like this.[761] Do you, my dear little ones, cry, aye, cry again and bleat forth the plaintive song of the sheep and of the stinking goats; follow me with erected organs like lascivious goats ready for action.

CHORUS. As for us, threttanello! we will seek you, dear Cyclops, bleating, and if we find you with your wallet full of fresh herbs, all disgusting in your filth, sodden with wine and sleeping in the midst of your sheep, we will seize a great flaming stake and burn out your eye.[762]

CARIO. I will copy that Circé of Corinth,[763] whose potent philtres compelled the companions of Philonides to swallow balls of dung, which she herself had kneaded with her hands, as if they were swine; and do you too grunt with joy and follow your mother, my little pigs.

CHORUS. Oh! Circé[764] with the potent philtres, who besmear your companions so filthily, what pleasure I shall have in imitating the son of Laertes! I will hang you up by your testicles,[765] I will rub your nose with dung like a goat, and like Aristyllus[766] you shall say through your half-opened lips, "Follow your mother, my little pigs."

CARIO. Enough of tomfoolery, assume a grave demeanour; unknown to my master I am going to take bread and meat; and when I have fed well, I shall resume my work.

CHREMYLUS. To say, "Hail! my dear neighbours!" is an old form of greeting and well worn with use; so therefore I embrace you, because you have not crept like tortoises, but have come rushing here in all haste. Now help me to watch carefully and closely over the god.

CHORUS. Be at ease. You shall see with what martial zeal I will guard him. What! we jostle each other at the Assembly for three obols, and am I going to let Plutus in person be stolen from me?

CHREMYLUS. But I see Blepsidemus; by his bearing and his haste I can readily see he knows or suspects something.

BLEPSIDEMUS. What has happened then? Whence, how has Chremylus suddenly grown rich? I don't believe a word of it. Nevertheless, nothing but his sudden fortune was being talked about in the barbers' booths. But I am above all surprised that his good fortune has not made him forget his friends; that is not the usual way!

CHREMYLUS. By the gods, Blepsidemus, I will hide nothing from you. To-day things are better than yesterday; let us share, for are you not my friend?

BLEPSIDEMUS. Have you really grown rich as they say?

CHREMYLUS I shall be soon, if the god agrees to it. But there is still some risk to run.

BLEPSIDEMUS. What risk?

CHREMYLUS. What risk?

BLEPSIDEMUS. What do you mean? Explain.

CHREMYLUS. If we succeed, we are happy for ever, but if we fail, it is all over with us.

BLEPSIDEMUS. 'Tis a bad business, and one that doesn't please me! To grow rich all at once and yet to be fearful! ah! I suspect something that's little good.

CHREMYLUS. What do you mean, that's little good?

BLEPSIDEMUS. No doubt you have just stolen some gold and silver from some temple and are repenting.

CHREMYLUS. Nay! heaven preserve me from that!

BLEPSIDEMUS. A truce to idle phrases! the thing is only too apparent, my friend.

CHREMYLUS. Don't suspect such a thing of me.

BLEPSIDEMUS. Alas! then there is no honest man! not one, that can resist the attraction of gold!

CHREMYLUS. By Demeter, you have no common sense.

BLEPSIDEMUS. To have to persist like this in denial one's whole life long!

CHREMYLUS. But, good gods, you are mad, my dear fellow!

BLEPSIDEMUS. His very look is distraught; he has done some crime!

CHREMYLUS. Ah! I know the tune you are playing now; you think I have stolen, and want your share.

BLEPSIDEMUS. My share of what, pray?

CHREMYLUS. You are beside the mark; the thing is quite otherwise.

BLEPSIDEMUS. 'Tis perhaps not a theft, but some piece of knavery!

CHREMYLUS. You are insane!

BLEPSIDEMUS. What? You have done no man an injury?

CHREMYLUS. No! assuredly not!

BLEPSIDEMUS. But, great gods, what am I to think? You won't tell me the truth.

CHREMYLUS. You accuse me without really knowing anything.

BLEPSIDEMUS. Listen, friend, no doubt the matter can yet be hushed up, before it gets noised abroad, at trifling expense; I will buy the orators' silence.

CHREMYLUS. Aye, you will lay out three minae and, as my friend, you will reckon twelve against me.

BLEPSIDEMUS. I know someone who will come and seat himself at the foot of the tribunal, holding a supplicant's bough in his hand and surrounded by his wife and children, for all the world like the Heraclidae of Pamphilus.[767]

CHREMYLUS. Not at all, poor fool! But, thanks to me, worthy folk, intelligent and moderate men alone shall be rich henceforth.

BLEPSIDEMUS. What are you saying? Have you then stolen so much as all that?

CHREMYLUS. Oh! your insults will be the death of me.

BLEPSIDEMUS. 'Tis rather you yourself who are courting death.

CHREMYLUS. Not so, you wretch, since I have Plutus.

BLEPSIDEMUS. You have Plutus? Which one?

CHREMYLUS. The god himself.

BLEPSIDEMUS. And where is he?

CHREMYLUS. There.

BLEPSIDEMUS. Where?

CHREMYLUS. Indoors.

BLEPSIDEMUS. Indoors?

CHREMYLUS. Aye, certainly.

BLEPSIDEMUS. Get you gone! Plutus in your house?

CHREMYLUS. Yes, by the gods!

BLEPSIDEMUS. Are you telling me the truth?

CHREMYLUS. I am.

BLEPSIDEMUS. Swear it by Hestia.

CHREMYLUS. I swear it by Posidon.

BLEPSIDEMUS. The god of the sea?

CHREMYLUS. Aye, and by all the other Posidons, if such there be.

BLEPSIDEMUS. And you don't send him to us, to your friends?

CHREMYLUS. We've not got to that point yet.

BLEPSIDEMUS. What do you say? Is there no chance of sharing?

CHREMYLUS. Why, no. We must first …

BLEPSIDEMUS. Do what?

CHREMYLUS. … restore him his sight.

BLEPSIDEMUS. Restore whom his sight? Speak!

CHREMYLUS. Plutus. It must be done, no matter how.

BLEPSIDEMUS. Is he then really blind?

CHREMYLUS. Yes, undoubtedly.

BLEPSIDEMUS. I am no longer surprised he never came to me.

CHREMYLUS. And it please the gods, he'll come there now.

BLEPSIDEMUS. Must we not go and seek a physician?

CHREMYLUS. Seek physicians at Athens? Nay! there's no art where there's no fee.[768]

BLEPSIDEMUS. Let's bethink ourselves well.

CHREMYLUS. There is not one.

BLEPSIDEMUS. 'Tis a positive fact, I don't know of one.

CHREMYLUS. But I have thought the matter well over, and the best thing is to make Plutus lie in the Temple of Aesculapius.[769]

BLEPSIDEMUS. Aye, unquestionably 'tis the very best thing. Be quick and lead him away to the Temple.

CHREMYLUS. I am going there.

BLEPSIDEMUS. Then hurry yourself.

CHREMYLUS. 'Tis just what I am doing.

POVERTY. Unwise, perverse, unholy men! What are you daring to do, you pitiful, wretched mortals? Whither are you flying? Stop! I command it!

BLEPSIDEMUS. Oh! great gods!

POVERTY. My arm shall destroy you, you infamous beings! Such an attempt is not to be borne; neither man nor god has ever dared the like. You shall die!

CHREMYLUS. And who are you? Oh! what a ghastly pallor!

BLEPSIDEMUS. 'Tis perchance some Erinnys, some Fury, from the theatre;[770] there's a kind of wild tragedy look in her eyes.

CHREMYLUS. But she has no torch.

BLEPSIDEMUS. Let's knock her down!

POVERTY. Who do you think I am?

CHREMYLUS. Some wine-shop keeper or egg-woman. Otherwise you would not have shrieked so loud at us, who have done nothing to you.

POVERTY. Indeed? And have you not done me the most deadly injury by seeking to banish me from every country?

CHREMYLUS. Why, have you not got the Barathrum[771] left? But who are you? Answer me quickly!

POVERTY. I am one that will punish you this very day for having wanted to make me disappear from here.

BLEPSIDEMUS. Might it be the tavern-keeper in my neighbourhood, who is always cheating me in measure?

POVERTY. I am Poverty, who have lived with you for so many years.

BLEPSIDEMUS. Oh! great Apollo! oh, ye gods! whither shall I fly?

CHREMYLUS. Now then! what are you doing? You poltroon! Will you kindly stop here?

BLEPSIDEMUS. Not I.

CHREMYLUS. Will you have the goodness to stop. Are two men to fly from a woman?

BLEPSIDEMUS. But, you wretch, 'tis Poverty, the most fearful monster that ever drew breath.

CHREMYLUS. Stay where you are, I beg of you.

BLEPSIDEMUS. No! no! a thousand times, no!

CHREMYLUS. Could we do anything worse than leave the god in the lurch and fly before this woman without so much as ever offering to fight?

BLEPSIDEMUS. But what weapons have we? Are we in a condition to show fight? Where is the breastplate, the buckler, that this wretch has not pledged?

CHREMYLUS. Be at ease. Plutus will readily triumph over her threats unaided.

POVERTY. Dare you reply, you scoundrels, you who are caught red-handed at the most horrible crime?

CHREMYLUS. As for you, you cursed jade, you pursue me with your abuse, though I have never done you the slightest harm.

POVERTY. Do you think it is doing me no harm to restore Plutus to the use of his eyes?

CHREMYLUS. Is this doing you harm, that we shower blessings on all men?

POVERTY. And what do you think will ensure their happiness?

CHREMYLUS. Ah! first of all we shall drive you out of Greece.

POVERTY. Drive me out? Could you do mankind a greater harm?

CHREMYLUS. Yes—if I gave up my intention to deliver them from you.

POVERTY. Well, let us discuss this point first. I propose to show that I am the sole cause of all your blessings, and that your safety depends on me alone. If I don't succeed, then do what you like to me.

CHREMYLUS. How dare you talk like this, you impudent hussy?

POVERTY. Agree to hear me and I think it will be very easy for me to prove that you are entirely on the wrong road, when you want to make the just men wealthy.

BLEPSIDEMUS. Oh! cudgel and rope's end, come to my help!

POVERTY. Why such wrath and these shouts, before you hear my arguments?

BLEPSIDEMUS. But who could listen to such words without exclaiming?

POVERTY. Any man of sense.

CHREMYLUS. But if you lose your case, what punishment will you submit to?

POVERTY. Choose what you will.

CHREMYLUS. That's all right.

POVERTY. You shall suffer the same if you are beaten!

CHREMYLUS. Do you think twenty deaths a sufficiently large stake?

BLEPSIDEMUS. Good enough for her, but for us two would suffice.

POVERTY. You won't escape, for is there indeed a single valid argument to oppose me with?

CHORUS. To beat her in this debate, you must call upon all your wits. Make no allowances and show no weakness!

CHREMYLUS. It is right that the good should be happy, that the wicked and the impious, on the other hand, should be miserable; that is a truth, I believe, which no one will gainsay. To realize this condition of things is as great a proposal as it is noble and useful in every respect, and we have found a means of attaining the object of our wishes. If Plutus recovers his sight and ceases from wandering about unseeing and at random, he will go to seek the just men and never leave them again; he will shun the perverse and ungodly; so, thanks to him, all men will become honest, rich and pious. Can anything better be conceived for the public weal?

BLEPSIDEMUS. Of a certainty, no! I bear witness to that. It is not even necessary she should reply.

CHREMYLUS. Does it not seem that everything is extravagance in the world, or rather madness, when you watch the way things go? A crowd of rogues enjoy blessings they have won by sheer injustice, while more honest folks are miserable, die of hunger, and spend their whole lives with you.

CHORUS. Yes, if Plutus became clear-sighted again and drove out Poverty, 'twould be the greatest blessing possible for the human race.

POVERTY. Here are two old men, whose brains are easy to confuse, who assist each other to talk rubbish and drivel to their hearts' content. But if your wishes were realized, your profit would be great! Let Plutus recover his sight and divide his favours out equally to all, and none will ply either trade or art any longer; all toil would be done away with. Who would wish to hammer iron, build ships, sew, turn, cut up leather, bake bricks, bleach linen, tan hides, or break up the soil of the earth with the plough and garner the gifts of Demeter, if he could live in idleness and free from all this work?

CHREMYLUS. What nonsense all this is! All these trades which you just mention will be plied by our slaves.

POVERTY. Your slaves! And by what means will these slaves be got?

CHREMYLUS. We will buy them.

POVERTY. But first say, who will sell them, if everyone is rich?

CHREMYLUS. Some greedy dealer from Thessaly—the land which supplies so many.

POVERTY. But if your system is applied, there won't be a single slave-dealer left. What rich man would risk his life to devote himself to this traffic? You will have to toil, to dig and submit yourself to all kinds of hard labour; so that your life would be more wretched even than it is now.

CHREMYLUS. May this prediction fall upon yourself!

POVERTY. You will not be able to sleep in a bed, for no more will ever be manufactured; nor on carpets, for who would weave them if he had gold? When you bring a young bride to your dwelling, you will have no essences wherewith to perfume her, nor rich embroidered cloaks dyed with dazzling colours in which to clothe her. And yet what is the use of being rich, if you are to be deprived of all these enjoyments? On the other hand, you have all that you need in abundance, thanks to me; to the artisan I am like a severe mistress, who forces him by need and poverty to seek the means of earning his livelihood.

CHREMYLUS. And what good thing can you give us, unless it be burns in the bath,[772] and swarms of brats and old women who cry with hunger, and clouds uncountable of lice, gnats and flies, which hover about the wretch's head, trouble him, awake him and say, "You will be hungry, but get up!" Besides, to possess a rag in place of a mantle, a pallet of rushes swarming with bugs, that do not let you close your eyes for a bed; a rotten piece of matting for a coverlet; a big stone for a pillow, on which to lay your head; to eat mallow roots instead of bread, and leaves of withered radish instead of cake; to have nothing but the cover of a broken jug for a stool, the stave of a cask, and broken at that, for a kneading-trough, that is the life you make for us! Are these the mighty benefits with which you pretend to load mankind?

POVERTY. 'Tis not my life that you describe; you are attacking the existence beggars lead.

CHREMYLUS. Is beggary not Poverty's sister?

POVERTY. Thrasybulus and Dionysius[773] are one and the same according to you. No, my life is not like that and never will be. The beggar, whom you have depicted to us, never possesses anything. The poor man lives thriftily and attentive to his work; he has not got too much, but he does not lack what he really needs.

CHREMYLUS. Oh! what a happy life, by Demeter! to live sparingly, to toil incessantly and not to leave enough to pay for a tomb!

POVERTY. That's it! Jest, jeer, and never talk seriously! But what you don't know is this, that men with me are worth more, both in mind and body, than with Plutus. With him they are gouty, big-bellied, heavy of limb and scandalously stout; with me they are thin, wasp-waisted, and terrible to the foe.

CHREMYLUS. 'Tis no doubt by starving them that you give them that waspish waist.

POVERTY. As for behaviour, I will prove to you that modesty dwells with me and insolence with Plutus.

CHREMYLUS. Oh! the sweet modesty of stealing and breaking through walls.[774]

BLEPSIDEMUS. Aye, the thief is truly modest, for he hides himself.

POVERTY. Look at the orators in our republics; as long as they are poor, both State and people can only praise their uprightness; but once they are fattened on the public funds, they conceive a hatred for justice, plan intrigues against the people and attack the democracy.

CHREMYLUS. That is absolutely true, although your tongue is very vile. But it matters not, so don't put on those triumphant airs; you shall not be punished any the less for having tried to persuade me that poverty is worth more than wealth.

POVERTY. Not being able to refute my arguments, you chatter at random and exert yourself to no purpose.

CHREMYLUS. Then tell me this, why does all mankind flee from you?

POVERTY. Because I make them better. Children do the very same; they flee from the wise counsels of their fathers. So difficult is it to see one's true interest.

CHREMYLUS. Will you say that Zeus cannot discern what is best? Well, he takes Plutus to himself ...

BLEPSIDEMUS. ... and banishes Poverty to earth.

POVERTY. Ah me! how purblind you are, you old fellows of the days of Saturn! Why, Zeus is poor, and I will clearly prove it to you. In the Olympic games, which he founded, and to which he convokes the whole of Greece every four years, why does he only crown the victorious athletes with wild olive? If he were rich he would give them gold.

CHREMYLUS. 'Tis in that way he shows that he clings to his wealth; he is sparing with it, won't part with any portion of it, only bestows baubles on the victors and keeps his money for himself.

POVERTY. But wealth coupled to such sordid greed is yet more shameful than poverty.

CHREMYLUS. May Zeus destroy you, both you and your chaplet of wild olive!

POVERTY. Thus you dare to maintain that poverty is not the fount of all blessings!

CHREMYLUS. Ask Hecaté[775] whether it is better to be rich or starving; she will tell you that the rich send her a meal every month and that the poor make it disappear before it is even served. But go and hang yourself and don't breathe another syllable. I will not be convinced against my will.

POVERTY. "Oh! citizens of Argos! do you hear what he says?"[776]

CHREMYLUS. Invoke Pauson, your boon companion, rather.[777]

POVERTY. Alas! what is to become of me?

CHREMYLUS. Get you gone, be off quick and a pleasant journey to you.

POVERTY. But where shall I go?

CHREMYLUS. To gaol; but hurry up, let us put an end to this.

POVERTY. One day you will recall me.

CHREMYLUS. Then you can return; but disappear for the present. I prefer to be rich; you are free to knock your head against the walls in your rage.

BLEPSIDEMUS. And I too welcome wealth. I want, when I leave the bath all perfumed with essences, to feast bravely with my wife and children and to break wind in the faces of toilers and Poverty.

CHREMYLUS. So that hussy has gone at last! But let us make haste to put Plutus to bed in the Temple of Aesculapius.

BLEPSIDEMUS. Let us make haste; else some bothering fellow may again come to interrupt us.

CHREMYLUS. Cario, bring the coverlets and all that I have got ready from the house; let us conduct the god to the Temple, taking care to observe all the proper rites.

CHORUS. [*Missing.*][778]

CARIO. Oh! you old fellows, who used to dip out the broth served to the poor at the festival of Theseus with little pieces of bread[779] hollowed like a spoon, how worthy of envy is your fate! How happy you are, both you and all just men!

CHORUS. My good fellow, what has happened to your friends? You seem the bearer of good tidings.

CARIO. What joy for my master and even more for Plutus! The god has regained his sight; his eyes sparkle with the greatest brilliancy, thanks to the benevolent care of Aesculapius.

CHORUS. Oh! what transports of joy! oh! What shouts of gladness!

CARIO. Aye! one is compelled to rejoice, whether one will or not.

CHORUS. I will sing to the honour of Aesculapius, the son of illustrious Zeus, with a resounding voice; he is the beneficent star which men adore.

CHREMYLUS' WIFE. What mean these shouts? Is there good news. With what impatience have I been waiting in the house, and for so long too!

CARIO. Quick! quick! some wine, mistress. And drink yourself, for 'tis much to your taste; I bring you all blessings in a lump.

WIFE. Where are they?

CARIO. In my words, as you are going to see.

WIFE. Have done with trifling! come, speak.

CARIO. Listen, I am going to tell you everything from the feet to the head.

WIFE. Ah! don't throw anything at my head.

CARIO. Not even the happiness that has come to you?

WIFE. No, no, nothing ... to annoy me.

CARIO. Having arrived near to the Temple with our patient, then so unfortunate, but now at the apex of happiness, of blessedness, we first led him down to the sea to purify him.

WIFE. Ah! what a singular pleasure for an old man to bathe in the cold sea-water!

CARIO. Then we repaired to the Temple of the god. Once the wafers and the various offerings had been consecrated upon the altar, and the cake of wheaten-meal had been handed over to the devouring Hephaestus, we made Plutus lie on a couch according to the rite, and each of us prepared himself a bed of leaves.

WIFE. Had any other folk come to beseech the deity?

CARIO. Yes. Firstly, Neoclides,[780] who is blind, but steals much better than those who see clearly; then many others attacked by complaints of all kinds. The lights were put out and the priest enjoined us to sleep, especially recommending us to keep silent should we hear any noise. There we were all lying down quite quietly. I could not sleep; I was thinking of a certain stew-pan full of pap placed close to an old woman and just behind her head. I had a furious longing to slip towards that side. But just as I was lifting my head, I noticed the priest, who was sweeping off both the cakes and the figs on the sacred table; then he made the round of the altars and sanctified the cakes that remained, by stowing them away in a bag. I therefore resolved to follow such a pious example and made straight for the pap.

WIFE. You wretch! and had you no fear of the god?

CARIO. Aye, indeed! I feared that the god with his crown on his head might have been near the stew-pan before me. I said to myself, "Like priest, like god." On hearing the noise I made, the old woman put out her hand, but I hissed and bit it, just as a sacred serpent might have done.[781] Quick she drew back her hand, slipped down into the bed with her head beneath the coverlets and never moved again; only she let go some wind in her fear which stunk worse than a weasel. As for myself, I swallowed a goodly portion of the pap and, having made a good feed, went back to bed.

WIFE. And did not the god come?

CAIRO. He did not tarry; and when he was near us, oh! dear! such a good joke happened. My belly was quite blown out, and I let wind with the loudest of noises.

WIFE. Doubtless the god pulled a wry face?

CARIO. No, but Iaso blushed a little and Panacea[782] turned her head away, holding her nose; for my perfume is not that of roses.

WIFE. And what did the god do?

CARIO. He paid not the slightest heed.

WIFE. He must then be a pretty coarse kind of god?

CARIO. I don't say that, but he's used to tasting shit.[783]

WIFE. Impudent knave, go on with you!

CARIO. Then I hid myself in my bed all a-tremble. Aesculapius did the round of the patients and examined them all with great attention; then a slave placed beside him a stone mortar, a pestle and a little box.[784]

WIFE. Of stone?

CARIO. No, not of stone.

WIFE. But how could you see all this, you arch-rascal, when you say you were hiding all the time?

CARIO. Why, great gods, through my cloak, for 'tis not without holes! He first prepared an ointment for Neoclides; he threw three heads of Tenian[785] garlic into the mortar, pounded them with an admixture of fig-tree sap and lentisk, moistened the whole with Sphettian[785] vinegar, and, turning back the patient's eyelids, applied his salve to the interior of the eyes, so that the pain might be more excruciating. Neoclides shrieked, howled, sprang towards the foot of his bed and wanted to bolt, but the god laughed and said to him, "Keep where you are with your salve; by doing this you will not go and perjure yourself before the Assembly."

WIFE What a wise god and what a friend to our city!

CARIO. Thereupon he came and seated himself at the head of Plutus' bed, took a perfectly clean rag and wiped his eye-lids; Panacea covered his head and face with a purple cloth, while the god whistled, and two enormous snakes came rushing from the sanctuary.

WIFE. Great gods!

CARIO. They slipped gently beneath the purple cloth and, as far as I could judge, licked the patient's eyelids; for, in less time than even you need, mistress, to drain down ten beakers of wine, Plutus rose up; he could see. I clapped my hands with joy and awoke my master, and the god immediately disappeared with the serpents into the sanctuary. As for those who were lying near Plutus, you can imagine that they embraced him tenderly. Dawn broke and not one of them had closed an eye. As for myself, I did not cease thanking the god who had so quickly restored to Plutus his sight and had made Neoclides blinder than ever.

WIFE. Oh! thou great Aesculapius! How mighty is thy power! (*To Cario.*) But tell me, where is Plutus now?

CARIO. He is approaching, escorted by an immense crowd. The rich, whose wealth is ill-gotten, are knitting their brows and shooting at him looks of fierce hate, while the just folk, who led a wretched existence, embrace him and grasp his hand in the transport of their joy; they follow in his wake, their heads wreathed with garlands, laughing and blessing their deliverer; the old men make the earth resound as they walk together keeping time. Come, all of you, all, down to the very least, dance, leap and form yourselves into a chorus; no longer do you risk being told, when you go home, "There is no meal in the bag."

WIFE. And I, by Hecate! I will string you a garland of cakes for the good tidings you have brought me.

CARIO. Hurry, make haste then; our friends are close at hand.

WIFE. I will go indoors to fetch some gifts of welcome, to celebrate these eyes that have just been opened.

CARIO. Meantime I am going forth to meet them.

CHORUS. [*Missing.*]

PLUTUS. I adore thee, oh! thou divine sun, and thee I greet thou city, the beloved of Pallas; be welcome, thou land of Cecrops, which hast received me. Alas! what manner of men I associated with! I blush to think of it. While, on the other hand, I shunned those who deserved my friendship; I knew neither the vices of the ones nor the virtues of the others. A twofold mistake, and in both cases equally fatal! Ah! what a misfortune was mine! But I want to change everything; and in future I mean to prove to mankind that, if I gave to the wicked, 'twas against my will.

CHREMYLUS (*to the crowd who impede him*). Get you gone! Oh! what a lot of friends spring into being when you are fortunate! They dig me with their elbows and bruise my shins to prove their affection. Each one wants to greet me. What a crowd of old fellows thronged round me on the market-place!

WIFE. Oh! thou, who art dearest of all to me, and thou too, be welcome! Allow me, Plutus, to shower these gifts of welcome over you in due accord with custom.

PLUTUS. No. This is the first house I enter after having regained my sight; I shall take nothing from it, for 'tis my place rather to give.

WIFE. Do you refuse these gifts?

PLUTUS. I will accept them at your fireside, as custom requires. Besides, we shall thus avoid a ridiculous scene; it is not meet that the poet should throw dried figs and dainties to the spectators; 'tis a vulgar trick to make 'em laugh.

WIFE. You are right. Look! yonder's Dexinicus, who was already getting to his feet to catch the figs as they flew past him.[787]

CHORUS. [*Missing.*]

CARIO. How pleasant it is, friends, to live well, especially when it costs nothing! What a deluge of blessings flood our household, and that too without our having wronged ever a soul! Ah! what a delightful thing is wealth! The bin is full of white flour and the wine-jars run over with fragrant liquor; all the chests are crammed with gold and silver, 'tis a sight to see; the tank is full of oil,[788] the phials with perfumes, and the garret with dried figs. Vinegar flasks, plates, stew-pots and all the platters are of brass; our rotten old wooden trenchers for the fish have to-day become dishes of silver; the very night-commode is of ivory. We others, the slaves, we play at odd and even with gold pieces, and carry luxury so far that we no longer wipe ourselves with stones, but use garlic stalks instead. My master, at this moment, is crowned with flowers and sacrificing a pig, a goat and a ram;[789] 'tis the smoke that has driven me out, for I could no longer endure it, it hurt my eyes so.

A JUST MAN. Come, my child, come with me. Let us go and find the god.

CHREMYLUS. Who comes here?

JUST MAN. A man who was once wretched, but now is happy.

CHREMYLUS. A just man then?

JUST MAN. You have it.

CHREMYLUS. Well! what do you want?

JUST MAN. I come to thank the god for all the blessings he has showered on me. My father had left me a fairly decent fortune, and I helped those of my friends who were in want; 'twas, to my thinking, the most useful thing I could do with my fortune.

CHREMYLUS. And you were quickly ruined?

JUST MAN. Entirely.

CHREMYLUS. Since then you have been living in misery?

JUST MAN. In truth I have; I thought I could count, in case of need, upon the friends whose property I had helped, but they turned their backs upon me and pretended not to see me.

CHREMYLUS. They laughed at you, 'tis evident.

JUST MAN. Just so. With my empty coffers, I had no more friends.

CHREMYLUS. But your lot has changed.

JUST MAN. Yes, and so I come to the god to make him the acts of gratitude that are his due.

CHREMYLUS. But with what object now do you bring this old cloak, which your slave is carrying? Tell me.

JUST MAN. I wish to dedicate it to the god.[790]

CHREMYLUS. Were you initiated into the Great Mysteries in that cloak?[791]

JUST MAN. No, but I shivered in it for thirteen years.

CHREMYLUS. And this footwear?

JUST MAN. These also are my winter companions.

CHREMYLUS. And you wish to dedicate them too?

JUST MAN. Unquestionably.

CHREMYLUS. Fine presents to offer to the god!

AN INFORMER. Alas! alas! I am a lost man. Ah! thrice, four, five, twelve times, or rather ten thousand times unhappy fate! Why, why must fortune deal me such rough blows?

CHREMYLUS. Oh, Apollo, my tutelary! oh! ye favourable gods! what has overtaken this man?

INFORMER. Ah! am I not deserving of pity? I have lost everything; this cursed god has stripped me bare. Ah! if there be justice in heaven, he shall be struck blind again.

JUST MAN. Methinks I know what's the matter. If this man is unfortunate, 'tis because he's of little account and small honesty; and i' faith he looks it too.

CHREMYLUS. Then, by Zeus! his plight is but just.

INFORMER. He promised that if he recovered his sight, he would enrich us all unaided; whereas he has ruined more than one.

CHREMYLUS. But whom has he thus ill-used?

INFORMER. Me.

CHREMYLUS. You were doubtless a villainous thief then.

INFORMER (*to Chremylus and Cario*). 'Tis rather you yourselves who were such wretches; I am certain you have got my money.

CHREMYLUS. Ha! by Demeter! 'tis an informer. What impudence!

CARIO. He's ravenously hungry, that's certain.

INFORMER. You shall follow me this very instant to the marketplace, where the torture of the wheel shall force the confession of your misdeeds from you.

CARIO. Ha! look out for yourself!

JUST MAN. By Zeus the Deliverer, what gratitude all Greeks owe to Plutus, if he destroys these vile informers!

INFORMER. You are laughing at me. Ho! ho! I denounce you as their accomplice. Where did you steal that new cloak from? Yesterday I saw you with one utterly worn out.

JUST MAN. I fear you not, thanks to this ring, for which I paid Eudemus[792] a drachma.

CHREMYLUS. Ah! there's no ring to preserve you from the informer's bite.

INFORMER. The insolent wretches! But, my fine jokers, you have not told me what you are up to here. Nothing good, I'll be bound.

CHREMYLUS. Nothing of any good for you, be sure of that.

INFORMER. By Zeus! you're going to dine at my expense!

CHREMYLUS. You vile impostor, may you burst with an empty belly, both you and your witness.

INFORMER. You deny it? I reckon, you villians, that there is much salt fish and roast meat in this house. Hu! hu! hu! hu! hu! hu! (*He sniffs.*)

CHREMYLUS. Can you smell anything, rascal?

INFORMER. Can such outrages be borne, oh, Zeus! Ye gods! how cruel it is to see me treated thus, when I am such an honest fellow and such a good citizen!

CHREMYLUS. You an honest man! you a good citizen!

INFORMER. A better one than any.

CHREMYLUS. Ah! well then, answer my questions.

INFORMER. Concerning what?

CHREMYLUS. Are you a husbandman?

INFORMER. D'ye take me for a fool?

CHREMYLUS. A merchant?

INFORMER. I assume the title, when it serves me.[793]

CHREMYLUS. Do you ply any trade?

INFORMER. No, most assuredly not!

CHREMYLUS. Then how do you live, if you do nothing?

INFORMER. I superintend public and private business.

CHREMYLUS. You! And by what right, pray?

INFORMER. Because it pleases me to do so.

CHREMYLUS. Like a thief you sneak yourself in where you have no business.
You are hated by all and you claim to be an honest man?

INFORMER. What, you fool? I have not the right to dedicate myself entirely to my country's service?

CHREMYLUS. Is the country served by vile intrigue?

INFORMER. It is served by watching that the established law is observed—by allowing no one to violate it.

CHREMYLUS. That's the duty of the tribunals; they are established to that end.

INFORMER. And who is the prosecutor before the dicasts?

CHREMYLUS. Whoever wishes to be.[794]

INFORMER. Well then, 'tis I who choose to be prosecutor; and thus all public affairs fall within my province.

CHREMYLUS. I pity Athens for being in such vile clutches. But would you not prefer to live quietly and free from all care and anxiety?

INFORMER. To do nothing is to live an animal's life.

CHREMYLUS. Thus you will not change your mode of life?

INFORMER. No, though they gave me Plutus himself and the *silphium* of Battus.[795]

CHREMYLUS (*to the Informer*). Come, quick, off with your cloak.

CARIO. Hi! friend! 'tis you they are speaking to.

CHREMYLUS. Off with your shoes.

CARIO. All this is addressed to you.

INFORMER. Very well! let one of you come near me, if he dares.

CARIO. I dare.

INFORMER. Alas! I am robbed of my clothes in full daylight.

CARIO. That's what comes of meddling with other folk's business and living at their expense.

INFORMER (*to his witness*). You see what is happening; I call you to witness.

CHREMYLUS. Look how the witness whom you brought is taking to his heels.

INFORMER. Great gods! I am all alone and they assault me.

CARIO. Shout away!

INFORMER. Oh! woe, woe is me!

CARIO. Give me that old ragged cloak, that I may dress out the informer.

JUST MAN. No, no; I have dedicated it to Plutus.

CARIO. And where would your offering be better bestowed than on the shoulders of a rascal and a thief? To Plutus fine, rich cloaks should be given.

JUST MAN. And what then shall be done with these shoes? Tell me.

CARIO. I will nail them to his brow as gifts are nailed to the trunks of the wild olive.

INFORMER. I'm off, for you are the strongest, I own. But if I find someone to join me, let him be as weak as he will, I will summon this god, who thinks himself so strong, before the Court this very day, and denounce him as manifestly guilty of overturning the democracy by his will alone and without the consent of the Senate or the popular Assembly.

JUST MAN. Now that you are rigged out from head to foot with my old clothes, hasten to the bath and stand there in the front row to warm yourself better; 'tis the place I formerly had.

CHREMYLUS. Ah! the bath-man would grip you by the testicles and fling you through the door; he would only need to see you to appraise you at your true value.... But let us go in, friend, that you may address your thanksgivings to the god.

CHORUS. [*Missing.*]

AN OLD WOMAN. Dear old men, am I near the house where the new god lives, or have I missed the road?

CHORUS. You are at his door, my pretty little maid, who question us so sweetly.[796]

OLD WOMAN. Then I will summon someone in the house.

CHREMYLUS. 'Tis needless! I am here myself. But what matter brings you here?

OLD WOMAN. Ah! a cruel, unjust fate! My dear friend, this god has made life unbearable to me through ceasing to be blind.

CHREMYLUS. What does this mean? Can you be a female informer?

OLD WOMAN. Most certainly not.

CHREMYLUS. Have you not drunk up your money then?

OLD WOMAN. You are mocking me! Nay! I am being devoured with a consuming fire.

CHREMYLUS. Then tell me what is consuming you so fiercely.

OLD WOMAN. Listen! I loved a young man, who was poor, but so handsome, so well-built, so honest! He readily gave way to all I desired and acquitted himself so well! I, for my part, refused him nothing.

CHREMYLUS. And what did he generally ask of you.

OLD WOMAN. Very little; he bore himself towards me with astonishing discretion! perchance twenty drachmae for a cloak or eight for footwear; sometimes he begged me to buy tunics for his sisters or a little mantle for his mother; at times he needed four bushels of corn.

CHREMYLUS. 'Twas very little, in truth; I admire his modesty.

OLD WOMAN. And 'twas not as a reward for his complacency that he ever asked me for anything, but as a matter of pure friendship; a cloak I had given would remind him from whom he had got it.

CHREMYLUS. 'Twas a fellow who loved you madly.

OLD WOMAN. But 'tis no longer so, for the faithless wretch has sadly altered! I had sent him this cake with the sweetmeats you see here on this dish and let him know that I would visit him in the evening....

CHREMYLUS. Well?

OLD WOMAN. He sent me back my presents and added this tart to them, on condition that I never set foot in his house again. Besides, he sent me this message, "Once upon a time the Milesians were brave."[797]

CHREMYLUS. An honest lad, indeed! But what would you? When poor, he would devour anything; now he is rich, he no longer cares for lentils.

OLD WOMAN. Formerly he came to me every day.

CHREMYLUS. To see if you were being buried?

OLD WOMAN. No! he longed to hear the sound of my voice.

CHREMYLUS. And to carry off some present.

OLD WOMAN. If I was downcast, he would call me his little duck or his little dove in a most tender manner....

CHREMYLUS. And then would ask for the wherewithal to buy a pair of shoes.

OLD WOMAN. When I was at the Mysteries of Eleusis in a carriage,[798] someone looked at me; he was so jealous that he beat me the whole of that day.

CHREMYLUS. 'Twas because he liked to feed alone.

OLD WOMAN. He told me I had very beautiful hands.

CHREMYLUS. Aye, no doubt, when they handed him twenty drachmae.

OLD WOMAN. That my whole body breathed a sweet perfume.

CHREMYLUS. Yes, like enough, if you poured him out Thasian wine.

OLD WOMAN. That my glance was gentle and charming.

CHREMYLUS. 'Twas no fool. He knew how to drag drachmae from a hot-blooded old woman.

OLD WOMAN. Ah! the god has done very, very wrong, saying he would support the victims of injustice.

CHREMYLUS. Well, what must he do? Speak, and it shall be done.

OLD WOMAN. 'Tis right to compel him, whom I have loaded with benefits, to repay them in his turn; if not, he does not merit the least of the god's favours.

CHREMYLUS. And did he not do this every night?

OLD WOMAN. He swore he would never leave me, as long as I lived.

CHREMYLUS. Aye, rightly; but he thinks you are no longer alive.[799]

OLD WOMAN. Ah! friend, I am pining away with grief.

CHREMYLUS. You are rotting away, it seems to me.

OLD WOMAN. I have grown so thin, I could slip through a ring.

CHREMYLUS. Yes, if 'twere as large as the hoop of a sieve.

OLD WOMAN. But here is the youth, the cause of my complaint; he looks as though he were going to a festival.

CHREMYLUS. Yes, if his chaplet and his torch are any guides.

YOUTH. Greeting to you.

OLD WOMAN. What does he say?

YOUTH. My ancient old dear, you have grown white very quickly, by heaven!

OLD WOMAN. Oh! what an insult!

CHREMYLUS. It is a long time, then, since he saw you?

OLD WOMAN. A long time? My god! he was with me yesterday.

CHREMYLUS. It must be, then, that, unlike other people, he sees more clearly when he's drunk.

OLD WOMAN. No, but I have always known him for an insolent fellow.

YOUTH. Oh! divine Posidon! Oh, ye gods of old age! what wrinkles she has on her face!

OLD WOMAN. Oh! oh! keep your distance with that torch.

CHREMYLUS. Yes, 'twould be as well; if a single spark were to reach her, she would catch alight like an old olive branch.

YOUTH. I propose to have a game with you.

OLD WOMAN. Where, naughty boy?

YOUTH. Here. Take some nuts in your hand.

OLD WOMAN. What game is this?

YOUTH. Let's play at guessing how many teeth you have.

CHREMYLUS. Ah! I'll tell you; she's got three, or perhaps four.

YOUTH. Pay up; you've lost! she has only one single grinder.

OLD WOMAN. You wretch! you're not in your right senses. Do you insult me thus before this crowd?

YOUTH. I am washing you thoroughly; 'tis doing you a service.

CHREMYLUS. No, no! as she is there, she can still deceive; but if this white-lead is washed off, her wrinkles would come out plainly.

OLD WOMAN. You are only an old fool!

YOUTH. Ah! he is playing the gallant, he is fondling your breasts, and thinks I do not see it.

OLD WOMAN. Oh! no, by Aphrodité, no, you naughty jealous fellow.

CHREMYLUS. Oh! most certainly not, by Hecaté![800] Verily and indeed I would need to be mad! But, young man, I cannot forgive you, if you cast off this beautiful child.

YOUTH. Why, I adore her.

CHREMYLUS. But nevertheless she accuses you ...

YOUTH. Accuses me of what?

CHREMYLUS. ... of having told her insolently, "Once upon a time the Milesians were brave."

YOUTH. Oh! I shall not dispute with you about her.

CHREMYLUS. Why not?

YOUTH. Out of respect for your age; with anyone but you, I should not be so easy; come, take the girl and be happy.

CHREMYLUS. I see, I see; you don't want her any more.

OLD WOMAN. Nay! this is a thing that cannot be allowed.

YOUTH. I cannot argue with a woman, who has been making love these thirteen thousand years.

CHREMYLUS. Yet, since you liked the wine, you should now consume the lees.

YOUTH. But these lees are quite rancid and fusty.

CHREMYLUS. Pass them through a straining-cloth; they'll clarify.

YOUTH. But I want to go in with you to offer these chaplets to the god.

OLD WOMAN. And I too have something to tell him.

YOUTH. Then I don't enter.

CHREMYLUS. Come, have no fear; she won't harm you.

YOUTH. 'Tis true; I've been managing the old bark long enough.

OLD WOMAN. Go in; I'll follow after you.

CHREMYLUS. Good gods! that old hag has fastened herself to her youth like a limpet to its rock.

CHORUS. [*Missing.*]

CARIO (*opening the door*). Who knocks at the door? Halloa! I see no one; 'twas then by chance it gave forth that plaintive tone.

HERMES (*to Carlo, who is about to close the door*). Cario! stop!

CARIO. Eh! friend, was it you who knocked so loudly? Tell me.

HERMES. No, I was going to knock and you forestalled me by opening. Come, call your master quick, then his wife and his children, then his slave and his dog, then thyself and his pig.

CARIO. And what's it all about?

HERMES. It's about this, rascal! Zeus wants to serve you all with the same sauce and hurl the lot of you into the Barathrum.

CARIO. Have a care for your tongue, you bearer of ill tidings! But why does he want to treat us in that scurvy fashion?

HERMES. Because you have committed the most dreadful crime. Since Plutus has recovered his sight, there is nothing for us other gods, neither incense, nor laurels, nor cakes, nor victims, nor anything in the world.

CARIO. And you will never be offered anything more; you governed us too ill.

HERMES. I care nothing at all about the other gods, but 'tis myself. I tell you I am dying of hunger.

CARIO. That's reasoning like a wise fellow.

HERMES. Formerly, from earliest dawn, I was offered all sorts of good things in the wine-shops,—wine-cakes, honey, dried figs, in short, dishes worthy of Hermes. Now, I lie the livelong day on my back, with my legs in the air, famishing.

CARIO. And quite right too, for you often had them punished who treated you so well.[801]

HERMES. Ah! the lovely cake they used to knead for me on the fourth of the month![802]

CARIO. You recall it vainly; your regrets are useless! there'll be no more cake.

HERMES. Ah! the ham I was wont to devour!

CARIO. Well then! make use of your legs and hop on one leg upon the wine-skin,[803] to while away the time.

HERMES. Oh! the grilled entrails I used to swallow down!

CARIO. Your own have got the colic, methinks.

HERMES. Oh! the delicious tipple, half wine, half water!

CARIO. Here, swallow that and be off. (*He discharges a fart.*)

HERMES. Would you do a friend a service?

CARIO. Willingly, if I can.

HERMES. Give me some well-baked bread and a big hunk of the victims they are sacrificing in your house.

CARIO. That would be stealing.

HERMES. Do you forget, then, how I used to take care he knew nothing about it when you were stealing something from your master?

CARIO. Because I used to share it with you, you rogue; some cake or other always came your way.

HERMES. Which afterwards you ate up all by yourself.[804]

CARIO. But then you did not share the blows when I was caught.

HERMES. Forget past injuries, now you have taken Phylé.[805] Ah! how I should like to live with you! Take pity and receive me.

CARIO. You would leave the gods to stop here?

HERMES. One is much better off among you.

CARIO. What! you would desert! Do you think that is honest?

HERMES. "Where I live well, there is my country."[806]

CARIO. But how could we employ you here?

HERMES. Place me near the door; I am the watchman god and would shift off the robbers.

CARIO. Shift off! Ah! but we have no love for shifts.

HERMES. Entrust me with business dealings.

CARIO. But we are rich; why should we keep a haggling Hermes?

HERMES. Let me intrigue for you.[807]

CARIO. No, no, intrigues are forbidden; we believe in good faith.

HERMES. I will work for you as a guide.

CARIO. But the god sees clearly now, so we no longer want a guide.

HERMES. Well then, I will preside over the games. Ah! what can you object to in that? Nothing is fitter for Plutus than to give scenic and gymnastic games.[808]

CARIO. How useful 'tis to have so many names! Here you have found the means of earning your bread. I don't wonder the jurymen so eagerly try to get entered for many tribunals.[809]

HERMES. So then, you admit me on these terms.

CARIO. Go and wash the entrails of the victims at the well, so that you may show yourself serviceable at once.

A PRIEST OF ZEUS. Can anyone direct me where Chremylus is?

CHREMYLUS. What would you with him, friend?

PRIEST. Much ill. Since Plutus has recovered his sight, I am perishing of starvation; I, the priest of Zeus the Deliverer, have nothing to eat!

CHREMYLUS. And what is the cause of that, pray?

PRIEST. No one dreams of offering sacrifices.

CHREMYLUS. Why not?

PRIEST. Because all men are rich. Ah! when they had nothing, the merchant who escaped from shipwreck, the accused who was acquitted, all immolated victims; another would sacrifice for the success of some wish and the priest joined in at the feast; but now there is not the smallest victim, not one of the faithful in the temple, but thousands who come there to ease themselves.

CHREMYLUS. Don't you take your share of those offerings?

PRIEST. Hence I think I too am going to say good-bye to Zeus the Deliverer, and stop here myself.

CHREMYLUS. Be at ease, all will go well, if it so please the god. Zeus the Deliverer[810] is here; he came of his own accord.

PRIEST. Ha! that's good news.

CHREMYLUS. Wait a little; we are going to install Plutus presently in the place he formerly occupied behind the Temple of Athené;[811] there he will watch over our treasures for ever. But let lighted torches be brought; take these and walk in solemn procession in front of the god.

PRIEST. That's magnificent!

CHREMYLUS. Let Plutus be summoned.

OLD WOMAN. And I, what am I to do?

CHREMYLUS. Take the pots of vegetables which we are going to offer to the god in honour of his installation and carry them on your head; you just happen luckily to be wearing a beautiful embroidered robe.

OLD WOMAN. And what about the object of my coming?

CHREMYLUS. Everything shall be according to your wish. The young man will be with you this evening.

OLD WOMAN. Oh! if you promise me his visit, I will right willingly carry the pots.

CHREMYLUS. Those are strange pots indeed! Generally the scum rises to the top of the pots, but here the pots are raised to the top of the old woman.[812]

CHORUS. Let us withdraw without more tarrying, and follow the others, singing as we go.[813]

* * * * *

FINIS OF "PLUTUS"

* * * * *

Footnotes:

[736] The poet jestingly makes Chremylus attribute two utterly opposed characteristics to his servant.

[737] Literally *sycophants* i.e. denouncers of figs. The Senate, says Plutarch, in very early times had made a law forbidding the export of figs from Attica; those who were found breaking the edict were fined to the advantage of the sycophant ([Greek: phainein], to denounce, and [Greek: sukon], fig). Since the law was abused in order to accuse the innocent, the name sycophant was given to calumniators and to the too numerous class of informers at Athens who subsisted on the money their denunciations brought them.

[738] A parody of the tragic style.

[739] Plutus, the god of riches, was included amongst the infernal deities, because riches are extracted from the earth's bosom, which is their dwelling-place. According to Hesiod, he was the son of Demeter; agriculture is in truth the most solid foundation of wealth. He was generally represented as an old blind man, halting in gait and winged, coming with slow steps but going away on a rapid flight and carrying a purse in his hand. At Athens the statue of Peace bore Plutus represented as still a child on her bosom as a symbol of the wealth that peace brings.

[740] A rich man, who affected the sordid habits of Lacedaemon, because of his greed. "More sordid than Patrocles" had become a byword at Athens. Even the public baths were too dear for Patrocles, because, in addition to the modest fee that was given to the bath-man, it was necessary to use a little oil for the customary friction after the bath.

[741] This catechizing is completely in the manner of the sophistical teaching of the times, and has its parallel in other comedies. It reminds us in many ways of the Socratic 'Elenchus' as displayed in the Platonic dialogues.

[742] Corinth was the most corrupt as well as the most commercial of Greek cities, and held a number of great courtesans, indeed some of the most celebrated, e.g. Laïs, Cyréné, Sinopé, practised their profession there; they, however, set a very high value on their favours, and hence the saying, "*Non cuivis homini contingit adire Corinthum*"—"it is not for every man to go to Corinth."

[743] This was the mild punishment inflicted upon the adulterer by Athenian custom. The laws of Solon were very indulgent to this kind of crime; they only provided that the guilty woman might be repudiated by her husband, but were completely silent concerning her accomplice.

[744] Cario means to convey that women often paid their lovers, or at all events made it their business to open up the road to fortune for them.

[745] In order to receive the *triobolus,* the fee for attendance.

[746] The richest citizens were saddled with this expense and were called trierarchs.

[747] Athens had formed an alliance with Corinth and Thebes against Sparta in 393 B.C., a little before the production of the 'Plutus.' Corinth, not feeling itself strong enough to resist the attacks of the Spartans unaided, had demanded the help of an Athenian garrison, and hence Athens maintained some few thousand mercenaries there.

[748] A civil servant, who had been exiled for embezzling State funds.

[749] No doubt an accomplice of Pamphilus in his misdeeds; the Scholiast says he was one of his parasites.

[750] An upstart and, through the favour of the people, an admiral in the year 389 B.C., after Thrasybulus; he had enriched himself through some rather equivocal state employments and was insolent, because of his wealth, 'as a well-fed ass.'

---

[751] A buffoon, so the Scholiasts inform us, who was in the habit of visiting the public places of the city in order to make a little money by amusing the crowd with ridiculous stories. Others say he was a statesman of the period, who was condemned for embezzlement of public money; in his defence he may well have invented some fabulous tales to account for the disappearance of the money out of the Treasury.

[752] The precise historical reference here is obscure.

[753] Laïs, a celebrated courtesan.—Of Philonides little is known, except that he was a native of Melita and a rich and profligate character.

[754] The reference is no doubt to a pretentious construction that had been built for the rich and over-proud Timotheus, the son of Conon. He was a clever general of great integrity; when the 'Plutus' was produced, he was still very young.

[755] Chremylus rises in a regular climax from love to military glory; the slave in as direct an anti-climax comes from bread, sweetmeats, etc., down to lentils.

[756] The son of Aphareus, the King of Messenia; according to the legends, he had such piercing sight that he could see through walls, and could even discover what was going on in heaven and in the nether world. He took part in the expedition of the Argonauts.

[757] A part of the victim which Cario was bringing back from the Temple; it was customary to present the remains of a sacrifice to friends and relations.

[758] As soon as Chremylus sees himself assured of wealth he adopts less honest principles.

[759] The citizens appointed to act as dicasts, or jurymen, drew lots each year to decide in which Court they should sit. There were ten Courts, each of which was indicated by one of the first ten letters of the alphabet, and the urn contained as many tickets marked with these letters as there were

dicasts. Cario means to say here that the old men of the Chorus should remember that they have soon to die themselves instead of bothering about punishing him.

[760] A word invented to imitate the sound of a lyre.

[761] The Cyclops let his flocks graze while he played the lyre; it was thus that Philoxenus had represented him in a piece to which Aristophanes is here alluding.—Cario assumes the part of the Cyclops and leaves that of the flock to the Chorus.

[762] In allusion to Ulysses' adventures in the cave of Polyphemus.

[763] Laïs.

[764] i.e. Cario, who is assuming the rôle of Circé of Corinth.

[765] This was the torture which Odysseus inflicted on Melanthius, one of the goatherds.

[766] A poet of debauched and degraded life, one of those who, like Ariphrades mentioned in 'The Knights,' "defiled his tongue with abominable sensualities," that is to say, was a *fellator* and a *cunnilingue.*

[767] It is uncertain whether Pamphilus, a tragedian, is meant here, who, like Euripides and Aeschylus, made the Heraclidae the subject of a tragedy, or the painter of that name, so celebrated in later times, who painted that subject in the Poecilé Stoa.

[768] Physicians at Athens were paid very indifferently, and hence the most skilled sought their practice in other cities.

[769] The Temple of Aesculapius stood on the way from the theatre to the citadel and near the tomb of Talos. A large number of invalids were taken there to pass a night; it was believed that the god visited them without being seen himself, because of the darkness, and arranged for their restoration to health.

[770] Like the Furies who composed the Chorus in Aeschylus' 'Eumenides.'

[771] A ravine into which criminals were hurled at Athens.

[772] During the winter the poor went into the public baths for shelter against the cold; they could even stop there all night; sometimes they burnt themselves by getting too near the furnace which heated the water.

[773] i.e. the most opposite things; the tyranny of Dionysius of Syracuse and the liberty which Thrasybulus restored to Athens.

[774] Crimes to which men are driven through poverty.

[775] The ancients placed statues of Hecaté at the cross-roads ([Greek: triodoi], places where three roads meet), because of the three names, Artemis, Phoebé and Hecaté, under which the same goddess was worshipped. On the first day of the month the rich had meals served before these statues and invited the poor to them.

[776] A verse from Euripides' lost play of 'Telephus.' The same line occurs in 'The Knights.'

[777] And not the citizens of Argos, whom agriculture and trade rendered wealthy.—Pauson was an Athenian painter, whose poverty had become a proverb. "Poorer than Pauson" was a common saying.

[778] There is here a long interval of time, during which Plutus is taken to the Temple of Aesculapius and cured of his blindness. In the first edition probably the Parabasis came in here; at all events a long choral ode must have intervened.

[779] The Athenians had erected a temple to Theseus and instituted feasts in his honour, which were still kept up in the days of Plutarch and Pausanias. Barley broth and other coarse foods were distributed among the poor.

[780] He was an orator, who was accused of theft and extortion, and who, moreover, was said not to be a genuine Athenian citizen.

[781] The serpent was sacred to Aesculapius; several of these reptiles lived in the temple of the god.

[782] Iaso (from [Greek: iasthai], to heal) and Panacea (from [Greek: pan], everything, and [Greek: akeisthai], to cure) were daughters of Aesculapius.

[783] He has to see, examine, and taste pill, potion, urine … and worse.

[784] An apothecary's outfit.

[785] Tenos is one of the Cyclades, near Andros.

[786] A deme of Attica, where the strongest vinegar came from.

[787] The Scholiast says that this was an individual as poor as he was greedy, and on the watch for every opportunity to satisfy his voracity.—The comic poets often had nuts, figs and other petty dainties thrown to the audience. It was a fairly good way to secure the favour of a certain section of the public.

[788] The ancients used oil in large quantities, whether for rubbing themselves down after bathing or before their exercises in the palaestra, or for the different uses of domestic life. It was kept in a kind of tank, hollowed in the ground and covered with tiles or stones. The wine-sellers had similar tanks, but of larger size, for keeping their wine.

[789] This was what was styled the triple or complete sacrifice.

[790] As evidence of the sorry condition from which he had been raised.

[791] The clothes a man wore on the day that he was initiated into the Mysteries of Eleusis had, according to custom, to be dedicated to the gods, but only after they had been worn. Most people only decided to do this when they were full of holes and torn; it is because his visitor's cloak is in such a sorry condition that Chremylus takes it to be the cloak of an Initiate.

[792] This Eudemus was a kind of sorcerer, who sold magic rings, to which, among other virtues, he ascribed that of curing, or rather of securing him who wore them, from snake-bites.

[793] The merchants engaged in maritime commerce were absolved from military service; the Scholiast even declares, though it seems highly unlikely, that all merchants were exempt from imposts on their possessions. When it was a question of escaping taxes and military service the informer passed as a merchant.

[794] At Athens 'twas only the injured person who could prosecute in private disputes; everyone, however, had this right where wrongs against the State were involved; but if the prosecutor only obtained one-fifth of the votes, he was condemned to a fine of 1000 drachmae or banished the country.

[795] A proverbial saying, meaning, *the most precious thing.*—Battus, a Lacedaemonian, led out a colony from Thera, an island in the Aegean sea, and, about 630 B.C., founded the city of Cyrené in Africa. He was its first king, and after death was honoured as a god. The inhabitants of that country gathered great quantities of *silphium* or 'laserpitium,' the sap of which plant was the basis of medicaments and sauces that commanded a high price. The coins of Cyrené bore the representation of a stalk of *silphium*.

[796] The old woman had entered dressed as a young girl. Or is it merely said ironically?

[797] A proverb, meaning, "*All things change with time.*" Addressed to the old woman, it meant that she had perhaps been beautiful once, but that the days for love were over for her.—Miletus, the most powerful of the Ionic cities, had a very numerous fleet and founded more than eighty colonies; falling beneath the Persian yoke, the city never succeeded in regaining its independence.

[798] Eleusis was some distance from Athens, about seven and a half miles, and the wealthy women drove there. It was an occasion when they vied with each other in the display of luxury.

[799] You are so old.

[800] The goddess of death and old age.

[801] Wineshop-keepers were often punished for serving false measure. Hermes, who allowed them to be punished although he was the god of cheating and was worshipped as such by the wineshop-keepers, deserved to be neglected by them.

[802] The greater gods had a day in each month specially dedicated to them; thus Hermes had the fourth, Artemis the sixth, Apollo the seventh, etc.

[803] This game, which was customary during the feasts of Bacchus' consisted in hopping on one leg upon a wine-skin that was blown out and well greased with oil; the competitor who kept his footing longest on one leg, gained the prize.

[804] The cake was placed on the altar, but eaten afterwards by the priest or by him who offered the sacrifice.

[805] An allusion to the occupation of Phylé, in Attica on the Boeotian border, by Thrasybulus; this place was the meeting-place of the discontented and the exiled, and it was there that the expulsion of the thirty tyrants was planned. Once victorious, the conspirators proclaimed a general amnesty and swore to forget everything, [Greek: m_e mn_esikakein], 'to bear no grudge,' hence the proverb which Aristophanes recalls here.

[806] A verse taken from a lost tragedy by Euripides.

[807] Hermes runs through the gamut of his different attributes.

[808] As the rich citizens were accustomed to do at Athens.

[809] This trick was very often practised, its object being to secure the double fee.

[810] He is giving Plutus this title.

[811] Within the precincts of the Acropolis, and behind the Temple of Zeus Polias, there stood a building enclosed with double walls and double gates, where the public Treasury was kept. Plutus had ceased to dwell there, i.e. the Peloponnesian war and its disastrous consequences had emptied the Treasury; however, at the time of the production of the 'Plutus,' Athens had recovered her freedom and a part of her former might, and money was again flowing into her coffers.

[812] In the Greek there is a pun on the different significations of [Greek: graus],_ *an old woman,* and the *scum*, or 'mother,' which forms on the top of boiling milk.

[813] In the 'Lysistrata' the Chorus similarly makes its exit singing.

INDEX[*]

C

Crime and poverty
Criticism, too low
Critylla
Crows, going to
Cuckoo, the
Curotrophos, meaning
Cuttle-fish
Cyclops, the, and lyre
Cycni, the two
Cynna, the courtesan
Cyrené, the courtesan

D

Dardanus, flute-girls from
Daughters, lent to strangers
Dead bodies on plants
Debts, in relation to women
Demagogues as drones
Demeter, Mysteries of
—how represented
—goddess of abundance
Democracy in Olympus
Demolochocleon, explained
Demos, a young Athenian
Depilation, for adultery
"Descend," term explained
Devil, to the, how expressed
Dexinicus, the greedy
Diagoras, a convert to atheism
Dicasts, insignia
Diitrephes, rich basket-maker
Dining stations
Diomedes, a brigand
Diomeia, temple at

Dionysus, not brave
Dionysus, temple
—the god
Diopithes, a diviner
Diopithes, the orator
Discontented, the rendezvous of
Division (the), of lands
Dog, backside of
Door-hinge, moistened
Drachma (the)
Draughts, rules of
Dreams, fee to interpret
Duck's domain, the

E

Eagle, symbol of royalty Egypt, soil of Ekkiklyma, the Elegants, effeminate Eleusis, mysteries of —women at Eleven (the), who they were Embezzling State funds Empusa, a spectre Engastromythes, explained Englottogastors, meaning of Epicrates, a demagogue Epigonus, a pathic Erasinidas, a general Erinnys, a fury Eryxis, noted for ugliness Ether (the), physical theory of Euathlus, a diffamer Eudemus, the sorcerer Euphemius, a flatterer Euripides, a verse from —date of his death —distich from —expressions from —verse from Orestes —origin —lost tragedies —verse from — heterodoxy —insipid style —"ghost" of —birth —stage-characters of — influence of his poetry —labour criticised —*versus* Aeschylus —rhythm — monologue —'Antigoné' quoted —'Telephus' and 'Meleager' quoted — 'Hippolytus,' line from —'Aeolus' and 'Phryxus' quoted —parodied — 'Aeolus,' —'Alcestis' quoted —'Menalippé,' —mother insulted — 'Sthenoboea,' —'Phoenix,' —'Palamedes,' —'Helen' quoted —how staged —son of —verse from Eurycles, the diviner Evaeon, poverty of Excrement, voiding —eating of, proverb Execestides, stranger at Athens —his tutelary deity Eyes, bad, proverb on

F

411

G

Grudge, bearing no
Gull, the voracious

H

Hades, leaders in Harmodius, statue of Hecaté, altars of —the poor fed —
goddess of death Hegelochus, an actor Heliasts, tribunal of —manner of
voting —daily salary —acrid temper —separated from public —choice
of *Hellé's sacred waves* Hellebore, for madness Hemlock, effect of
Heracles, gluttony of —descends to Hades Heracles, Temple of Hermes,
attributes of Hesiod on Plutus "Hestia, addressing first" Hiero, of Syracuse
Hieronymus, the argive Hippias, tyranny of Hippocrates, theories of
Hipponicus, the orator Homer's text corrupted "Horse, the," an erotic
posture Horses, devoured by Hydriaphoros, the alien

I

Ibycus, the poet
Ilithyia, goddess of child-birth
Illyrians, the
Incest, in the 'Aeolus,'
Informer, business of
Ino, metamorphosis of
Intercourse, sexual
Interrupters, how dismissed
Invoke the god
Iophon, son of Sophocles

J

Jar of wine comp. to ass
Jest, obscene
Jocasta, married by son
Jokes, coarse
Jurymen, fees of

—tricks of
Justice, slowness of

K

Kimos, top of voting urn Kite, the, and springtime

L

Laches, an Athenian general
—comic trial of dog and
—ref. to his peculations
Laespodias, a general
Laïs, the courtesan
Lamachus, better opinion of
Lamia, transformed
Lamiae (the)
Lamias, unknown
Lampadephoria, the
Lampon, a diviner
—prediction of
Lasus, the poet
Laurium, the mines of
Leather, allusion to old
Leogaras, an epicure
Leotrophides, his leanness
Lesbian women, tricks of
Literature, heavy
Locksmiths, Spartan
Lots, drawing
Love exercises, ref. to
Love's Labour's Lost
Lovers, gifts of
—paid
Lycabettus
'Lycimnius,' a tragedy

Mysteries, insulting the
—of Eleusis

N

Nausicydes
Naxos, island of
Neoclides, an orator
Nephelococcygia, meaning
Nicias, grandson of
Nicias, the general
—his slackness
Nightingale, song of
"Niobe," tragedies of
Nysa, a town of Dionysus

O

Odeon (the), by whom built Odysseus, manner of escape —as spy —how
he tortured Odyssey, the, quoted Offal, human, tasting Oil, extensive use of
Olive leaves Olophyxians, the Omen, word for —satire on —starting on
journey Onions, as aphrodisiac Oracles, trees as Orators, infamous —venom
of —wear chaplets —rapacity of "Orestes," prologue of the Orestes, the
robber —cave alluded to Origanum, used for corpses Ornaments, worn by
girls Orneae, a town —alluded to by prophet Owls, as omen —at Athens
Ox-fat, syn. for people

P

Palamedes, the inventor
Pamphilus, two of the name
Pan, the god
"Pankration" (the)
Pantacles, unknown
"Parsley and the rue"
Pathos and bathos

Q

R

Shoemakers, women as
Shoes, etc., where left
Sight, extraordinary
Simois, city of the
Singing, exit whilst
Slaves
—branding of
—names
Smaeus, the debauchee
Socratic, the, "Elenchus"
Socrates, etc.
—comp. to vampires
—the accuser of
Soldier, as ambassador
Solon, laws of
Son, marries mother
Sophocles
—mentioned
—parodied
—the Laocoon of
Sore throat and bribery
"Sows, little," obscene pun
Sparta
—play on word
—alliance against
Sperchius, the
Sphettian vinegar
Spintharus
Sporgilus, a barber
State funds, embezzled
State, prosecuting the
Statutes, how protected
Sthenelus, an actor
Sthenoboea, an amorous queen
Stool, position at

Strangers, enjoy host's daughters
Streak, the red
Strouthian, the poulterer
Sun, the, parodied
Sunburnt, how to get
Sunshade carrier
Surnames of characters
Swearing, by the birds
Sybaris, the town of
Sycophants, origin of word
Syllables, seventy-seven
Syrmea, a plant

T

Tablets and scrolls
Taleas, a citizen
Talent, value of
Tartessus, a town
Taxes on slaves
Tenian garlic
Tereus, legend of
Terminus, the god
Testicles
—play on word
—tortured
Teucers
Thales, his fame
Thallophores (the)
Tharelides, the jay
Theagenes, his farting
Theogenes, a boaster
Theognis
Theorus, comp. to crow
Theramenes

U

Ulysses' adventures
Urns, the two
—threatened
Versatile people, proverb
Verse, a borrowed
Verses, sung by maidens
Vine-prop (the), a comparison
Vote, of juryman, how given

W

Wealth, and principle Wild pears and sore throats Wine-skir, hopping on
Wine-pits, the Wineshop-keepers punished Woman and carding —"to go
with," pun on word —debt in relation to —old woman, pun on Women, at
funerals —secret loves of —in child-bed —period of gestation —love of
strong drink —their form of oath —addressed as men —yellow tunics of —
pale-faced —pay their lovers —display of luxury Word, a wonderful Wren,
play on word —in French and German

X

Xenocles, an inferior poet

Y

Yellow tunics
Young men, how seduced

Z

Zeus, the Deliverer

The End